CAMBORNE TOWN BAND

By

Tony Mansell

Cover design by Dan Benney

Published by Trelease Publications

First Published October 2005

Published by:
Trelease Publications
An Avallennek
Mithian
St Agnes
Cornwall TR5 0QF
tony@manselltrelease.wanadoo.co.uk

ISBN 0-9545583-5-9

Printed by R. Booth Ltd
Printers & Bookbinders
Antron Hill
Mabe
Penryn
Cornwall TR10 9HH

For Isabelle & Chloe

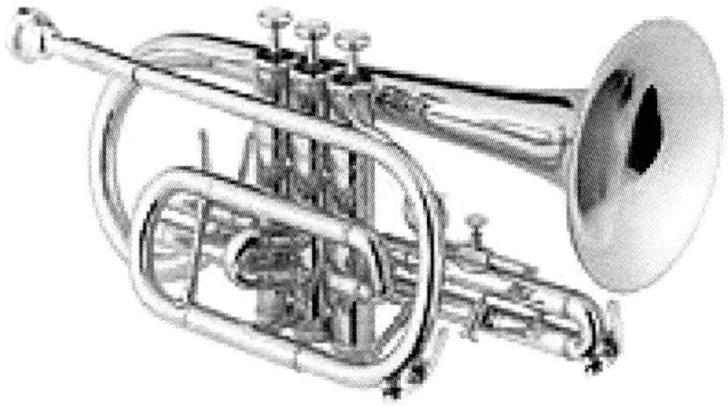

Goin up Camborne Hill, comin down
Goin up Camborne Hill, comin down
The horses stood still, the wheels went around
Goin up Camborne Hill comin down

I knawd er old father old man
I knawd er old father old man
I knawd her old man, he blawed in the band
Goin up Camborne Hill comin down

Contents

Introduction

Brass bands were once at the heart of every community and in constant demand at every sort of event. Even a casual glance at the history of Cornish villages in the nineteenth and the first half of the twentieth century, shows that life would have been extremely dull without this form of entertainment. It is therefore surprising that so little has been written about them – particularly in Cornwall.

This then, is an attempt to redress the situation by producing the history of the Duchy's most famous and consistently successful brass band – Camborne Town Band.

Having written the history of St Agnes Band I was asked by Tom Ruse, a former Camborne player, to write about Camborne Town Band. I said I would think about it but before I could do much thinking, he telephoned me to say he'd discussed it with the Band Committee and they would like me to get on with it. Tom, a former tutor of mine, was always quite persuasive and this book is the result of his persuasion. His involvement didn't stop there however and he, like so many others, helped by providing information, photographs, concert programmes and other material which has made my research easier than it might otherwise have been. Alongside this was the enthusiasm and encouragement of the people connected with the Band – both currently and in the past. Writing is a solitary task but I was sustained by those who were as keen as I to see the history of their Band in print; I hope they are pleased with the result.

I started with the advantage of being an ex player, not of Camborne but of St Agnes. I played during the 1950s to the early 1970s when the band was very tidy, as they say, and contesting in the Championship Section locally. But for some non-playing decisions we may have progressed further but that is the subject of another book and you'll have to read *St Agnes and its Band* to find out more about that.

Camborne Town Band emanates from an equally well-known town with a mining and industrial heritage second to none. It was the home of Richard Trevithick, Holman's Engineering and the world famous School of Mines.

The Band has an unrivalled contest record dating from the late 1800s and many of its results are covered in this book; it is truly remarkable, unsurpassed by any other in Cornwall. It has been a local Championship Section band since its formation and on the national stage since the 1920s. Having won the National Second Section Championship in 1945 it was promoted to the Championship Section the following year – a position it has retained ever since. It has contested on BBC Radio, BBC Television, at entertainment contests as well as local, regional and national contests and it is still at the top; competing with the best in the country. Put simply, it is what other bands aspire to be.

We cannot deny the north of England its claim to be the birthplace of brass bands when workers from the pits and the mills formed an affinity with brass and reed instruments. It provided them with an opportunity to create music with their workmates; a chance to partake in something of contrast to their days of hard graft. With hands that were probably too coarse for more delicate instruments they found these robust versions ideal. In many cases support from employers was forthcoming; those who were prepared to invest in recreation for employees while at the same time promoting their companies. In other cases small groups of musicians gathered together to play in the churches and chapels and these grew into the dozen or so members playing a variety of instruments. Over the years the quality of instruments and playing skills improved and bands evolved into groups of musicians providing an incredibly high standard of music – amateurs performing like professionals.

We cannot be certain when the first brass band was formed but it has been claimed that a Newcastle colliery band was established as early as 1809. A few years later, Besses o' th' Barn and Black Dyke Mills Band came into being and the movement was really under way. The early bands were certainly a combination of brass and reed and we know these still existed in the 1890s, when they were competing against pure brass bands. In the late 1800s, the rise in popularity of the all-brass sound saw the gradual demise of these combination bands.

There was vigorous growth from the mid 1800s when contesting was on a more organised footing. Gradually, music began to be scored for brass and voice and even the famous orchestral conductors were beginning to take the movement seriously.

Music has been a part of Cornish life for as long as anywhere else and it wasn't long before the success of the northern bands spread to other areas and in Cornwall it was the miners, the fishermen and the farmers who embraced it.

It's impossible to say when the first brass band was formed in Cornwall; here again, the issue is clouded by the existence of brass and reed bands which were certainly in place during the 1830s. We do know that contests were definitely being held in the early 1880s and maybe earlier.

We can imagine the difficulties faced by the early bands. Times were hard and money was in short supply and it must have been a struggle to purchase instruments and music. Many bands fell by the wayside having given up the unequal struggle while others managed to cling on through the good and the lean years. Much more than today, brass bands were at the very heart of the community, performing a great social service to their village or town. There was a pride in taking part, a satisfaction in being a member of such an important group. A former player in Camborne Town Band remembered one of his proudest moments, not when he played at the Royal Albert Hall but when, as a member of the Band, he returned to his own village to take part in a parade.

One of my earliest banding memories is of marching back through Bugle after the contest. We passed under the railway bridge which used to cross the road; it was thronged with people. Filled with emotion, I had to stop playing.

Brass bands no longer hold the pivotal position in society but the movement is still thriving. With so many other casual attractions it's surprising that so many people are still willing to devote so much time and effort to maintain this great movement – long may they continue to do so. Hobbies can be all consuming but surely brass banding is more than a hobby, more than something to be picked up or discarded at will. The best description I have for brass banding is that it is a way of life and although a playing career may not last a lifetime the affect it has on the player certainly does.

Perhaps the old Cornish tea-treat epitomises what banding is all about. Sitting on hard wooden forms or marching along country lanes where the only audience is the occasional cow who chooses to look over the hedge to check which band is playing this year. It is grass roots stuff and leaves a lifetime of memories.

The History

1841 – A band was formed in Camborne.

Many sources refer to a band being formed in 1841 in the thriving mining area of Camborne. Bands of that time consisted of a hotchpotch of instruments – mainly brass and woodwind with the odd string "thrown in" for good measure. These groups provided an enjoyable pastime for players and entertainment for the listener regardless of the mix of instruments.

It has not, however, been possible to form a link with this early band with what we now know as Camborne Town Band. So we begin with an uncertainty. Was the band of 1841 the forerunner of the current band? Or was it just another group of musicians from Camborne that shared its name with its modern counterpart? Indeed, this early band may have been one of many that started and played through the second half of the 1900s. The connection remains unproven and my view is that the sequence of events in the 1890s suggests there is no direct link.

I commenced my research with an open mind and if I'm guilty of anything it is in trying to prove a link rather than to disprove one. Some of the Band's promotional material refers to a commencement date of 1841 and the 150-year anniversary celebrations in 1991 strengthened that theory.

Other sources refer to 1896 as the date when the band was re-formed, but re-formed from what? In trying to trace the start of the present band I came across a newspaper report in the *West Briton* which suggests Camborne had two bands in 1896. Firstly, the Camborne Choral Society and Philharmonic Band which, *" gave a most successful rendering of Judas Maccabaeus in the Public Rooms on Tuesday ...... The band was led by Mr H V Pearce Mus. Bac., and Mr R White of Penzance ably discharged his duties of conductor"* (presumably of the whole ensemble).

I also discovered that Troon Brass Band (Mr W Gribben) gave a concert in Redruth in May 1896 but that's another story.

At the same time as the Philharmonic Band was doing its stuff, Camborne Volunteer Band was practising on Tuesdays and Thursdays and taking part in various parades. There are many notices in the newspapers advising the band, buglers and fighting personnel when training would take place and it seems the *West Briton* was the major avenue of notification.

1888 – Mr W J Uren became Bandmaster of Camborne Voluntary Band.

1896 – Camborne *"Independent"* Town Band formed with Mr W J Uren as Musical Director (The term Bandmaster was used in those days).

In August 1896 a crisis hit the town which would reverberate around the streets - and in the newspapers - for some time to come. The *West Briton* reported, *"Camborne Volunteer Band have been requested to hand in their kit and to consider themselves no longer members of the company. This step has been taken by the Commanding Officer in consequence of the action of the band in taking part in the band contest at Trevenson Park on Bank Holiday without permission. They obtained the first prize at the contest."* This action must be measured against the times in question when we were preparing for war with the Boars and patriotism, and not a little jingoism, filled the air. Additionally, men tended to doff their cap and do as they were told and here we have the entire band being dismissed for contravening orders. The *West Briton*, in what would now be called the editorial, debates the issue. *"At last Camborne Band have broken through all restraint and, having defied authority, has been thrown adrift. The more or less casual onlooker is uncertain as to which party is the aggrieved one and deserves sympathy.*

One feels inclined sometimes to admire the feeling of conscious ability displayed by the bandsman, and also the daring to infringe a regulation they considered too binding; but then orders are orders and if the band desire to wear the Queen's uniform they must learn to take the bitter with the sweet. The mischief has now been done; and on Friday the conquering heroes returning from camp, bronzed with exposure, paraded the streets without the strains of music which were want to herald their approach. Tramp! Tramp! Tramp! They went, but only to cause people to liken them to a funeral. Truly we might exclaim when we consider the trifling matters which breed discontent, and put friends at variance. What fools we mortals be."

It seems that the company marched down the street in comparative silence and that the marching rhythm was not helped by a group of young "musicians" who gathered at the side of the street playing imitation drums.

The *West Briton* completes its report by saying, *"The solution of the band difficulty is awaited with much interest"*.

Within a few days many young men from Camborne and the surrounding area went to the headquarters of the company and volunteered to fill the vacancies caused by the dismissal of the members of the band. At the same time, the dismissed musicians gave their first appearance as an "independent" band when they played in Commercial Square and a considerable number of people were there to hear them. The players must have moved with some speed to beg or borrow instruments and music but I'm sure they were determined to show it was business as usual.

It's interesting to note that the Band won the Trevenson Park Contest, something which it has been doing ever since with amazing consistency. But for that precipitous action, and the subsequent dismissal, who knows if the band, as we know it, would have been formed.

1887 - The 2nd Company Camborne Volunteer Band (The Rifles Band) before the changes of 1896 when it became "independent". Current bass player Eric Thomas identified his great grandfather, William John Thomas, in the back row and second from right. Eric thinks this band practised in a building at the junction of Eastern Lane and North Roskear Road.
Back row: Dickie Kendall, Dick Smitheram, Joe Holman, Dick Hicks, William John Thomas and Joe Wearne.
Front row: George Rosevear, Arthur Richards, Phil Collins, W J Bennetts, William Trudgeon (Bandmaster), Jack Angove, Alfred Jewell, J Gay, and W J Curry.
The drummer is Sam Pascoe.

The Band in the 1890s

1897

Back row: Gaby Pascoe, P Collins, G Rosevear, J Paul, W Hendy and W Jones.
Middle row: J Belman, J Bawden, R Osborne, W Uren (Musical Director), R Osborne, R Osborne, F Collins and J Berryman. (The name R Osborne appears three times - not sure if this is correct)
Front row: R Pascoe and J Tresidder.

1889 to 1903 - Camborne Town Band - The uniforms appear to be ex-Army, perhaps Boer War
Back row: W J Thomas (great grandfather of Eric Thomas), H Harris, G H Victor, J Paull and J Wearne.
Middle row: G Rosevear, F Collins, W Thomas, Wm Uren (Bandmaster), J Bawden, H Rosevear, W Jones and J Berryman.
Front row: J Southcote, E Wills, J Tresidder and J Belman.

1890s - W J Uren's Band

Camborne Town Band gradually involved itself in the life of the town giving concerts and leading processions including the celebration for the Relief of Ladysmith in 1900.

In 1901 the Band led a parade in honour of a local man who achieved national and international fame. In very heavy rain, eight traction engines steamed around the town to mark the 100th anniversary of Richard Trevithick's historical run of his "steam carriage," which took place on Christmas Eve 1801.

In January 1902 W Uren conducted the Band in a concert at the Mission Buildings, Trelowarren Street, Camborne. The Uren family played a leading role in the early Band and Mr W Uren was its first Musical Director. One report states he remained in position for nearly 20 years while another said J Uren was first in post and W Uren was appointed Musical Director in 1902. Could the two men have been related or were they, as I believe, the same person. I know that doesn't explain the 1902 appointment but reporting was not always accurate in those days and that could have been a reference to his re-appointment at an annual general meeting. As ever, if you know different, then please let me know.

1905 - A photo-call at a tea-treat
(Both of the photographs on this page are by courtesy of David Thomas of Camborne)

The Band in 1910

1913 - the first band to be presented with the Royal Trophy at the West of England Band Festival at Bugle

Inset: W Uren (Bandmaster) and Walter Nettle (Trainer - conducted the Band at the contest).

Back row: William John Uren (soprano), Ernie Wills (cornet), ? Pender, ? Jenkin (cornet), Edgar Pearce, Martin Oates, Fred Uren and Harry Uren.

Middle row: Johnny Major, Arthur Pollard (horn), Jim Tregellas, Joe Volante, Arthur Paul, Walter Tregellas (baritone) and Alfred Tresidder.

Front row: Jimmy Tresidder, Jack Eustace, Phil Collins (cornet/euph - played from the 1880s to the 1920s), George Rosevear (trombone), Jimmy Carter, John Collins (trombone), Bill Eustace, Gus Rhilman and Bill Jones. (Photo by W J Bennetts & Son of Camborne)

1912 – Camborne Town Band won first prize at the first West of England Bandsmen's Festival (Bugle Contest).

1913 - W Nuttall (possibly Nettle) appointed Musical Director.

1913 – Camborne Town Band won first prize at the West of England Bandsmen's Festival (Bugle Contest) and became the first band to be presented with the H R H The Prince of Wales Challenge Cup (The Royal Trophy).

1914 – Mr Will Layman appointed Musical Director.

Circa 1918 – Mr E J Williams appointed Musical Director.

1913 - Mr Uren's last year as MD

Howard Phillips, was trained by Edwin Williams and played with Freddie Roberts in the 1920s. When young, Howard and his two sisters were each given £25 by their father to, *"Further their musical enjoyment,"* and Howard bought a new cornet and joined the Band. At one particular contest Mr Parker asked him to play flugel and it seems he'd played beautifully until he missed the final high note. He missed it again at the second attempt and after a third failure he said, *"Bugger it,"* and gave up. Despite the slip, Camborne won first prize and Howard was awarded a special (for perseverance I should think). It seems Mr Parker never missed an opportunity to tease him about it. Howard's son, John Phillips, still has the cornet he played in the Band and in a local orchestra run by Dr Rivers.

Sometime around 1900 Jimmy Tresidder (Barry Tresidder's great uncle) took over the drum from Gaby Pascoe and played it until 1903, when he moved to E flat bass. His brother, Alfred Tresidder (Barry Tresidder's grandfather), then took over and played it until 1956.

During the latter period Richard Tresidder, "Drummer Dick" (Barry's father), undertook the marching role and Alfred played in the indoor concerts. Dick had started his banding career in the Junior Band and continued playing until his retirement in 1968. The drum, in his day, was much heavier than the modern instrument and he is said to have turned purple as a colleague tightened the supporting straps. When the drum was in place the pressure eased and Dick gradually returned to his normal colour.

Richard's brother, Alfred John Tresidder, played E flat bass for about 30 years and their brother-in-law, Leonard Wills, played E flat bass for over 30 years - up to the early 1960s.

The three drummer members of the Tresidder family all managed to split the skin on the bass drum or, in technical terms, to "put it in". Alfred was none too pleased when he discovered some kind soul had kicked in his drum while the players were celebrating their performance at the St Ives Band Contest. The triumphal march down Trelowarren Street had to be accompanied by a drummer running on only one cylinder! Richard's moment of embarrassment was at Bolenowe tea-treat when the drum skin had tautened in the heat. The double hit to signal the end of playing did not go quite as planned as the drumstick went straight through. A replacement instrument had to be borrowed from the Salvation Army for the evening concert.

Richard said courting was difficult because of the commitment required to play in a brass band and it seems his wife always warned young girls, "*Never marry a bandsman. You'll never see anything of him in daylight*".

Before the days of easy transportation it was usual for bandsmen to travel to contests and concerts by horse and wagon or even by shank's pony. An event was taking place at St Keverne and an E flat bass player was walking home with his instrument on his back. The story goes that he realised his pipe needed re-lighting and he turned around to shelter the match from the wind. He then continued walking and ended up back in St Keverne again. I can't be sure he played for Camborne but Kingsley Hitchens told the story and said, "*Well, he could've*".

1919 - With conductor E Williams. This photograph of the band was printed in postcard form and was actually sent through the post with a message on the reverse. The postmark is the 8th March 1927 and the card is addressed to Mr James Opie, Stithians Row, Four Lanes, Redruth. It reads, "Dear Jim, There will be no practice tomorrow night (Wednesday) send word to Reed (Cecil Reed) as I don't know his address.
M Oates".

The Band suffered a severe blow in 1919 when William J Uren (soprano), who had joined in 1912, and Harry Uren (Principal Cornet), who had joined in 1913, emigrated. Their father, William Uren, had been Musical Director from 1888 to 1913. Another brother, Fred Uren joined in 1913 and was a playing member for 25 years. When home on holiday in 1951, Harry played in a joint concert with St Dennis Silver Band and Camborne.

Cecil Reed (cornet) joined just after Bugle Contest in 1919 when Edwin Williams was Musical Director. He played until 1930 and always spoke of the win at Bugle in 1925 as being his most memorable occasion; it was Mr A W Parker's first contest with the Band.

Three members of the Roberts family played in the Band. Fred and Sam are mentioned later in the book but Reggie Roberts also played cornet. His career was somewhat shorter than his brothers as he moved to Australia and I don't know if he continued playing over there; he died in 2001.

Reg Toy was born at Praze in 1911 and started playing the piano when he was eight years old. In 1923 his family moved to Camborne where he attended Roskear School and went on to serve an apprenticeship in Holman's pattern shop. He joined Camborne Junior Band (baritone) under Jack Eustace when it started in 1925 and played with them until about 1933. Jack Eustace was an E flat bass player who had been with the Band from about 1913. Reg then played with Rame Cross Band (bass trom), Perranporth Town Band (tenor trom) in 1932 under Jack Eustace, Bodmin Town Band (tenor trom) and with Hayle Band for a while.

He joined Camborne Town Band in the late 1930s and played until the early to mid 1950s. Reg said, *"Sidney Keen (bass) was probable the oldest player when I joined. We had lots of engagements in the 1930s but the Band was so large that we could split in order to cover them all. I remember Townshend tea-treat before the Second World War when half the band was having tea while the others went to play outside the house of a bed-ridden man. Players were paid a small amount for playing at engagements as most of them had to take time off work – even Saturdays were work days back then."*

Ernie Yeoman (trombone) joined in 1923 when he was 11 years old, his daughter, Barbara, recalled some of her memories. *"We used to accompany them on lots of trips, especially the tea-treats; Townshend was my favourite. My cousin, Sylvia Berryman (John Berryman's sister) and I would join in the procession. Another favourite was Bugle Contest when we would arrive home in Camborne at about 9.00pm and march down Trelowarren Street in front of the Band with all the cups. The Square would be packed with supporters; the cheering was tremendous. My skin would tingle and I'd feel so proud. Dad loved Bugle and always looked forward to meeting old friends, particularly Eddie Williams. Dad was quite stocky and had to pull himself in so my brother and I could quickly fasten the braids. I never knew how he managed to blow the trombone trussed up like that. Many concerts were held at Holman's Canteen and the place was always full. I remember one concert, when I was about nine years old, the Band was playing and one by one they left the stage leaving just Mr Parker. The first time they did it everyone was taken by surprise."*

Ernie Yeoman and Jack Berryman were brothers-in-law and, of course, John Berryman (cornet) was Ernie's nephew. Glen Loze was a brother to Ernie's wife and played cornet during the 1950s and 1960s before transferring to Constantine Band. Health problems caused Ernie to finish playing in 1953 but he occasionally returned to help out when there was a shortage of trombone players.

1924 – Mr George Rosevear appointed Musical Director (see note under Musical Directors).

1925 – Mr A W Parker appointed Musical Director.

1925 – Camborne Town Youth Band formed under Jack Eustace.

1926 – First attendance at a National Contest (Crystal Palace).

In his year-end report in December 1926, Mr Donald W Thomas, President, stated that the Band had just completed its fifth year under its new constitution. He appreciated the splendid spirit and the players' continued happy relations with the Committee. He continued, *"As intimated in last year's report the arrangement between Mr Henry Nettle and Mr A W Parker came to an end at Easter last. The public spirit shown by Mr Nettle in retaining the services of Mr Parker for a period of 12 months laid the foundation of the Committee's efforts in putting the Band on a sound financial basis. The Committee is happy to state that through Mr Parker having obtained employment with Messrs Holman Bros Ltd, the expense of retaining his services will not be anything like the financial burden*

Circa 1925 – The Band with a young A W Parker.

1925 – The Royal Trophy Band

1926 – The Band pose for this photograph during a break in playing
Note the old delivery van to the right of the picture

it has hitherto been." Although the Band had not been amongst the winners at Crystal Palace it was agreed that its performance had been one of the best in its history.

In his report as Bandmaster, Mr Parker said membership stood at 27 plus three learners and that it had been a good year but fell a bit short of 1925 in terms of contest results. *"No stone will be left unturned to try and bring back the Royal Trophy next August."* The instruments were said to be sound and in good condition but several players needed new uniforms.

William Floyd conducted Four Lanes Brass Band where his three sons started their playing careers before transferring to Redruth and then to Camborne circa 1928 when there was a waiting list to join. Jack Floyd (cornet) was the eldest but when his brother, Gordon, died in 1933, he felt unable to continue playing. Gordon was only 23 when he died; he was an outstanding euphonium player and the conductor of Gweek Brass Band. Camborne Town Band led the walking funeral from his home to Pencoy Church. The third brother, Edgar, went on to make a considerable impact on the brass band movement in Cornwall and there is more about him later in the book. W Blackeney (euphonium), John Major (percussion) and W Pearce (cornet) also played in the early Band.

J P (Jack) Trounce was born with no left forearm and with only one finger and a thumb where his elbow should have been. Despite this incapacity, and the fact that he was a very shy person who hated being in the limelight, he developed into one of the finest cornet players in the country. His brother "Joe," who was 14 years older, bought him his first cornet – the instrument which he could most easily hold. Jack joined Camborne Town in 1930 and held the position of Principal Cornet for approximately 17 years. He entered the *Daily Herald All-Britain Solo Championship* (Cornet Section) in 1946 and was placed first in the qualifying contest and seventh in the national final at Belle Vue.

He featured in an advertisement for Besson instruments under the heading *Leading Cornet Soloists of today*. Harry Mortimer tried to persuade him to join one of the top bands – Black Dyke or Munn & Feltons - but he didn't want to leave Camborne. In his final years as a player he was plagued by teeth troubles. He tried to overcome the problem by filling the odd gap with the compound Gutta-

Percha which would set and remain in place for an hour or so but this was no long-term solution and he gave up playing in 1957.

Adrian King (cornet) once asked Jack how he developed such a fine tonguing technique and he told him Johnnie Bawden had him spitting out peas and then transferring the skill to his playing.

Some players from the early years: George Henry (cornet - seems to have joined circa 1931) / G Loze / S Rowe (cornet - seems to have joined circa 1929) / D Semmens / A Thomas (trombone - seems to have joined circa 1928) / Joseph Arthur Williams (bass trombone - was a Camborne man who probably played in the 1920s).

1931
The Uren Brothers: Fred, William J, Richard B and Harry.

1934 - Camborne Town Band Quartet - Willie Harris (cornet), Edgar Floyd (horn), Walter Pryor (baritone) and Roy Cruze – all from Four Lanes

1936 – Camborne Town Band moved into a new purpose-built bandroom.

The "old Bandroom" 1936 to 2005 - built by Olley Ruse.

A former bandroom was located in Wesley Street, in an old, two-storey barn belonging to Harry Jory but this became a bit shaky and unsafe and it was necessary to move.

Tom Ruse recalled practising in Holman's small canteen near No. 1 works (now at the rear of Tesco's) and as he started playing in 1936, it seems likely this was in use immediately prior to the move to the premises behind the Community Centre. It may even have been a temporary arrangement pending completion of the new building. Tom also remembered the Band using a room over an electrical store near Commercial Square. This was before he started playing, possibly circa 1930.

George Oliver (Olley) Ruse played tenor horn and baritone from the late 1920s to 1947. He started his playing career at Hayle where he had lived before moving to Camborne. His son, Tom Ruse, was born in 1925 and his first period of membership was from 1936 to 1943, when he left to serve in the RAF. Tom played at his first contest in 1939, at Bugle when, "*We won the Royal Trophy*".

The Band was short of a euphonium player for the National Championship at the Albert Hall Contest in 1946 and Mr Parker asked Olley Ruse if Tom would be available. Tom was fortunate to have an enthusiastic Commanding Officer who was happy to shuffle his duties and provide the neces-

During the 1930s with a host of cups

1936 West of England Champions
Back row: C Dower, G O Ruse, A K Williams, C V Williams, F Skinner, S Keen, L Wills, A J Tresidder, W A Trounce, E Yeoman, J Berryman and H Eddy.
Front row: T Rule, J C Nicholas, J P Trounce, J Volante, J Curnow, D Chinn (soprano), R Lugg, A W Parker (Musical Director), L Bussey, E Floyd, H Pascoe, J P Mooney, W J Nancarrow, T H Gilbert and A Tresidder.
(photo by W J Bennetts & Son, Camborne)

Ernie Yeoman

Alfred Tresidder

sary leave to enable him to take his place as second euphonium. He recalled the contest stage layout as, *"very open"* and quite unlike the preferred compact formation. *"It took a bit of getting used to but we quickly adapted and felt that we played very well. It seems the adjudicators thought so as well and we were delighted when Idris Stone caught up with us at Paddington Station and told us we were sixth."*

When he left the forces in August 1947 he re-joined the Band and played until 1955 - mostly on first baritone. For a short period during his time in the services he played in the RAF Radio School

1939 in what became known as the Lion Tamer's uniform
Back row: Telfer Rule (soprano and Bandmaster), Johnnie Bawden, Jervis Curnow, Archie Hancock, Kenny Williams, Joe Volante. Basses - Sid Keen, Fred Skinner, Leonard Wills, Alfie John Tresidder, Trombones - Toe Trounce, Ernie Yeoman and Jack Berryman.
Front row: Sammy Roberts (Principal Cornet), Jackie Trounce, Gordon Nicholas (cornet - played during the 1920s-1930s and maybe later), Idris Stone, Leonard Bussey, Glen Loze, Eddie Williams, Olley Ruse (second baritone), Tom Ruse (first baritone), Ronnie Lugg and Henry Gilbert (solo euph - commenced playing in 1936 and continued on into Freddie Robert's era).
Alfie Tresidder (Bass Drum), Harry Eddy (Side drum). A W Parker (Musical Director)
(Photo by W J Bennetts & Sons of Camborne)

Unit Band but said he only volunteered to get out of fire watching!

Tom said, *"I took part in some of the Gala Evening Mass Band concerts following the Contest and was thrilled to play under Sir Malcolm Sargeant. Playing was a lot of fun, we got up to a bit of mischief but it was nothing malicious. I recall playing under Harry Mortimer and during a rehearsal in the bandroom I played a wrong note. It was a bit embarrassing but he just looked across at me and smiled."*

Many national and local bands closed for the duration of the Second World War when the movement suffered from the loss of players – sadly many never returned.

Summer 1939 – Fourteen year-old Tom Ruse playing solo baritone

1945 – Placed first in the National Brass Band Championship of Great Britain (Second Section).

1946 – Placed sixth in the National Brass Band Championship of Great Britain (Championship Section).

In January 1946 the *Musical Progress and Mail,* which had then been publishing for 100 years, reflected on the turmoil of the Second World War and its affect on brass banding. It took a positive line and wrote of the resurgence of the movement in 1945 saying, *"Contesting has been given a fillip by the action of a national daily paper on the basis of a local-cum-national festival. The new National Championship at the Royal Albert Hall".* It also bemoaned the continuation of conscription saying it was, *"a constant leakage of young fellows between the ages of 18 and 19 from our bands, lads who have become very useful bandsmen during the war years".* It seems there was a Ladies Band Association and a letter from a Miss O'Connell said that it

A W Parker receiving a cup - early 1940s

was hoped to organise a series of contests in connection with the women's movement. I'm not sure if this ever came to be as it was not long before ladies were accepted into what had been male bastions. From what I gather, it may have taken a little longer in Camborne than elsewhere!

A letter in the correspondence section of the same publication discusses the merits and demerits of high and low pitch for brass bands – apparently various bands had claimed the distinction of being the first to adopt low-pitch – initially, no doubt, by the use of conversion kits with their associated tuning problems. The kits consisted of short lengths of tubing placed on the tuning slides to lower the pitch by a semi-tone.

Under the heading of *Bands on the Air* it was reported that Camborne Town had broadcast on West Country Bandstand on two occasions in November 1945.

A Boosey & Hawkes advertisement on the back page of the *Musical Progress and Mail* of 1946 provides a full price list for all sorts of instruments. A Hawkes Excelsior Bb cornet and case would set you back £18 while the best quality euphonium was £28.10.0 (£28.50p). A trombone was £18.18.0 and a Besson B flat bass was £39.10.0. According to my calculations a set of 25 instruments, excluding percussion, would have cost about £570 plus carriage.

Fred Waters recalled the rising fortunes through the 1940s and said, *"Unlike most top bands, we did not lose players to the war – most working at Holman's in reserved occupations.*

On one occasion Mr Parker must have felt that some of the players were not paying sufficient attention to his beat and he looked at Johnnie Bawden and said, "*You must keep your eyes on me Johnnie"*.

The bandroom is a wonderful place for repartee, and spontaneous ripostes will often cause great hilarity. On this occasion Johnnie, using his broadest mid-Atlantic drawl, came back with,

"Well, you ain't no oil painting are you Mr Parker?" I have no idea of Mr Parker's response but I fondly think it may have been a chuckle.

1945 - Holders of the Prince of Wales Trophy, Winners of the Daily Herald Western Area Championship and winners of the Daily Herald Championship of Great Britain (2nd Section)
Standing: T Rule, J P Trounce, J G Nicholas, J C Harris, W Oliver, O G Rihlman, C Dower, Charlie Osborne (presented with a long-service certificate from the Cornwall Brass Band Association), R Tresidder, A Tresidder, P Stevens, J Bawden, J A Hancock, J Volante, C A Hancock, W A Trounce, W E Yeoman, J Berryman and A W Parker (Musical Director).
Seated: S A E Keen, F C Skinner, A J Tresidder, R C Toy, J F Weeks, G O Ruse, W Uglow (Chairman), A E Old (President), R B Britton (Treasurer), E Floyd, E P Cock, J D Cock, J E G Fletcher, S Oliver and T H Gilbert.
(Photo by W J Bennetts & Sons of Camborne)

The Band of 1948

Celebrating another win – with a "cup tea".

1949

Back row: A Tresidder, K Williams, Eddie Williams, W A (Joe) Trounce, Ernie Yeoman, Jack Berryman, Edgar Floyd, J J Rule, Dick Tresidder.
Middle row: Sidney Keen, A J Tresidder, Stanley Oliver, Tom Ruse, Donald Cock, R J Thomas, L Wills, F. C. Skinner (bass - played in the Junior Band of the 1920s and then in the Senior Band up to about 1960).
Front row: Jack Trounce, Clifford Harris, Willy Oliver, Idris Stone, Johnnie Bawden (Bandmaster), A W Parker (Musical Director), Sam Roberts, T Jory, Charlie Dower, Archie Hancock.
(Photo by W J Bennetts & Son of Camborne)

Gerald Fletcher (baritone and euphonium) learnt to play in Camborne Salvation Army and joined Camborne Town Band in 1946. Apart from his absence for National Service he played until 1962 when he moved to India to help set up a factory for Holman's. He returned after three years and occasionally helped with concerts and contests. He recalled the difficulty he had combining home practice and bringing up a young family. Rather than disturb the youngsters he went to the bandroom at 7.00am each day for an hour's practise before starting work.

Percy and Donald Cock were Gerald's cousins. Percy (horn) played from 1946 for about six or seven years and Donald (baritone), from 1946 for about 10 to 12 years until he went to work in South Africa. Donald joined again in the mid 1970s (bass trombone) and played until 1985. Nigel Cock (solo cornet & euphonium) was Donald's son and played from the mid 1970s to the early 1980s when he joined the Metropolitan Police.

Percy Thomas (horn), Garfield Thomas (horn) and Jim Thomas (euphonium) were all uncles of Gerald Fletcher and played in the years immediately prior to the Second World War.

Leslie Fletcher (Gerald Fletcher's father) was Secretary from the early 1950s to the late 1960s and Jim Chappel, his brother-in-law, was Entertainment Secretary for about the same period. They were involved in bringing the National Band of New Zealand to Camborne in the 1960s.

David Saunders, a life-long supporter, recalled that a fishing boat was run down off Porthleven in 1948 and two brothers from the Richards family were killed. Camborne Town Band gave a concert in Bertram Mills Circus tent in Rodda's Field (where the fire station now stands) and the proceeds went to the families of the deceased. He recalled the emotion when the Band played a part of the piece *Sailor's Life*. Gerald Fletcher said, *"The concert was the finest of that era. My first time on stage at the Royal Albert Hall was tremendous but that concert was the most emotional. We finished with the William Tell overture and I've never known such a reaction from an audience."*

David Saunders joined the committee in 1946 for a few years and then again in 1970. He was very ill at one stage and was proud to be made a life member. He joked, *"They only did it because they thought I was going to die".*

At one of the Area Championship at Exeter during the late 1940s/early 1950s Camborne took part in the evening concert. Mr Parker decided to put on a fresh shirt and enlisted the help of Dick Tresidder (bass drum). Unfortunately Dick had not washed his hands since he had rolled tobacco for his pipe and the replacement shirt ended up dirtier than the one it was replacing.

1949 – Hat-trick of wins at Bugle Contest.

1950 – Hat-trick of wins at the Area Championship.

1951 – Mr A W Parker died.

In the autumn of 1951 the players and committee members mourned the passing of a great man. Mr A W Parker had succumbed to his illness and the stability of the last 25 years had come to an end. Within a short period a former player was at the helm; Mr F J Roberts began his period as Musical Director which was to last almost 20 years.

1951 – Mr F J Roberts appointed Musical Director.

1951 – Placed sixth in the National Brass Band Championship of Great Britain (Championship Section).

Johnnie Bawden played at Camborne from 1896 to 1906 and again from 1935 to 1953. He toured the World with the famous Besses o' th' Barn Band 1906-1908.

1950s - Jack Trounce, Roy Cock (percussionist) and Donald Cock.
Roy was a good xylophone player in the 1950s, before he moved to Canada.

Toni Volante joined in 1951, aged 14, just after the Band achieved one of their best results at the National Final. He played bass trombone for about eight years and remembered Freddie Roberts as, *"A very strict Musical Director. The playing was very intensive with lots of engagements and contest work taken very seriously."* Toni's grandfather was Joe Volante (horn) who had played many years previously. Toni had private lessons from Joe Trounce whose bass trombone role he later took over. He was Treasurer for one year and admits that he had no idea how much work was involved and how much trouble he would have in balancing the books.

1952 – Double hat-trick of wins at Bugle Contest.

Monica Orchard (now Dean) started cornet lessons with Fred Roberts in 1952 at the age of nine. She's not really sure if it was her intention to join a brass band but in 1954 she did so. Her father, David Orchard, had been Band Chairman for some time – probably from the 1940s – and held the post until circa 1960.

She played in Cornwall Youth Brass Band from the mid 1950s and attended the first residential course, with Dr Dennis Wright, held under canvas at Pentewan, St Austell, in 1959. She also joined the National Youth Brass Band of Great Britain – and was there at the same time as Desmond Burley, Reg Bennetts and Roy Wearne - but was aware that Mr Roberts was not really in favour of them becoming members.

Monica was the first female player at Camborne and her presence caused some concern at first. This was no reflection on her, she simply became a female entering into this male gathering. The players had to agree to moderate their language in the bandroom. A vote was taken before she was allowed to travel with them on the coach and even then, she had to sit at the front while some of the older and more vociferous members sat at the back and tried to refrain from swearing but she said, "*They often forgot*". The reaction to the same situation at St Agnes, albeit a few years earlier, was that the bandroom was no place for a girl but, as with Camborne, common sense prevailed. She recalled playing in a number of solo contests and gaining a first place at the St Austell Music Festival in 1955 and, a bit nearer to home, in the Cornwall Brass Band Association contest held at Holman's in 1957 where, *"I think I played Schubert's Serenade; Mr Roberts was keen on that"*.

She said tea-treats were enjoyable; at places like Troon and Townshend and, *"I remember the BBC recordings at Camborne Wesley when Mr Roberts had to use a stop-watch to make sure the times fitted in with the required schedule"*.

One of her funniest memories was accepting a lift from Dennis Bennett and Mary Allen (cornet), in their Isetta Bubble-car, to an engagement at St Ives. Dennis (bass and trombone) had previously played in the Band of the Coldstream Guards. With three of them and two cornets in this tiny car (luckily the trombone went on the coach) they made their way to the engagement never really sure if they were going to make it up the hills.

Fred Roberts liked the piece of music *Three Blind Mice;* the Band had played it on a broadcast and he often tried to include it in a concert. It was not so popular with the E flat bass players as it included a rather difficult cadenza for them. Barry Tresidder and Toni Volante were librarian and assistant librarian and no matter how much Freddie asked for the music, they couldn't seem to find it.

1954 – Double hat-trick of wins at the Area Championship.

It was no surprise that Jack Pascoe (flugel) took up music as his father had also played in a brass band and when Jack started, it was with St Stythians. He played with them at Belle Vue in 1951, at King's Hall, in a boxing ring. He recalled Mr A W Parker spending some time helping them prepare for the contest. Jack joined Camborne in 1954, when invited by Telfer Rule. He played in the National Final on 13 occasions and particularly remembered the test piece *Freedom* when Eric Ball thanked them for playing the last movement as a scherzo and not a march. He recalled Derek Johnston being a stickler on tuning and said he thoroughly enjoyed playing under Derek Greenwood, *"It was with him that we had our best results in the National Final. I remember him on stage wearing a uniform with no coat pockets; he had nowhere to keep his cigarettes and matches and he looked lost without them. We all loved contesting and I remember one April in the 1970s when we practised nearly every day for one contest or the other."*

I'd been primed to ask Jack about the name of his house and, with a smile, he told me it was *Aspera.* Apparently he couldn't think of a name so he took it from the Italian manufacturer of his lawn-mower engine.

Jack was with Camborne for 28 years and when he left, in 1983, he had a short break before taking up the baton and conducting Wendron Band for 22 years. He only recently relinquished this role and said, *"I enjoyed that period and saw it as putting something back for all the pleasure I'd derived from my playing days"*. He recalled with pride his medal from the Cornwall Brass Band Association for 50 years service to the movement.

Toni Volante recalled that the Duke of Cornwall's Light Infantry wanted to take over Camborne Town Band during the 1950s. He said, *"I was all in favour as I could see we would be better off financially and could have whatever instruments and uniforms we needed. There was a vote taken and many of the older players had had enough of being involved with officialdom and didn't want to sign up to it so the idea was rejected."*

Stanley Pope commenced his playing career in 1943, at the age of 14. He played bass for Carharrack & St Day and has wonderful memories of playing at Stenalees Contest in his late teens. After completing his military service he played for Truro City Band and in 1955 he moved to Camborne Town Band (bass). He said, *"I didn't stick it there for very long, I had to walk from Nine Maidens and in the winter that was no joke"*. He moved back to Truro City for a while but is now involved with Camborne again, *"Carrying the collector's bucket for the Youth Band."* He seems to be a collector extraordinaire and the takings are always lower when he isn't there. He also helps his son, Alan, on occasions with, *"A bit of training with the basses"*. He said, *"I remember an occasion in 1946, when Camborne was playing in a field near the Seven Stars Pub at Carharrack. Mr Parker was con-*

A pause for a photo:

Faces from the left: Fred Skinner, Tom Ruse, A Tresidder, Leonard Wills, Ken-Williams, Jack Trounce (seated), Donald Cock, Ernie Yeoman, Jack Berry-man, Stanley Oliver and Idris Stone.

The bass section:

Sid Keen, Fred Skinner, Leonard Wills and Alfie John Tresidder (Invariably referred to as Alfie John)

(photo by Randall & Hosking, Camborne.)

ducting 'Deep Harmony'. I'd never known a standing ovation at the end of a hymn but the playing was so wonderful, everyone stood up."

Christmas was always a busy time as the Band contributed to the festive mood of the community. The staff and patients of Tehidy Sanatorium appreciated its visits to play carols and the younger players were made really welcome when they made additional visits as they travelled the district. Some of the young players of that era have said their visits were not without some trepidation as they recalled the fear surrounding tuberculosis. From a mercenary point of view, this was also a good time to bolster the funds and any money collected would help finance appearances at far-away contest venues. In the town, a stage was erected in Commercial Square for carol playing.

Eddie Ashton recalled an occasion when rehearsing for Bugle Contest. *"Freddie Roberts noticed that one of the cornet players was using a trumpet mouthpiece; he told him to get it changed before the next practice. When we met again Freddie noticed he was still using the same mouthpiece and he was out."*

1953 - Treve Jory was a state trumpeter and played at the Coronation of Queen Elizabeth II.

Monica Orchard – the first female member of Camborne Town Band.

1958 – Triple hat-trick of wins at the Area Championship.

Some players from the 1950s/1960s: Jack Collins (percussion - he didn't play for long and seemed more interested in dance and orchestral music) / Barry Davis (bass - joined in the mid 1960s from Helston for two or three years and left due to work pressures) / Leonard Dunstan (tenor horn - played in the All-Star Brass Band) / John *"Smiler"* Floyd (tenor horn) / Henry Freeman (horn - joined from Morris Motors, for about one year, in the mid 1950s) / Raymond Haley (cornet - played in the early 1950s and is said to have had a lovely tone) / Ralph Kenward (cornet) / Morley Knight (second trombone) / Eric Richards (baritone - joined from Carharrack & St Day and left in January 1965. He was a publican) / Eric Richards (euphonium) / Owen Richards (bass trombone – brother to Eric - moved to Australia) / Jeff Smith (horn - played for about one year before returning north to play with Crossley Carpets) / Robin Thomas / Stanley Truan (cornet – ex Salvation Army) / Ken Williams (horn - part time during the 1950s).

In Easter 1960 Fred Roberts took up a two-week appointment tutoring a brass band in Dun Laoghaire, near Dublin. The minute book states,*" The Executive Committee wish Mr Roberts to be aware of its pleasure on the appointment. We consider the recognition as a compliment to him and to Camborne Town Band and wish him to know he goes with our full blessing."*

The Camborne Salvation Army had a full band and would often play in the Square and then march down to the citadel for a service. A number of its players later played with the Town Band.

Paul Bourdeaux (E flat bass) cycled to practice from Praze-an-Beeble with the bass strapped to his back. He later became the headmaster of St Merryn School. Idris Stone drove a blue Austin "7" which he nicknamed the *Blue Flash* and Paul drove a silver one which he called the *Silver Bullet.*

Mid 1950s
The bass section

Reg Toy
Paul Bourdeaux
Barry Tresidder
Eric Thomas

(Photo by Henry Parkinson)

Having previously played at Gweek Silver under Tom Chainey, Desmond Burley was invited by Freddie Roberts to join Camborne. He played from 1957 to 1972, mostly cornet, and remembered Freddie Roberts as a good conductor, well respected as a musician but a very hard man to play under.

From time to time small groups of players teamed up to play together – usually as quartets. One such group in the 1950s comprised youngsters Toni Volante (bass trombone), Fred Waters (tenor trombone), John Roberts (horn) and John Berryman (cornet). It was an extremely good quartet with three of them playing in the National Youth Brass Band of Great Britain – according to Toni they were the first from the South-West to do so. Fred Waters had chosen to go down an academic route otherwise John Berryman is sure he would have also been a member. He joined Camborne in 1948 under A W Parker and continued to play until his studies forced him to resign in 1955. Fred said, *"In addition to being a good trainer Freddie Roberts was keen to foster the younger members and under his direction the Camborne Town Band Junior Quartet was formed. He turned this quartet into an unbeatable combination and within a year we were the West of England junior and under 18 champions. I even remember going to one solo and quartet contest at Bodmin where the Band had also entered a senior quartet. We had entered the Open Class in addition to the under 16 and under 18 Classes. As the senior group entered the stage their solo cornet, Jacky Trounce – the Band's Principal Cornet - was heard to say, 'What happens if they boys beat us!' Fortunately for them we didn't – we only came second beating senior quartets from St Dennis and Falmouth! We also broadcast with the Band on BBC's Bandstand as well as giving charity concerts with Ben Luxon – the international singer."*

My own period of playing was from 1954 to 1971 when St Agnes Band was in the ascendancy. During the latter stages of that period we played in the top section but that was very much on a local basis, as even the most optimistic amongst us would not have suggested we could hold a candle to Camborne. Having said that, we did have a couple of memorable results which St Dennis Band may wish to forget. I played first baritone and learnt only recently, from Toni Volante, that it was referred to as the *"bastard instrument"*. I understand this was to do with the fact that its music took it around the band to play with every section rather than anything to do with me personally. Tom Ruse

1954/1955 The three players holding on to their hats are Barry Tresidder, Derek Kemp (cornet) & Toni Volante.

Jack and John Berryman
father and son

Circa 1955 at Gladys Holman House.
Back row: T Rule (Bandmaster), C Harris, J Pascoe, S Truan, A King, D Kemp, A Hancock, E Thomas, F Skinner, L Wills, B Tresidder, T Volante, R Toy, J Berryman Snr and J Collins.
Middle row: J Berryman Jnr, J Trounce, W Oliver, I Stone, R Thomas (horn), A Toy, J Smith, E Pearce, G Weeks, A Oliver, G Fletcher and R Tresidder.
Seated: W Head (Secretary), J T Holman (President), F J Roberts (Musical Director) and W A Trounce (Youth Tutor).
(Photo by W J Bennetts & Sons, Camborne)

said he'd never heard it called that but when he told Derek Greenwood he played baritone Derek said, "*Oh yes, in the euphonium graveyard!*"

Reg Bennett started learning to play the cornet in 1958, under Freddie Roberts. He recalled, *"There were many occasions when I went home in tears. On one occasion I awoke from a nightmare at 4.00am in the morning; it had involved a music lesson with Mr Roberts. My mother decided to ring Fred and the conversation went something like:*

'Is that Mr Roberts?'
'Yes'

Circa 1960 - Young players from Cornwall who had qualified for membership of the National Youth Brass Band of Great Britain.
Malcolm Yelland (St Dennis), Roy Wearne (CTB), Desmond Burley (CTB), Andre Heluer (St Austell), Paul Hiley, Dickie Dale (Bodmin), Phil Harris (Bodmin), Mr Trudgian, unknown, Reg Bennett (CTB), Monica Dean (née Orchard of CTB) and unknown.

'Well Reg has just had a nightmare about you and now I can't sleep so I thought, why should you?'"

In fairness to Freddie Roberts, I could tell many a similar story about my music lessons at St Agnes under Frank Moore.

Bill Johnson (bass) from Blackwater played with most bands in the area. He always kept his trilby hat on and in his wardrobe were to be found the uniforms of a number of bands for whom he played and it was not unknown for him to turn up for an engagement wearing the wrong one.

Reg Bennett played until just after the London Final in 1965. He recalled his proud parents taking a photograph of him as he marched through Camborne. Fred Roberts caught sight of the resultant prints and immediately turned on Reg and said, *"There you are, just what I've been telling you, you don't hold your instrument high enough".*

Reg had been playing for about a year, and was about 16 years old, when the players were travelling to a contest by coach. He was sitting behind the driver and it seems he fell asleep and was having a nightmare. He said, *"The coach driver, Freddie Tremain, was kidnapping Barbara, my sister, and when I awoke I was grabbing him around the throat – while the coach was moving".*

Warren Bennett, Reg's son, also played with Camborne for about a year in the mid 1990s; he'd learnt under Albert Chappell and had also played with Redruth Band.

Early 1960s - Fred Roberts conducting.

Fred Roberts with the Band in the early 1960s - on his left is Ken Haynes

Reg spent many years working for the Band and was elected Chairman of the Society in the late 1990s and, with the exception of one year when Roy Kelynack - a long-serving member of the committee - took over, held the post to 2005.

David Bray started playing at the age of 14 and joined the Senior Band in about 1962, when Freddie Roberts was conducting. David said, *"You were not considered a full member until you'd played at a contest and in 1964, at The Royal Albert Hall, I achieved that distinction"*. David played until 1975 when he finished after playing at Bugle under Bernard Bygrave. He remembered Derek Johnston's period as Musical Director with much pleasure," *Coming after Freddie Roberts, Derek was a complete contrast and would even join us in playing football before practice. He used to refer to us as World Champions and although that may have been an exaggeration, he somehow managed to make us feel we were."*

I remember attending a concert by the New Zealand National Band during the early 1960s. It was arranged by Camborne Town Band and held at the Recreation Ground. It featured a marching display but the highlight for me was their performance of *Rhapsody in Brass* by Dean Goffin. Reg Bennett hosted two of the players, Gill Evans and Trevor Bremner, and is still in contact with them. Trevor went on to become the World Champion cornet player.

David Reed (cornet) played in the Junior Class under Telfer Rule and Clifford Bolitho before graduating into the Senior Band in 1963. He left in 1979, after Yeovil Contest, but joined again in 1989 for a couple of years when Stephen Sykes was Musical Director. He said, *"My best memory was probably in 1965 when Camborne came sixth in the National Final and beat Black Dyke but winning the Royal Trophy and playing in the Square at Bugle takes a lot of beating. I think our best performance while I was playing was at the Area Contest in 1977 when we played 'Pageantry'."*

Barbara Yeoman recalled the early 1960s as a busy time for fund-raising. *"We were never flush with money and every penny was valuable whether it was from the playing efforts or from events organised by the committee. But there was also the day-to-day activity and I remember helping Secretary Desmond Mitchell with typing and keeping the membership forms up to date."*

Russell Kellow (bass) began playing in 1964, when Fred Roberts was Musical Director. He left in 1971 and has since played with St Erth, Porthleven, Penzance Silver and the Camborne "B" Band. His daughter, Vicki Kellow, currently plays in the Senior Band.

1965

Back row: Peter Tresidder (baritone/bass - took over from Barry Davis and played for a while under Derek Johnston), Edwin Willcocks (euphonium/baritone - joined from Helston Band and played until the 1980s), Bill Horton, Frank Woods (euphonium - moved down when his employers transferred to Cornwall in the 1960s), George Ansell, Gerald Weeks, John Collins, Russell Kellow, Malcolm Quintrell (baritone – famous for trying to stop an electric fan with his finger), Owen Richards, Douglas Piper, Edward Ashton and Freddie Roberts.
Front row: Desmond Burley, Monty Ray, David Parsons, Robert Rennard, unknown, Alan Toy, Dennis Treloar, John Morrisey, David Bray, Clyde Keverne (cornet – played for about five years in the 1960s), Jack Pascoe and David Reed.

Mid 1960s

Back row cornets: Desmond Burley, Robert Rennard, Jack Pascoe, Malcolm Quintrell.
Inner semi-circle: Monty Ray, Idris Stone, Reg Bennett, Clifford Harris, Alan Toy, John Floyd, Dennis Treloar, David Bray, David Reed and Clyde Keverne.
Baritones/Euphoniums: Edwin Willcocks, unknown, Frank Woods and Roderick Facey.
Basses: Peter Richards, Gerald Weeks, David Boase and Alfie John Tresidder.
Trombones: Owen Richards, Doug Piper and Eddie Ashton.
Standing: Fred Roberts, Dick Tresidder and Mervyn Charleston.

In June 1964 the condition of the bandroom was causing concern. Gerald Fletcher prepared a report on the state of the roof and a number of committee members were enlisted to undertake the re-decoration of the building. At a subsequent meeting Messrs Fletcher, Weeks, Laity and others were thanked and told that their efforts meant the cost was six pounds and a few shillings instead of about £120.

During the early to mid 1960s, and maybe longer, the Band experienced the twin problems of a lack of players and money. To the other bands in Cornwall, Camborne Town Band was an institution and I'm now surprised to find it suffered the same problems that bedevilled lesser bands. Fred Roberts talked of players being needed otherwise, *"The Band would be in deep water"* and his firm view was that the Junior Band should be a feeder band. That seems a reasonable strategy although it could be argued that as long as the youngsters played somewhere then they could infill behind experienced players who *"gravitated upwards"* to Camborne Town Band.

1965 – Placed sixth in the National Brass Band Championship of Great Britain (Championship Section).

George Ansell (bass) joined on New Year's Day in 1966 and played for 11 years. He learnt to play with Kimbolton Comrades Silver before joining the armed forces and playing with the 9th Queen's Royal Lancers. While he was in the Army he met Peter Richards who re-joined Camborne on completion of his National Service and then mentioned a vacancy in the bass section when he bumped into George at the National Championship in 1965. George recalled, *"I came down on New Year's Day 1966 and Monty Ray met me at the station. He took me to meet Mr Roberts at Holman's on the 1st January - it wasn't a Bank Holiday in those days. Peter had vouched for my playing and I was in. The Band found me some lodgings and a job and I moved to Cornwall."* It seems George must have liked the place as he married a Cornish girl, learnt the language and was made a Bard in 1978 taking the Bardic name Caradok (amiable). In 1991 he became the Grand Bard of Cornwall, a post he held until 1994.

Idris Stone (cornet) resigned in late 1967 due to health problems and Fred Roberts expressed his regret and said, "After so many faithful years of service this was a big blow" (I'm sure no pun was intended).

(Photo by W J Bennetts & Son of Camborne)

In the late 1960s new uniforms were required and an appeal was made to local businesses and townspeople for financial support. One particular anonymous gift was very welcome and was to be used, principally, for buying new uniforms. An order was placed in March 1967 and it was hoped they would be available for the forthcoming Area Contest but it seemed doubtful as, *"Only 21 bandsmen had succumbed to measurement"*.

Income from carol playing seems to have been very low around the late 1960s and fund-raising was becoming a priority.

During a rehearsal, Dennis (Jim) Treloar (bass) lost one of his valve caps. It hit the floor and carried on rolling and in a desperate attempt to retrieve it he put his instrument down, went on his hands and knees, and crawled after it. As it continued to roll he followed it and Jack Pascoe said, *"The music stands were falling like dominos, it was like a dog chasing a rabbit. The players thought it hilarious but Fred Roberts was not so amused.*" A short while later Jim was moved to the cornet rank and then to the trombone section. He was told it was a good idea to practise in front of a mirror but he clearly misjudged the length of the slide and that was the end of the wardrobe mirror.

While rehearsing a piece of music involving the tubular bells, Mervyn Charleston was told to, "*Hit them harder"*. Mervyn obliged but the head of the hammer flew off and struck one of the bass players in the back of the neck. Once again, it seems, the players found it funnier than Freddie Roberts.

On another occasion they were rehearsing the *Blue Danube* Waltz and the Davids, Bray and Reed, had a few bars rest and started to hum the tune. Freddie stopped the Band and said, *"I hope you two can play it better than you can sing it"*.

Roy Nancarrow's introduction to Camborne Town Band came in 1968 when Stanley Pope invited him along to the practice room and then to the Area Championship. His first job was shaking the box (collecting) at a rugby match and he was soon invited to join the committee. Since then he has held a number of posts and has been a prodigious worker. Born at Carn Marth, his family moved to Frogpool when he was two years old. He reckons he became hooked on brass bands at a very young age, when his father walked him from his home to Frogpool to attend a concert. Roy's wife, Dorothy, was a daughter of Jack Floyd and a niece of Edgar and Gordon Floyd who all played at Camborne.

Robert Cook (tenor horn) and Barrie Trevena (cornet) commenced playing at Carharrack & St Day Band. Barrie recalled the new Besson cornet which his parents bought him, *"They were not very amused when I dropped it the first time I took it to practice. I recall Leonard Adams telling me I would be daft if I went to Camborne but Robert and I decided that was where our future lay and we made the move in December 1968. Leonard wasn't very pleased but, despite that, it was only about a year before he followed us"*.

Barrie and Robert joined Peter James (ex St Erth Band) and John Morrisey on cornet but Robert soon moved along the line to soprano. He said, "*It wasn't really my instrument and I transferred to tenor horn in March 1970 joining Alan Toy, David Bray and Ian Facey"*. When Alan left in 1975, Robert took over the solo position. Barrie Trevena stayed on cornet and during his period at College in 1975-6 he played with the City of Bristol Band and when he returned home he played at Helston Town. Ian Facey also moved from Carharrack & St Day and played at Camborne until the 1980s.

Barrie recalled carol playing at Tehidy hospital and afterwards having a game of snooker when, *"Dougie Piper had us in stitches by moving the balls around, unbeknown to Monty Ray who tended to take the game a bit seriously"*.

At the AGM in April 1970 Mrs M J Morrissey reported, *"The Five Women Committee members had given the Band £100"*. Mr Eric Townsend was elected President, the Revd Basil Brown - Chairman, Mr A J Earnshaw - Vice-Chairman, Mr Roger Johnson - Secretary and Mr F J Roberts – Musical Director,

Michael Seymour learned and played at Camborne. He left in the mid 1970s but his father, Bob Seymour, stayed and served on the committee for many years. Bob had a continuing interest and was asked to join the committee and become Secretary. He received the usual story of it being only a small commitment with one meeting per month and a few letters to write and did not seem at all embarrassed when he told me he'd believed it. He served on the committee for 23 years (left in 2000), as Secretary for most of that time. With Mrs Sylvia Morcom (Treasurer) he was very involved in registering the organisation with the Registrar of Friendly Societies in 1974 and in building the new constitution for the *Camborne Town Band Music Society*. His biggest disappointment was in not obtaining a Lottery Grant for new premises in the 1990s.

One of the Secretary's jobs was to arrange transport and he recalled a particular coach journey to the Regional Championship at Bristol. The coach had been parked at Four Lanes and it had snowed overnight – in April! The snow had built up under the roof ventilators and as it thawed it began to drip on to one seat – that of Mrs Reg Toy. Unfortunately Bob was unable to move her to another seat because the coach was full.

Freddie Tremain drove for Grenville Motors and tended to drive a bit fast for some people's liking. Courtney Berryman was not a good traveller and moved to the front of the bus where he sat on the engine casing. Ronnie Weeks shouted, *"If you don't slow down Freddie, those bloody pistons are going to come up through Courtney's Ass".*

At one of the Regional Contests at the Colston Hall, Bristol, Bob Seymour was given charge of the cup in its wooden box when everyone went out to celebrate. Having carefully carried it all evening he suddenly saw a similar cup on the bar being filled with drink. It was only then he realised he'd been guarding the empty box.

When Eddie Ashton left in 1969 Doug Piper was asked to take over as principal trombone. He declined the invitation but Mr Roberts was quite insistent and asked him to play a delicate melody at practice night. Doug promptly played it in George Chisholm style which left Fred Roberts seething. Doug's response was, *"Well I told you so, let's go and get a bag of chips Barry (Clift)".*

John Phillips lives at 18 Enys Road; the house where Mr A W Parker once lived. He remembered his grandfather having a variety of instruments, in particular, a B flat instrument like a small euphonium which they nicknamed the *bump-de-boo.* It was high-pitch and re-tuning it to low-pitch was never easy when John started learning at North Parade Chapel in the "B" Band, in the early 1970s. Eric Thomas persuaded him to have a go in the Band when he discovered John had taught himself to play. At that time the "B" Band consisted mostly of youngsters and ex players and was conducted by Keith Rowe. In 1974 the Band competed at Bugle Contest with John playing second euphonium on his ancient *bump-de-boo.* Leonard Adams took the baton and Keith Rowe, the usual conductor, played horn.

Freddie Roberts suggested a transfer to trombone and John bought a Yamaha tenor trombone and set about learning the shifts. At the age of 40, he was a little older than most of the other beginners but he was keen and stuck at it. Training under Freddie Roberts, he soon learnt that music was not just about playing the notes; *he said, " He was not a man to give much praise but he was a brilliant teacher".*

He joined the Senior Band in 1976, just after a 12 hour sponsored blow. Derek Greenwood heard him playing and invited him into the trombone section, then led by David Parsons who seems to have played in most positions. David had joined from Truro City Band and played up until circa 1980. John became librarian, responsible for the storage and issue of music from the extensive library - it then contained 3000 sets of music. When he left Camborne, in 1989, he joined Barry Tresidder and Eric Thomas at Porthleven where he said he was the solo trombone and the sole trombone. After about seven years he joined Hayle where he still plays.

At the player's AGM in April 1970 (not the organisation as a whole) Ian Facey was elected Secretary, Basil (Barry) West - Chairman, Leonard Adams - Public Relations Officer, Monty Ray - Treasurer, Alan Toy - Bandmaster and Peter James and Barrie Trevena - *"assistant drum-kit carriers!"*

A Sponsored Walk in May 1970 raised £120 with Denis Treloar recording the fastest time and Barrie Trevena raising the most sponsorship. Mrs Ray and Miss D James were the first women to finish.

1971 – Mr F J Roberts resigned as Musical Director.

In 1971 Mr F J Roberts tendered his resignation and after a stable period of 20 years, the Band was faced with finding a new Musical Director.

1971 - Alan Toy conducted until a new Musical Director could be appointed.

As part of the process of finding a new Musical Director a Mr O'Connell from St Ives auditioned on the 15th January 1971. The following evening it was the turn of Derek Johnston who Barrie

Trevena remembered as *"quite impressive"*. However, he was not appointed immediately and Mr O'Connell was back for a second session in early February.

1971 – Derek Johnston appointed Musical Director.

In March 1971 an appeal was launched to raise almost £5,000 for a complete set of instruments; some of the old ones dated back to before the First World War and urgently needed replacing. Secretary Ron Kellow described them as, "*Really ropey*". It seems that instruments were being borrowed from other bands which was said to be, *"A sad state of affairs for a Championship Section band"*.

The appeal was successful and a new set of Yamaha instruments was purchased. Under the heading of *"New instruments"* in the Brass Band News of July 1972 Monty Ray, George Ansell, Neil Peters and Derek Johnston Jnr appeared in an advertisement for Yamaha instruments.

A record was made with the intention of promoting the tonal qualities of Yamaha instruments and in the July 1974 edition of Brass Band News, Keith Edwards was very glowing in his opinion of the tone and the playing in general. Alan Toy had a mention for his *"very good playing"* and Neil Peters was said to have made a splendid job of *The Wedding.* The only criticism relates to an unusual aspect, *"In this era of long hair why did you wear hats!"*

Camborne's most famous son was born in April 1771 and on the 10th April 1971 a huge gathering celebrated the 200 years anniversary of his birth. Richard Trevithick was the toast as Camborne Town Band led a procession of 27 steam traction engines and rollers past his memorial statue in front of Camborne Library. His great-grandson, Captain Richard E Trevithick, laid a laurel wreath at the base of the bronze statue with a card which read: *"Richard Trevithick. Inventor of the steam locomotive. Born April 13th 1771."*

Trevithick's success at producing both road and railway locomotives is an achievement of which Camborne and the whole of Cornwall are rightly proud and this event was a fitting tribute to the great man. One of Barrie Bennetts' articles in the *West Briton* was headed, *"Big day for town band"*. It read, *"Not all the admiration from the thousands of spectators who packed Camborne was for the gleaming traction engines. Some was for the smartly uniformed Camborne Town Band, playing in public for the first time under the baton of new musical director, Mr Derek Johnston, who has recently come to Cornwall to take up the position."*

Michael Weeks had previously played in Camborne Salvation Army Band when he joined Camborne Town Band in 1971. He was continuing a family tradition as eight members of his family have played for Camborne Town over the past 70 years or so – mostly in the bass section.

Michael (bass) played from 1971 to 1992 and brothers - Gerald (horn, baritone and bass) from the 1950s to 1983, Ronald (bass) from circa 1983 to circa 1986, Brian (baritone) circa 1955 to circa 1965 and Desmond was mace carrier circa 1972 to circa 1975. His father Thomas Arthur Weeks (bass) played for many years, uncle Fred Weeks (bass) played in A W Parker's time and Michael's son Steven (percussion) played from the 1970s to circa 1990.

Michael also served as Band Chairman for 12 years (1979 to 1990) and as Vice-Chairman of the Camborne Town Band Music Society when he undertook a tremendous amount of work. In 2005 he was elected Chairman of the Society.

In May 1971 a sponsored walk was arranged. I don't have a list of the finishers but I do know George Ansell completed the 20 Kilometre route in three hours and five minutes. His treasured certificate was amongst the programmes he lent me.

In July 1972 Alan Toy knocked on Courtney Berryman's door and asked if he would like to play for Camborne. Courtney's first contest was at the National Final in 1972 for which Derek Johnston held some "secret" rehearsals in a factory near Carn Brea; apparently he didn't want visitors on those occasions. Courtney said, *"I remember it well, it was bloody freezing"*.

Prior to joining Camborne, Courtney played at St Agnes for 21 years before taking a year off. He was at Camborne for eight years after which he played with St Stythians, Bugle and then Lostwithiel where he and his wife, Sue, currently play euphonium. In 2004 he was awarded a long service medal at Bugle Contest in consideration of his fifty plus years as a player.

Mr Harold Stewart was elected President at the annual general meeting in July 1972 and the Revd Basil Brown was re-elected Chairman. Other positions were: Vice-Chairman – Reg Warren, Secretary – Roy Nancarrow, Assistant Secretary – David Saunders, Treasurer – Mrs S M Morcom, Assistant Treasurer – Bill Head and Publicity Officer – M J Smith. Accommodation was high on the agenda and the need for space to accommodate both bands was stressed.

In 1972 John Berryman and Fred Waters, former Camborne players from the 1950s, were concerned at the quality of brass band recordings and decided they would produce some themselves. With the help of Eric Ball, 28 of the country's top players were assembled and became the Virtuosi Brass Band of Great Britain leading to the production of a number of long-playing records (later CDs).

Some players from the 1970s: Barry Clift (bass trom - played with Truro City before joining Camborne) / Glenn Jones (percussion - left to join the Band of the Royal Army Medical Corps) / Graham Mitchell (horn) / Ronald Stephens (cornet). Ian Armstrong was Chairman circa 1970s/1980s and Harold Stewart took the role a little later.

1973 – Placed fifth in the National Brass Band Championship of Great Britain (Championship Section).

1973 – Change of name to the Camborne (CompAir-Holman) Band.

Derek Johnston announced the name change but stressed it would remain a public subscription band and not a sponsored works' band. *"It will still be very much Camborne's town band,"* he said, *"we are simply associating the area's main works with the Band's name. A lot of people have always associated the Band with Holman's because over the years many of the bandsmen have worked there."*

In January 1974 the Camborne-Redruth Packet quoted committee member Ronald Hosking in saying the Band had competed in the National Championship on 18 occasions and had finished in the top half on 12. Ronnie served the Band for many years and became its unofficial historian and when he died in 1980, his colleagues at Holman's purchased a cup – *the Ronnie Hosking Memorial Cup* – and presented it to the Band.

Derek Johnston Jnr

They say it's the memory that goes first! It's amazing the number of stories I've heard about Camborne players forgetting their instruments, their music or even their uniforms. Well I'm sure the problem is not restricted to this Band. I can remember from a young boy of about nine years old up to when I finished playing in my late twenties, obsessively checking that I had my mouthpiece, my music and my clothes-pegs (bandsmen will know that they're for holding the music in place and not for hanging out the clothes). These days it would probably be given a name but then I just thought of it as keeping on the right side of Frank Moore. Anyway, the list of items is spread throughout the book but there was also a forgotten trombone but I was not told by whom or at which contest. (Actually I lie, I was asked not to divulge the name. It just shows that even I can be bought!)

There are many instances of succeeding generations of families playing at Camborne and a glance through the photographs will reveal a number of Urens, Tresidders, Weeks, Collins, Roberts and others. Derek Johnson introduced his sons Derek on trombone, Leon on euphonium and son-in–law Peter Goldsworthy on soprano and when he left in 1974 they resigned as well and there was some rapid reorganising necessary.

1974 – Placed first in the Brass Championship at the World Music Festival in Kerkrade.

Following the 1973 National Championship the Band was invited to take part in the Brass Championship of the World Music Festival at Kerkrade and in July 1974 Camborne Town Band travelled to Holland to compete in this prestigious event. The tour included a marching and test piece contest as well as some concerts. The contest aspect appears later but the event as a whole sounds like an enjoyable, if occasionally hair-raising, experience. The return trip took them to Le Havre to catch the ferry. It seems the coach was already running late when the driver, Freddie Tremain, followed a direction sign off the main route on to a narrow country road. The dust was flying but he could see the port in the distance so he knew he couldn't go far wrong.

Approaching a narrow bridge he ploughed on and the coach bounced across the surface of what seemed like sleepers. It was only when the passengers looked back that they realised it was only supported by poles and was intended for bicycles and pedestrians. Even with the short cut the coach arrived late and found queues of other vehicles waiting to board. Freddie's reaction to the whole debacle was, *"Thank God that's over, now I can get 20 Senior Service; I hate foreign fags"*.

On one of Adrian King's visits back to Camborne he called on Freddie Roberts who had a surprise for him. Quite apart from their association at Camborne Town Band, they played together in a number of local shows when Freddie would invariably play what he referred to as, his Bach Aida trumpet. This was a very long brass instrument that could be broken down into three parts when being transported. It had externally sprung valves with old-fashioned round caps. Freddie was making a present of it to Adrian but not before Reynolds, the instrument repairers, had refurbished it. Adrian was clearly touched by this gesture and still treasures the instrument.

When the players switched allegiance from the bar at the Camborne Rugby Club to the Railway Hotel they set about getting to know their new landlord. He had a friend who owned a hotel in St Mawes and he arranged a concert for about 10 players there. It finished with the players marching through the village (or is it a town) and shaking the box. In failing light they floated out of the harbour busking *A Life on the Ocean Waves* and arrived back in Falmouth - to find their dinghy had been knicked.

The 1976 Camborne Town Band Annual Gala Day was set for Monday the 30th August at the Recreation Ground, Camborne. There was to be a fancy dress parade, donkey and pony rides, children's sports, a dog show, comic football match and a piano-smashing contest. A host of events and competitions were arranged to which could be added, musical entertainment by the Band. And then, with supreme optimism, it said, *"If wet, at the bandroom"*.

In whatever period I have researched I find Camborne Town Band ably supported by its committees. Toni Volante recalled, *"We had good leadership and a dedicated hardworking committee. I recall people like Reg Parnell and Leslie Fletcher and a host of others like them. There were catering, travel arrangements, chairs to carry and all the other things that make an event go like clockwork. We even had a stage, usually transported by Holman's, which had to be erected and dismantled. I think we were sometimes so busy with our playing that we overlooked the massive contribution made by the helpers."*

No band can flourish without its helpers, those people who work in the background with refreshments and fundraising so that the players can enjoy their hobby. Often these are parents or spouses of members but there are also people who just want to support the Band of which they are so proud. I know from my own playing career how important these workers are. A good Ladies' Committee is worth its weight in Cornish tin. Their unstinting efforts are a boon to any band. Betty Fletcher (née Allen) was Secretary of the Ladies' Committee during the 1950s and Roma Cock was a member from about 1955 to the late 1980s and Secretary for about seven years during the 1970s. She said, *"We used to have a lot of fun as well as raising much needed cash. We organised whist drives, jumble sales, beetle drives, fetes and even a sponsored silence."* As quick as a flash she turned on me

Desmond Weeks leading the parade celebrating the re-opening of Trelowarren Street after weeks of work there.

1973

Back row: P Goldsworthy, J Pascoe, M Roberts, D Weeks, B Horton (in front of pillar), M Weeks , P James, G Weeks, G Ansell, M Hocking, B Clift (trom), P Wicks, I Uren and D Bray (D Reed absent at time of photograph)
Middle row: M Ray, L Adams, B Trevena, R Stevens, C Berryman, E Willcocks, L Johnston, N Peters, D Piper, D Parsons and D Johnston Jnr.
Front row: G Mitchell, I Facey, R Cook and A Toy.

and said, *"You can smile, we all did it and there's nobody worse at yapping than you men"*. That was me put in my place and she went on to recall some of her colleagues: *"Pam Whear, Chairman for about seven years, Joyce Hitchens, Verna Weeks, Rosie Weeks, Joyce Saunders, Mrs Trevena, Mrs Cook and a lot of others"*. Melba Roberts was a member for many years and Secretary from 1960 to 1963.

One of the fund-raising activities was the weekly Bingo Club which helped raise a lot of money: Lesley Fletcher and Melba Roberts were among the organising stalwarts.

At a meeting in April 1963 Mrs Morcom reported that the Ladies' Committee had decided to discontinue their work. Recent attendance had been disappointing and the poor health of the President, Mrs Tresidder, had not helped. The ladies were thanked for, *"Many years of excellent work, support and service and the unequalled amounts of money collected"*.

From time to time attempts to re-start the committee were made. It was active again during the 1970s and in July 1972 Mrs J James reported that they had seven hard-working members.

1974 July – *The Reason Why* LP released.

Featuring Camborne (CompAir Holman) Band, the Holman-Climax Male Voice Choir and Redruth born baritone Alan Opie, the record included a feast of Cornish music; *Going up Camborne Hill, The Flora Dance, The Blackbird Song, The Oggie Song, The White Rose* and, of course, *Trelawny*. There were also many hymn tunes and marches by St Day composer, Kenneth Pelmear. The RNLI received some of the income from the record which was on sale for £1.94.

1974 September - Derek Johnston resigned as Musical Director.

1974 – Leonard Adams conducted until a new Musical Director could be appointed.

1974 - Camborne Town Band was re-constituted and became the Camborne Town Band Music Society.

The Society was registered under the Friendly Societies Act 1974 and became the over-arching organisation for Camborne Town Band, Camborne Youth Band, Camborne "B" Band and the Training Band.

1974 December - Bernard Bygrave appointed Musical Director.

1975 – Return visit to Kerkrade in Holland.

The Band visited Kerkrade a second time in October 1975 when it was invited back as winners of the World Championship. Derek Johnston had left by then and Bernard Bygrave had taken over as Musical Director. Lester Ashton was unwell and his father, Eddie, was invited to take his place.

The crossing was very rough and Courtney Berryman is not the best sailor. He decided to build himself up with a fried breakfast so he wouldn't be sick on an empty stomach and sure enough, he and the breakfast parted company before long. He said that the sight of George Ansell eating a roast meal didn't help.

The Band took part in the Gala Concert the programme of which included the *Barber of Seville, La Boutique Fantastique, Symphony of Marches, Slavonic Dance No. 8, Ruy Blas, Les Preludes, and Sicilian Vespers.* At another concert some of the same pieces were chosen to which was added *Knight Templar, William Tell, Nimrod, Date with a Square* and *Padstow Lifeboat.*

There were two drivers, Freddie Tremain and Trevor Berryman, and Trevor decided to get off the coach and check for directions. He'd obviously forgotten that they were driving on the right and jumped out of the door in front of a cyclist. The rider was thrown from his bike but picked himself up, muttered a few indecipherable words and rode off. Trevor was shaken but also very relieved at the realisation it could have been a car.

Memories are a bit hazy but it is thought that the problem at Customs relates to this trip. Although Paul Wick was wearing his new watch, officers discovered the packaging and receipt and insisted on searching everybody and everything including looking down the slides of the instruments.

Although not taking part in the National Championship in 1975, some of the Camborne players and supporters travelled to London to attend the contest. Roy Nancarrow, Stanley Pope and Bernard Bygrave stayed in a near-by bed and breakfast establishment. It was a case of shared facilities and Roy recalls that the toilet door opened out and had no lock. Stanley popped along the corridor but soon returned saying that it was occupied. Roy said, *"It's a bit stiff Stanley, you've got to give it a bit of a pull"*. So Stanley did just that, not realising that Bernard was inside holding on like grim death. Finally, the door gave way and Bernard was pulled off the seat with his trousers around his ankles - still holding on to the door. Stanley returned to his room where he lay on his bed and laughed so much that one of his room mates thought he was having a fit.

The annual Band Dinner with the in-house entertainment was always popular and it seems many of the players loved dressing up (no comment). This mid 1970s photograph of a beauty contest at The Membley Hall, Falmouth, is slightly blurred but just had to be included. It wasn't until I asked for the telephone number of the gorgeous young lady on the right that John Phillips revealed who it was – thank goodness! From left to right: Ronnie Weeks, Michael Weeks, Jimmy Gribben, Barrie Trevena, John Phillips and, with a pose to dream about, Leonard Adams.

In a Persian Market at Lowenac Hotel, Camborne. John Phillips as the juggler but the Sand Dancer (Leonard Adams again) to the left looks as though he has decided to do the Dance of the Seven Veils. After this, whenever 'In a Persian Market' was played, Gerald Weeks would collapse in hysterics after only a few bars.
Other themes were Uncle Tom Cobley and Snow White and the Seven Dwarfs which, I'm told, will bring back memories – of what, I'm not sure.

1975 – The Camborne (CompAir-Holman) Band reverted to its original name of Camborne Town Band.

1975 – Bernard Bygrave resigned as Musical Director.

1975 – Leonard Adams conducted until a new Musical Director could be appointed.

1976 January – Robert Oughton decided not to accept the position of Musical Director.

In January 1976 Camborne Town Band was advised that the man who was due to take over the baton as Musical Director would not be joining them. Robert Oughton had decided to accept a position with a Scottish band and the search had to start all over again.

The newspaper headline read, *"Monty signs off after 18 years with town band"*. Monty Ray, Principal Cornet for many of those years, decided to leave banding altogether in 1976. At the age of 11 he'd responded to an advertisement to learn a brass instrument; he saw it as a way of avoiding piano lessons. His father had played with Camborne during the early 1930s so there was no objection

Early 1970s - Camborne Town Band with Derek Johnson
Back row: Peter Goldsworthy, Jack Pascoe, Derek Johnston, Dougie Piper, Barry Clift, Ian Facey, David Bray, Robert Cook and Alan Toy.
Middle row: Monty Ray, Leonard Adams, Barrie Trevena, David Reed, John Morrisey, Paul Wicks, Leon Johnston, Barry West (baritone - left early 1970s), and Edwin Willcocks.
Front row: George Ansell, Gerald Weeks, Bill Horton, Neil Peters, Derek Johnston (Musical Director), Michael Weeks, Peter Tresidder and Russell Kellow.

1974 at Praze Cricket Ground

Alan Toy, Robert Cook, Ian Facey and David Bray with their new Yamaha instruments

from that quarter. He developed into a superb player and there were many who regretted his decision to retire.

During the mid 1970s to early 1980s *The Hot Foundation Big Band* was formed. This was a jazz/big band and included many Camborne players: Robert Cook (bass guitar), Jimmy Gribbin (trombone), Lester Ashton (trombone), Monty Ray (trumpet), Ivor Uren (trumpet) and Edward Ashton (trombone) who helped on occasions.

1973 - Prize-winning horn quartet led by Alan Toy. Graham Mitchell, Robert Cook, Sharon Toy holding the cup, Ian Facey and Alan. They played at many concerts and won every quartet contest that they entered and many people have said that the rapport gained from playing in the quartet was of great benefit to the Band as a whole in its contest performances.

1974 - taken in front of Veor House. The building was demolished and the stone used to build the nearby homes for the elderly.

1976 May - Derek Greenwood appointed Musical Director.

For the princely sum of 5p you could attend a *Sponsored Blow* at the bandroom on Saturday the 15th May 1976. For a small additional charge you could have a request played or even conduct. No, this wasn't a way of finding a new MD, it was a 12-hour playing session to try and raise some much-needed funds. It involved players from the Senior and Junior Bands and even Secretary Bob Seymour joined in with a four-hour stint on percussion and together they raised about £450 in spon-

Monty Ray

sorship. Meanwhile Roma Cock, Valerie Rowe, Pam Whear and others kept the players' lips moist with cups of tea.

An incident-packed year was how 1976 was described at the annual general meeting. A change of Musical Director, the loss of Holman's Canteen for concerts due to fire regulations and the failure to purchase the Literary Institute because the asking price was too high. The financial results were described as remarkable and the Treasurer, Mrs S M Morcom, said they were the best set of figures she had presented.

Kingsley Hitchens began helping when his son, John, joined in 1976. He served as a committee member for three or four years before taking over as Secretary when Bob Seymour stepped down. Kingsley held this post for almost 15 years including the occasion of the 150 years celebration. During his period of office his wife, Joyce, was Treasurer having taken over from the long-serving Mrs Morcom. Joyce was in post for four or five years before handing over to Trevor Goninan.

In mid 1976 the Band was featured on the BBC Radio programme, *As Prescribed;* presented by Dudley Savage it played requests for hospital patients. In addition, recording was soon to start for two other BBC programmes, *Among your Souvenirs* and the *Reginald Dixon Show*.

1977 – Placed fourth in the National Brass Band Championship of Great Britain (Championship Section).

The Band formed a guard of honour at the funeral of William (Bill) James Langdon Head (tenor horn) in October 1977. Bill had been a founder member of the Junior Band of the 1920s before joining the Senior Band and holding the posts of Secretary and Treasurer.

Never one to hold back with a comment, Derek Greenwood was standing next to a cow-pat in a field at a tea-treat when he came out with, *"You wouldn't get Harry Mortimer doing this"*. Those who were there may remember the language as more colourful than that.

In the late 1970s there was a concerning newspaper headline which read, *"Out of tune! So band will spend £10,000 on new instruments"*.

It reflected the disappointment that, after only five years, the Yamaha instruments were deteriorating and needed to be replaced. They were difficult to tune and needed constant repair and for a top section band that was not acceptable. Donations were being requested and loans were arranged to purchase a new set of British Boosey and Hawkes instruments.

In 1978 a long playing record was released and in a review in December of that year, Tim Mutum of the British Mouthpiece said that he enjoyed the marches and *The Flora Dance* which, *"Was played as written and does not omit the opening bars as the Brighouse recording. Leonard Adams proved himself a worthy Principal Cornetist with his fine playing of 'Napoli' and Robert Cook played his part with great feeling."* The record concluded with *Journey into Freedom*, *"Played with all the fervour and tenderness the composer intended. A fine conclusion to an enjoyable record"*. It was on sale for £3.42.

Eric Trerise joined in 1978, having previously played with St Stythians Band and the Band of the Duke of Cornwall's Light Infantry (DCLI) under Major Peter Parkes. His early memories are of first playing when he was eight years old, moving to solo cornet at the age of 10 and, a year later, playing in the same concert as Dudley Savage at Killigrew Chapel in Falmouth. He'd been invited to join Morris Motors and Camborne sometime before he left St Stythians but felt the time wasn't right.

Not long after moving to Camborne he became Bandmaster and he told me that he recalled 13 players leaving due to sickness, work and moving from the area. Eric was very involved in trying to fill the vacant positions and it's remarkable to think that within a couple of years the Band achieved one of its best ever results in the National Championship. He said, *"We seemed to gel and we had a superb reputation at the National where we were referred to as the 'Blue Devils'".*

In 1988 Eric was diagnosed with cancer of the throat and the prognosis was not good but he recovered and, against the odds, returned to play in late 1989. After a short period with St Dennis Silver he returned to Camborne in 1992 where he played for a further 18 months. He enjoyed the social side at Camborne where, he said, *"We were like one big family. The music side was taken seriously but there was more to it than that. We had a darts, football and a cricket team. Tim Joslin was a good bowler and Derek Greenwood was pretty good with the bat. We played at Wendron and Praze and were a good team; we even beat Praze on one occasion."*

Another "Sponsored Blow" in July 1979 and another £500 in the bank. As the Town Clock struck 8.00am, Derek Greenwood lifted his baton and the 12-hour playing stint commenced. The Youth Band, under Phil Tonkin, took over completely for an hour in the morning and, following an afternoon engagement, the youngsters returned to continue helping. Musical Director Derek Greenwood commented that given the choice of a sponsored walk or a blow, he would choose the blow anytime.

In December 1979 Pam Whear and Roma Cock, on behalf of the Ladies' Committee, presented the Band with a new drum kit costing £850. This replaced the old, second-hand kit and was played by percussionist Andrew Perkin who had joined from Penzance Silver.

Some players from the 1970s/1980s: Kathryn Bygrave (in 1975 when her father was conducting) / Tanya Ferris (cornet) / Eve Greenwood (horn) / Graham Hooper (euphonium and baritone - later joined the Royal Air Force) / Alan Ralph Richards (a member in 1975) / Ivor Uren (cornet - who played at the National Championship in October 1973).

Robert Tanner joined in 1980, having moved from Hayle Band where he'd been Principal Cornet. He said, *"I can still recall the sense of awe as I walked into the wooden band hut behind the railway station, with its pictures of past players and successes hanging on the walls and with the committee members and supporters sitting to the right and to the left. The atmosphere in that wonderful bandroom, surrounded by dedicated and skilled players, is one that I shall never forget nor equal.*

I became Principal Cornet in 1981, replacing the illustrious Leonard Adams, and held the position until I left to study medicine in 1986. I recall my first two contests as Principal Cornet, playing Edward Gregson's 'Essay' at Bristol and Gilbert Vinter's 'Spectrum' at Brean Sands. We won on both occasions and embarked on a wonderful year that saw us take fourth place at the Nationals playing Wilfred Heaton's 'Contest Music', and appear on BBC 2's Best of Brass competition.

The energy was always harnessed towards competitions and we were very successful. Underpinning this competition success was the enormous effort of the players and committee in performing concerts throughout the year to raise funds to pay for the trips away to the big competitions. It is only now that I fully understand the dedication and sacrifice required to keep the organisation financially sound and musically successful.

I can picture the face of each and every one of my fellow players, even if some of their names now elude me. I feel I owe them all a huge thank you for their support and friendship during my time there. I would like to particularly thank Derek Greenwood who nurtured my musicianship and who made a huge leap of faith in appointing a 13 year-old lad to the end chair. I am immensely proud of having played my part in the success of Camborne and I know my pride was shared by my wonderful dad and I would like to save my last thank you for him."

Jack Pascoe recalled a concert at Exmouth when Harry Mortimer conducted. "*We were preparing to play 'Facilita' and he looked along the cornet line to see who was going to play the solo. He seemed surprised that it was going to be a very young Bobby Tanner but I think he was impressed after."*

Sometime around 1980 the Band was preparing for the National Final and Derek Greenwood received a telephone call from *The British Bandsman* to check what Camborne had been up to recently. He could imagine Black Dyke and Brighouse listing all the major concerts they had given but all he was able to say was, *"Frogpool and Skinners Bottom tea-treats"*.

John Coggins, Band Chairman and Manager of Home World Store, attended a rehearsal just prior to a contest during the 1980s. His purpose was to encourage the players and to ensure them that they had the best wishes of their supporters. He said how good it would be if they could bring back some silverware and went on to say how he had taken his two dogs to a show and won two cups. In a response that is so familiar to bandroom banter some bright spark asked, *"And how did the dogs get on?"*

Ashley White (bass) joined in 1981 having given up the solo euphonium role at Newquay Town Band about six months earlier. He said, *"Leonard Adams knocked on my door and asked if I could play E flat bass for Camborne at the Albert Hall. At first I felt it was too big a step, the standard of play and time demands would be so much greater than required at Newquay. But I must have wavered because the next thing I knew, Leonard had fetched an instrument from his car and said, 'See you at practice on Tuesday'. I arrived for practice in a state of trepidation but needn't have worried – the welcome was so good. I already knew Leonard, Alan Toy, David Reed and a number of other Camborne players in fact, Derek Greenwood occasionally played at Newquay – on euphonium next to me – just to keep his 'lip in'."*

Ashley played for a couple of years until personal circumstances made it difficult to devote the necessary time and very reluctantly, he handed in his notice. His memory is of a band with a truly close-knit, family atmosphere never more apparent than on the band and the supporters' coach when travelling to an engagement or contest.

At the 1981 annual general meeting the Treasurer, Mrs Sylvia Morcom, stepped down after many years. Other appointments were: President - The Revd Basil Brown, Chairman - Mr I W Armstong, Vice-Chairman – Mr J Phillips, Secretary – Mr R T Seymour and Musical Director – Mr Derek Greenwood..

A Camborne Town Band ensemble scored the highest mark in the Camborne Music Festival in November 1981. Derek Greenwood conducted the group, assembled especially for the competition, when it played *Prelude and Rondo* by Ronald Hanmer. It comprised bass - Michael Weeks; solo cornet - Robert Tanner; cornet – Chris Parkin; tenor horn – Stephen Williams; euphonium – Simon Williams; baritone – John Phillips and trombone – James Gribben. Both Stephen Williams and his brother, Simon, also played horn in the Band.

Lester Ashton (trombone) joined in August 1982 having started his playing career at Helston. *"Moving from a Third Section band to Camborne was a big step and, as events turned out, I found myself playing solo trombone within a couple of months. It all happened so quick that my registration transfer came through just one day before my first contest."* After seven busy years he was seeking a reduced commitment and returned to Helston in May 1989 where he is still a playing member.

Albert Chappell attended a pre-contest concert by Camborne ahead of the National Championship at London. The highlight of the programme was the test piece but just as it was about to be played an announcement called him out to move his car. As he rushed out of the hall he called back over his shoulder, *"Don't start before I get back"*.

1982 – Placed fourth in the National Brass Band Championship of Great Britain (Championship Section).

A Donkey Derby was held in August 1983 to raise much-needed funds. The event was held at Bassett Junior School and donkeys Minstrel, Heidi, Dillon, Dougal, Georgie, Sinbad, Polly, Nellie, Sam, Adam and Trigger (the West of England Shay-Racing Champion) all did their stuff. Some volunteers were visitors but it seems that quite a few members of the Junior Band were *"volunteered"* by their sadistic older colleagues.

1983 - 1,000 Voices Concert in London.

In November 1983 Camborne Town Band helped fly the flag for Cornwall when it took part in a concert at the Royal Albert Hall. Presented by Richard Radcliffe, *1,000 Cornish Male Voices* was a celebration of Cornish music and an outstanding success. The concert was conducted by Vilem Tausky and featured over 30 Male Voice Choirs, Wendy Eathorne (soprano), John Treleaven (tenor), Alan Opie (baritone), Geoffrey Pratley (accompanist), John Winter (organist of Truro Cathedral), the Camborne Town Band and Richard Radcliffe as Master of Ceremonies. The Band's contributions included the overture from *The Pirates of Penzance*, *Memory from Cats*, *YMCA*, *Trelissick Gardens* (by Vilem Tausky), *Introduction to Act 3 Lohengrin*, *High on a Hill* (featuring Robert Tanner), *Padstow Lifeboat* (by Malcolm Arnold) and *The Lost Chord.* The event was brought to a close by a rousing performance of – what else – *Trelawny.* John Phillips recalled the line of red-coated players being applauded on to the stage. He said, *"The emotion was so great that I couldn't feel my feet touching the ground and I was afraid I was going to fall over. It was a superb event and the huge audience so appreciative."*

By contrast, a concert at the Prince's Pavilions at Falmouth a month later attracted just 30 people. Lester Ashton recalled a huge crash during the playing of the National Anthem. *"The chairs were positioned on blocks and as Michael Weeks stood up, his toppled over and he finished up lying on his back under his bass."*

Continuing its association with Brenda Wootton the Band went to Paul Church in November 1983 to record a Christmas video with her.

In support of the 1983 Remembrance Sunday, Wayne Brown played at the Camborne gathering while Michael Pritchard went to Marazion.

In the week prior to Christmas in 1983 the Band was giving a concert at Redruth and when it had finished, Jonathan Bond and his bass needed a lift back to Camborne. There were no offers from anyone else so, despite having to make a detour, Lester Ashton volunteered – he still wishes he hadn't. Travelling back along Illogan Highway with the rain hammering down, he failed to see the red light by the Railway Inn. Jonathan shouted and pulled on the handbrake and Lester braked hard but the car aquaplaned right over the crossing. As it happens he was being followed by a police car and the vehicle he hit was also a police car – lucky old Lester! He was asked to produce his driving licence and insurance but discovered he'd left them back in the changing room at the concert venue. He said the police were very good about it but what really wound him up was the other players on their

Prize winning quartet
Robert Cook
Simon Williams
Eve Greenwood
Ian Facey
Derek Greenwood
(MD)

The Band in the late 1970s

Back row: David Whear, Jack Pascoe, Eric Trerise, Barrie Trevena, Kevin Goninan, Leonard Adams, Nigel Cock, Stephen Williams, Michael Roberts, Michael Couch and Chris Parkin.

Middle row: Eve Greenwood, Ian Facey, Simon Williams, Robert Cook, Jimmy Gribben, unknown, John Phillips, Donald Cock and Andrew Perkins.

Front row: Eric Thomas, Courtney Berryman, Susan Rowe, Edwin Willcocks, Derek Greenwood (Musical Director), A Kemp, Neil Peters, Michael Weeks and Gerald Weeks.

Mid to late 1970s.

A Retallack and Glen Jones are at the back.

Full back row: L Adams, B Trevena, A Kemp, E Greenwood, R Cook, K Goninan, D Reed and D Tonkin.

Middle row: C Parkin, D Whear, N Cock, D Cock, J Phillips, J Gribbon, S Walkley, Chris Verryon, A Faraway and J Pascoe.

Front row: E Thomas, R Weeks, G Hooper, C Berryman, Derek Greenwood (MD), E Willcocks, N Peters, M Weeks and G Weeks.

way home who wound down their windows to ask if he was all right. Any one of them could have taken Jonathan home. Fifty pounds lighter and with four penalty points to his name he met one of the policemen in Helston a few weeks later who asked him if he'd written off any police cars lately.

Camborne Town Band formed a guard of honour at the funeral of Pam Whear in January 1984; she had died suddenly at the age of 55. Chairman of the Ladies' Committee for a number of years, she had been a committed supporter and hard worker for the Band.

Circa 1978 - The Ladies' Committee outside the bandroom
Back row: Susan Nancarrow, Anne Nancarrow, Jean Trevena, Lorraine Weeks, Mrs Tonkin, Rosie Weeks, Sylvia Dunstan, Verna Weeks, Dorothy Nancarrow and Margaret Goninan.
Front row: Sylvia Morcom, Gwyneth Adams, Pamela Whear, Mrs James, Joyce Saunders, Roma Cock, Eileen Cook and Mrs Scriven.

The Barber Shop Four (five actually) in cabaret at the Membley Hall Falmouth early 1980s.

Michael Weeks
Ronnie Weeks
John Phillips
Steve Walkley
Leonard Adams

Jack Hosking and Reggie Mills having a natter sometime in the late 1980s. Jack was a committee member and a good helper and Reggie "shook the tin" and supported the Band for many years. Reg was often referred to as "French Resistance" because of his black beret.

At the 1984 annual general meeting the talk was of mixed fortunes on the contest stage but the retiring Treasurer reported a *"good set of accounts"*. Michael Williams was the new Treasurer and John Phillips was elected Vice-Chairman.

Marcus Dunstan joined in 1984 after having been a guest player at the 1,000 Voices Concert at the Royal Albert Hall the previous year. He commenced his playing career in 1962, at St Stythians, where he played baritone and then cornet under Edgar Floyd – an ex Camborne player - and was principal for a number of years. Marcus ceased playing in Camborne Senior Band in 2001 but extended his career by joining the "B" Band. Apart from playing, he held a number of administrative posts including that of Treasurer since 2001. His son, Simon (cornet), was a member of Camborne Youth Band since the early 1990s and part of the successful team that became the Junior Champions of Great Britain in 2004.

1980 at Penwith Contest
Back row: D Whear, N Cock, Jack Pascoe, E Trerise, K Goninan, L Adams, B Trevena, Michael Hocking, S Williams, N Johns and C Parkin.
Middle row: I Facey, Simon Williams, R Cook, D Cock, J Phillips, unknown, J Gribben, D Weeks and A Perkins.
Front row: E Thomas, N Wills, Susan Rowe, E Willcocks, Derek Greenwood (MD), Simon Jackson, N Peters, M Weeks and G Weeks.

Robert Tanner playing a solo with Carn Brea Castle in the background (Photo by Donald Williams)

June 1981

Back row: R Tanner, D Whear, B Trevena, N Cock, L Adams, K Goninan, E Trerise, C Parkin, J Pascoe and M Medlyn.
Middle row: J Rutter, S Williams, R Cook, J Phillips, D Cock, unknown, J Gribben and A Perkins,
Front row: M Weeks, S Williams, E Willcocks, D Greenwood (MD), N Peters, A White and E Thomas. (Photo by Donald Williams)

The Paris Trip. Alan Farraway (guest from Sunlife but had previously played with Camborne) Marcus Dunstan and Ralph Rowden (guest from Sunlife). Lyndon Baglin from Sunlife also guested.

1984 – Brenda Wootton tour of Paris.

The headline *"Band win French hearts"* summed up the trip to Paris. The article goes on to say, *"Cornish singer, Brenda Wootton, took Camborne Town Band to Paris where they won the acclaim and hearts of millions of French people. Brenda, her group and the Band were well received at daily concerts in the Bobino Theatre, Paris, and enjoyed by millions over radio and television."*

Barrie Trevena thinks the French were surprised at the quality of the music; perhaps expecting *"oompah"* they heard pieces like *Memory*, *Shepherd's Song*, the *Flora Dance* and even the *Can-Can.*

Eddie Ashton had left by then but joined the tour due to illness amongst the trombone ranks. The schedule was so tight that players had to change into their uniforms as the coach was travelling. Brenda ran through the pieces in the dressing room and all went well.

Lester Ashton was the only player who could speak fluent French and became the compère for each concert. He proceeded to make gentle fun of the players and Derek Greenwood, which the French audience loved and his colleagues could not understand. A visit to the Palace of Versailles was included in the itinerary for which one hour was allocated – hardly enough to do it justice! Derek Greenwood managed to cause a bit of a stir when he went on French radio and referred to their beloved saxophone as an agony bag.

Jason Smith said, *"There were fourteen concerts in nine days - a live radio broadcast at 2.00am on Europel, a live television broadcast, a champagne reception, a concert in the Casino de-Paris, the Amnesty International concert and seven concerts at the famous Bobino Theatre".*

The highlight had to be the Amnesty International Concert in the Zenithe Stadium with an audience of 6,000 people. Marcus Dunstan said, *"We came on stage at midnight; the other performers were mostly rock bands but despite the type of concert we were well received. One thing that really surprised me was how well known Brenda Wootton was in France; her name was plastered all over the place."* Whilst there, the Band took part in a lager advertisement featuring Charlene Tilton of Dallas fame.

Second Brenda Wootton tour of Paris.

The first trip was so successful that Brenda invited the Band to accompany her again a few months later when the concerts were performed in the open air.

During 1984 and 1985 the Band made a number of BBC recordings including one at Lanhydrock House for a new series, *Music at the Manor* when John McAvoy (percussion) stepped in at short notice.

At the 1985 annual general meeting Bob Seymour considered it was time to stand down as Secretary but no replacement was immediately available. It seems he was not able to relinquish the post until the 1988 annual general meeting when Mrs Joyce Hitchens was Treasurer and Jonathan Bond was elected as the first ever Engagement Secretary.

1985 December – Derek Greenwood resigned as Musical Director.

1985 – Edward Ashton appointed temporary Musical Director.

Darren Hendy joined Camborne from Porthleven Band in 1986, at the age of 14. Three years later he moved to Rigid Containers (formerly GUS Footwear and later Travelsphere) where he played for about a year. Returning to Cornwall, he played at St Dennis, under Derek Greenwood, for about three years before re-joining Camborne in 1993. He soon took over the role of Principal Cornet and

Circa 1986 – Eddie Ashton conducts while Lester Ashton plays a solo at a Trevarno Estate concert.

The Band in the late 1980s taken at Camborne School.
Back row: Mark Medlyn, Norman Johns, Chris Parkin, Eric Trerise, Michael Pritchard, Marcus Dunstan, Vivian Smitheram, Dylan Herbert, Darren Hendy and Andrew Sutton.
Middle row: Wayne Brown, Andrew James, Graham Christophers, Neil Rutter, Ian Sutton, Brenda Wootton, Steve Sykes (Musical Director), Stuart Chappell, Andrew Teague, John Phillips, David Nicholas and Lester Ashton.
Front row: Jason Smith, Michael Weeks, John Hitchens, Tim Joslin, Steve Weeks, Andrew Tellam, David Wilton, Shaun Thomas, Terry Tonkin and Jonathan Bond.

won many awards during his seven or eight years in that position.

He recalled the occasion when he guested for Brighouse and Rastrick in a concert at the Hall for Cornwall circa 2000 and when he did likewise for Grimethorpe when recording a CD. It seems that Darren acquired a reputation for being late for engagements and he must have found a Gwennap Pit concert a tad embarrassing when he arrived one piece into the concert and had to make his entrance through the large crowd down to the centre of the pit.

On another occasion he was on his way to Bugle Contest – running a bit late – when he spotted James Knight by the roadside - his car had broken down. He said, *"I asked James if he was worried but he said he wasn't because he knew I'd be along sooner or later".* A similar incident happened when travelling to a Plymouth contest when James had missed the bus and decided to wait for Darren. He said, *"I don't think Derek Greenwood was too pleased that his Principal and second Principal Cornet players were arriving, more or less, by chance".*

Some of the "old timers" who returned to play at Treswithian Fete in the late 1980s
Faces left to right: unknown, Ian Facey, Robert Cook, David Parsons, David Pascoe, Andrew Kemp (leaning forward), Eric Thomas (back row), Leon Johnston, Barry Tresidder and Neil Peters (front).

1987 – Stephen Sykes appointed Musical Director.

Lester Ashton was delighted to win the raffle at a Prince's Pavilion concert but it turned out to be an embarrassing experience. In his eagerness to collect his winnings he almost toppled into the orchestra pit and when he'd collected his prize from Brenda Wootton - and a big hug - Stephen Sykes played the old trick of holding the curtains together as he tried to get back on the stage.

The DEAL Quartet was made up of four trombone players: Donald Waters, Eddie Ashton, Adrian Waters and Lester Ashton. When they took part in the South West Brass Band Association Quartet Contest people imagined it was something to do with the Royal School of Music based at Deal and only later discovered that the name was made up of the first letters of their first names. Donald Waters also played with Perranporth, Truro City and Newquay Town.

Before Ian Sutton (tenor horn and Bandmaster) joined in 1986 he had previously played with Drayton, in Norfolk, the 308 Regiment of Loyal Hussars, Royal Artillery and St Austell Town. In 1991, his playing career was temporarily interrupted when he suffered a heart attack but after a couple of years he had two spells of helping out and returned to play in the 2004 National Championship. He

Camborne Town Band circa 1990
Very back row (in front of doors): Steve Weeks and Andrew Tellam.
Back row: Steve Uren, Sarah Hooper, Marcus Dunstan, Ryan Hollow (cornet), Dylan Herbert, James Knight, Paul Bilkey, Stuart Chappell, Ian Hooper, Karen Triggs and Michael Pritchard.
Middle row: John Mitchell, Andrew Teague (bass trom - became involved in organising Bugle Contest), Alan Caddy, Kevin Dower (bass/tenor trombone - was the librarian and played until circa 1990), David Nicholas, Stephen Sykes (Musical Director), Wayne Brown, Ian Sutton, Richard Knight, Andrew "Farmer" James (horn - came up from Youth Band in mid-1980s and played until about 1990) and David Wilton (baritone - joined from Redruth in the 1980s and left to join the RAF. His brother, Derek, played bass for a short while in 1995.)
Front row (seated): Jason Smith, Michael Weeks, John Hitchens, Alan Toy, Russell Kellow and Jonathan Bond. (Photo by Malcolm Jenkin B. A. 22 Greenfield Terr., Portreath)

said, *"Have I ever left Camborne Band? Who knows?"* His son, Andrew (cornet), also played at Camborne in 1989/1990.

Over the years many Camborne players have successfully taken part in solo and quartet contests and January 1988, at Helston, was no exception. John Hitchens won the slow melody and air varie class for the second year running and bass players Michael Weeks, Stephen Sykes, Jason Smith and Jonathan Bond won the Open Championship Quartet competition.

More recordings: during the early part of 1988 the Band was recording for Radio Cornwall and for the BBC Radio programme, *Listen to the Band.*

A rota was prepared to spread the load of doing various jobs like loading the percussion and other equipment. Lester Ashton said, *"We arrived for a concert at the Guildhall in St Ives, to discover we had no music stands. Stephen Sykes was not pleased and Steve Trelease was slightly red-faced".* Steve (cornet) left in the mid 1990s and later played flugel for Lanner & District.

St Ives is a popular venue for summer concerts but there are disadvantages in using a beachside location. Lester Ashton said, *"Mark Medlyn was playing soprano and Chris Parkin was on repiano when we heard the splat. A seagull had scored a direct hit on both of them; they just sat there with a resigned look on their faces."*

During the early 1990s four young men from Camborne Band were in the National Youth Brass Band of Great Britain at the same time. Mark Leigh (cornet), John Mitchell (percussion), James Knight (cornet) and Richard Knight (tenor horn) all became either principal or vice-principal in their respective sections. Many other Camborne players have been accepted for this honour and I remember Desmond Burley being auditioned at the same time as my brother, David Bunney from St Agnes, in 1959. Desmond attended nine courses and thoroughly enjoyed the involvement. Like so many of the Camborne players, Desmond played in the Cornwall County Youth Band and remembered the many friendships and associations.

James Knight (cornet) was the Principal Cornet at the National Youth Brass Band of Great Britain for two years and his brother, Richard (horn) later played with Flowers. John Mitchell (percussion) left in mid 1993 when offered a place at Trinity College London to study music.

In 1991 a CD was recorded to celebrate the 150th Anniversary and included: *Royal Trophy, Embraceable You* (trombone soloist David Nicholas), *Oklahoma, Sommerkveld* (cornet soloist Stuart Chappell), *Manhattan Skyline, In this hour of Soften'd Splendour* (featured Stuart Chappell, Ian Sutton, Wayne Brown and John Hitchens), *Aspects of Andrew Lloyd Webber, Next to Silence* (soprano soloist Paul Bilkey), *Three King's Swing, Rhapsody for Euphonium* (soloist John Hitchens), *Eloise* and *Deep Harmony*. Ginsters Pasties Ltd sponsored the recording, Stephen Sykes conducted and Alan Knight was thanked for his help and support. Alan was an excellent worker for the band and was tragically killed in a car accident near Chiverton Cross.
The players were:
Solo cornets: Stuart Chappell, Ian Hooper, Michael Pritchard and Karen Triggs.
Soprano cornet: Paul Bilkey. Repiano cornet: Dylan Herbert. Flugel: Wayne Brown.
Second cornets: Ryan Hollow and Marcus Dunstan. Third cornet: Sarah Hooper (née Lenton).
Tenor horns: Ian Sutton, Mark Bray, Andrew James and Elaine Bray. Euphoniums: John Hitchens, Shaun Thomas and Jonathan Law. Baritones: Timothy Joslin and David Wilton.
Trombones: David Nicholas, Kevin Dower, Alan Caddy and Andrew Teague (bass).
E flat basses: Michael Weeks and Phil Blake who was not a regular member but helped out when required. B flat basses: Jonathan Bond and Jason Smith.
Percussion: Steven Weeks, John Mitchell and Derek Thomas.

1991 – Stephen Sykes resigned as Musical Director.

(Photo by Cornwall & Isles of Scilly Press)

1991 - Practising for the 150th Anniversary Event
Back row Clockwise: Desmond Burley, unknown, Michael Couch, David Bray, Michael Weeks, unknown, unknown, Terry Tonkin, unknown, unknown, Andrew Teague.
Front row clockwise: Eric Trerise, Chris Parkin, Barrie Trevena, Edwin Willcocks, Andrew Kemp, Gerald Fletcher and Simon Williams. Percussion at rear - Michael Hocking.

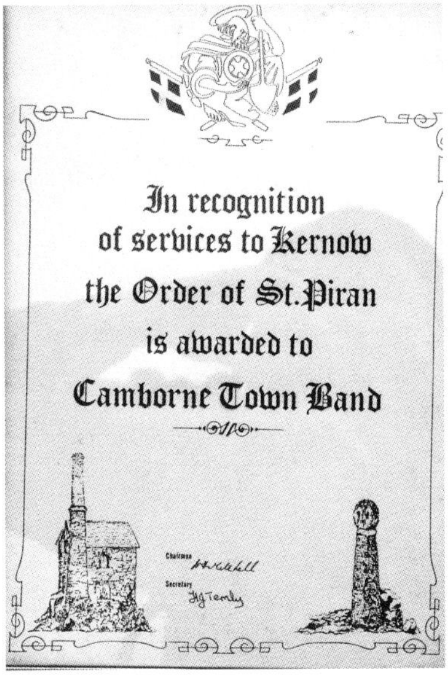
In recognition
of services to Kernow
the Order of St.Piran
is awarded to
Camborne Town Band

1991 – John Hitchens conducted until a new Musical Director could be appointed.

In August 1991 Camborne Town Band was awarded the Cornish Gorsedd Brass Band Trophy.

1991 (October) - Holland trip

Prior to his departure, Stephen Sykes had arranged an exchange visit to Holland with Brassband de Bazuin from Oenkerk. Derek Greenwood returned to conduct the tour which released John Hitchins, the temporary Musical Director, to play euphonium.

On Sunday the 8th December 1991 a Former-Members Band and the Camborne Town Youth Band (Jim Richards) joined Camborne Town Band (Derek Greenwood) to celebrate the 150th anniversary. The three bands played their individual programmes, the future represented by the Youth Band, the past, by about 50 former members, and the present, by the current Band. Former flugel player Jack Pascoe conducted a piece by the "old boys," - sorry, players - some of whom hadn't played for 15 years. It was a concert which provided a fitting celebration of Camborne Town Band's illustrious history. The event concluded with a buffet, a slice of anniversary cake and a whole plateful of reminiscences.

1991 – Derek Greenwood appointed Musical Director.

In 1992 it was time to decorate the bandroom again but on this occasion a contractor undertook the exterior work while the members took care of the inside. Additionally, the bandroom roof was beginning to cause problems and Marcus Dunstan was asked to, "*Have a look at it*".

1992 – South Western Electricity Board sponsorship commences.

Stephen White (bass) joined in 1992 having previously played with St Agnes, St Stythians and St Austell and subsequently with Kernow Brass. He played for about six years and also conducted at St Agnes, Newquay and St Austell.

In 1992 the uniforms changed but not the colour or style. Trevails of Truro was the supplier and it was good that an order could be placed locally.

An anonymous donation was received for the repair and refurbishment of the photographs in the bandroom. The Band hold an impressive set of historical photographs, some of which appear in this book. This was duly undertaken and the committee agreed that a bottle of sherry and a CD be given to the anonymous donator (just how anonymous was it?).

1993 – Placed first at the Yeovil Entertainment Contest.

Chris Netherton (cornet) joined Camborne in 1993 and his parents, Angela and Roy Netherton, soon became involved in committee work. Angela has been an Executive Committee member since about 1994 with two years as Assistant Secretary and the last five years as Secretary which involved arranging transportation, accommodation (for players and supporters) concerts and venues as well as general secretarial duties. Roy has been an Executive Committee Member for about seven years and also serves on the Band Committee.

Mid 1990s
Back row: Jeremy Squibb, Karen Triggs, Stuart Chappell, Chris Netherton, Sarah Lenten, Stephen Trelease, Rob Brokenshire, Steve Weeks, Jason Smith, Jonathan Bond, Stephen White, Michael Pritchard, Gary Lannie, Tim Joslin, Kevin Dower, David Nicholas and David Nicholas.
Front row: Darren Hendy, James Knight, Wayne Brown, Mark Leigh, Graham Barker, Derek Greenwood (Musical Director), Richard Knight, Ian Sutton, Marcus Dunstan, Stuart Butt and John Hitchens. (photo by Brian Errington)

Conducted by Howard Snell, Camborne Town Band, Bodmin Town and Foden's combined for a Gala Concert in the Plymouth Pavilions at the conclusion of the European Championship in May 1993.

In July 1993 the *West Briton* and *Royal Cornwall Gazette* carried the headline "*Band get a new sound*". It went on to say, *"Christmas came early for SWEB Camborne Town Band players on Saturday when they unpacked an almost full set of new instruments."* The Band received a £17,500 grant towards the cost from the Foundation for Sport and the Arts on condition that the existing 15 year-old instruments were passed to the Youth Band. As the *West Briton* said, *"Now members can get down to 'blowing them in' so that they are ready for their performance at the October National Brass Band Championship in London"*.

In 1994 the SWEB Camborne Town Band under Derek Greenwood, recorded the CD, *The Invisible Force,* which included the march *Punchinello, Zampa, You Needed Me* (flugel soloist Stuart Chappell), the hymn tune *Dear Lord and Father of Mankind*, *The Invisible Force* by Goff Richards, *Introduction to Act 3 Lohengrin, Carnival Cocktail* (euphonium soloist – John Hitchens), the hymn tune *Holy, Holy, Holy, Toccata in D Minor* and *Jubilation.*

John Coggins was Chairman and the players were:
Solo cornets: Darren Hendy, James Knight, Wayne Brown and Mark Leigh.
Soprano cornet: Jeremy Squibb. Repiano cornet: Karen Pritchard. Flugel: Stuart Chappell.
Second cornets: Ryan Hollow and Chris Netherton.
Third cornets: Sarah Lenten and Steve Trelease.
Tenor horns: Graham Barker, Ian Sutton and Marcus Dunstan.
Euphoniums: John Hitchens and Stuart Butt.
Baritones: Timothy Joslin and Gary Lannie.
Trombones: David Nicholas, David Nicholas and Kevin Dower (bass).
E flat basses: Michael Pritchard and Stephen White.

B flat basses: Jason Smith and Jonathan Bond.
Percussion: Steven Weeks and Andrew Tellam.

David Nicholas (solo trombone) moved from Hayle and played during the 1980s and 1990s. David (Diddy) Nicholas (trombone) moved from Gweek in the 1990s. Jonathan Bond joined Camborne Junior Band in 1975 and played in the Senior Band from 1981 to 1994 and again from 2001 to 2002. He later became a member of Helston Town.

Brenda Wootten died in 1994 and there were many players who had fond memories of her from the two trips to Paris.

1998 Cornwall Quartet Champions

Mark Leigh
Wayne Brown
Terry Sleeman (conductor)
Graham Barker
John Hitchens

In October 1994 Redruth Town Band was considering building solid walls around the outside of its bandroom and it was suggested that Camborne should do the same. Having a construction man on the team is always useful and Marcus Dunstan was again enlisted to consider the feasibility. His view was that the structure was actually quite sound but a new roof and, possibly, new windows would be required. A short while later Marcus had prepared a specification for a replacement roof and was inviting quotations for the necessary work - it was undertaken during late 1995.

Camborne Town Band took part at the re-opening of the town's library on the 31st May 1995; Queen Elizabeth II performed the ceremony.

On the 6th Oct 1995, the Band took part in the Radio 2 programme, *Cousin Jacks.*

1995 – South Western Electricity Board sponsorship ends.

The South Western Electricity Board had sponsored the Band for three years but that arrangement came to an end in 1995. Many attempts were made to find replacement sponsors but it proved to be very difficult and the financial position of the Music Society was causing great concern. Financial projections by the Treasurer, Trevor Goninan, painted a gloomy picture and urgent action was needed if the Band was to retain the services of a professional Musical Director. Many players and members of the Society responded to the situation and at the annual general meeting in May 1996 it was considered that the worst of the crisis was over. In particular, Trevor Goninan was thanked for keeping everyone informed of the financial situation and Michael Weeks for his efforts in holding the Society together. Derek Greenwood too, was glad to leave 1995 behind; a year which would be remembered for the gloomy financial situation and a scarcity of good contest results. The Revd Basil Brown resigned as President; he'd been Chairman for 12 years and President for 18 years; an exceptional service to the Band, and he was later made a Life Member. David Roberts was elected the new President. Michael Weeks was asked if he would become Chairman but he preferred to remain in his present role of Vice-Chairman. Philip Robinson was then elected Chairman.

The CD, *In Harmony,* featured the Band (Derek Greenwood) and Four Lanes Male Voice Choir (Ronald Brown). It was made in 1996 and included *Glemdene, Let's Face the Music and Dance, You'll Never Walk Alone, Two Little Boys, Soldiers Farewell, The Newquay Fishermen's Song, and Soldiers Chorus.*

1996 – Derek Greenwood resigned as Musical Director.

1996 – John Hitchens appointed Acting Musical Director.

1997 January – John Hitchens appointed Musical Director.

1997 June – John Hitchens resigned as Musical Director.

1997 – Leonard Adams appointed Musical Director.

Trevor Goninan had helped steer the organisation through some difficult financial waters and in 1997, the Treasurer's job passed to Pat Farr who undertook the role until 2003. Pat and his wife have been members of the committee since the early 1990s.

During the mid to late 1990s there was a great deal of interest in obtaining the Trevithick School (the old girls' grammar school) in Trevu Road as a bandroom but after much discussion the idea was shelved.

In 1997 Michael Pritchard (cornet/euph/bass) had been playing for 17 years and received a presentation at the Dinner/Dance.

Don McGeorge was a former writer in the Royal Navy and served on the Band Committee. He initiated the idea of forming a link with HMS Cornwall whereby the Band would play at some official functions and the ship's crew would sell CDs as it travelled the world. Don, Leonard Adams and Marcus Dunstan visited the ship when she was in Plymouth and Marcus said he couldn't remember when he'd had a better meal (lucky them!).

Terry Sleeman (baritone) had the distinction of achieving a hat-trick of wins at Bugle with Camborne, St Dennis and St Austell; he later played for Mount Charles.

Some players from the 1980s/1990s/2000s: David Barnes (cornet) / Robert Brokenshire (percussion - left April 1995) / Robert Commons (cornet - also played at St Dennis and St Austell) / Graham Christophers (horn - came from Helston and later joined Flowers) / Felicity Denning (left in August 1997 to attend college) / Vaughan Denning (Felicity's father, also left in August 1997) / Adrian Dower (bass trombone) / Clive King (cornet) / Charlotte McCaffrey (horn) / Wayne MacCarthy (joined in 1995) / Alan Penrose (cornet) / Megan Pinsent, / Alan Retallack (percussion) / Rachel Retallack (horn) / Alison Richards (tenor horn - played during the 1990s) / Juliette Richards (cornet - played during the 1990s and later moved to Sellers) / Kelly Roberts (cornet) / Denise Repper (tenor horn) / Stephen Wearne (E flat bass - 1998 but left soon after and joined an RAF Band) / Sharon Wearne (tenor horn - wife of Stephen Wearne, left Sept 1998).

1999 – Alan Pope appointed Youth Training and Development Officer.

In February 2000 Camborne Town Band presented a concert by Yorkshire Building Society Brass Band, the European, British Open and All England Masters Champions at that time.

Another CD was recorded in 1999, *Song to the Moon* included: *The Avenger*, Rusalka's *Song to the Moon* (cornet soloist Darren Hendy), *Cruella De Vil, Plenteous Grace, May Dance, Skelter* (tenor horn soloist Graham Barker), *Pops for Brass, Montreal Citadel, Bilitis* (soprano soloist Jeremy Squibb), *Tresavean, Blue Bells of Scotland* (euphonium soloist John Hitchens), *Padstow Lifeboat, Folks on the Hill* (flugel soloist Stuart Chappell) and *Wagner's Procession to the Minster.*
Leonard Adams conducted; he'd recently been made a Cornish Bard for his services to Cornish music.

The players taking part on the CD were:
Solo cornets: Darren Hendy, Mark Leigh, Ian Harvey and Andrew Mitchell.
Soprano cornet: Jeremy Squibb. Repiano cornet: Christopher Leonard. Flugel: Stuart Chappell.
Second cornets: Christopher Netherton and Joanne Ryder-Pollard.
Third cornet: Marcus Dunstan and Rachel Jenkin.
Tenor horns: Graham Barker, Wayne Brown and Tracy Smith (formerly of Lanner & District Band).
Euphoniums: John Hitchens and Tim Joslin.
Baritones: Terry Sleeman and Aldene Button.
Trombones: Shaun Vercoe, Gareth Cottrell and Andrew Rice (bass).
E flat basses: David Coad and Andrew Kemp.
B flat basses: Jason Smith and Simon Hooper.
Percussion: Mark Rosewarne, Nigel Chadd, Steven Weeks and Julie Squibb.

2000 – Leonard Adams resigned as Musical Director.

Graham Boag and the Band with Puffing Devil.
(Photo Mike Saynt James Photography)

2000 - Chris North appointed Musical Director.

2000 – Chris North resigned as Musical Director.

2001 – Graham Boag appointed Musical Director.

In 2001 Camborne Town Band and the Holman-Climax Male Voice Choir combined to record a CD celebrating the first journey of Trevithick's self-propelled road vehicle; the idea for the recording came from Reg Bennett. *Proper Job* was conducted by Graham Boag and included many Cornish tunes.

2002 - Graham Boag resigned as Musical Director.

2002 - Derek Greenwood returned to conduct the Band for a few months.

David Hocking of Camborne painting the bandroom in the late 1990s.

Tramway cyclists in 2002 - Lee Trewhella and Mark "Pob" Leigh.
Andrew "L Plate" Mitchell and Rob Jose took a wrong turning at Rodda's Creamery and ended up in Porthtowan and had to climb the steep hill to get back on course!

2003 - Reg Bennett (Chairman) presenting a framed photograph of Camborne Town Band to Cyril Waterhouse, the Mayor of Camborne, for the Council Offices.

There was a surprise guest at the Band's *Brass on the Grass* event in July 2002. England rugby international Jason Robinson was on holiday and enjoyed a few hours entertainment as the Senior and Junior Bands were put through their paces.

In 2002 the Band recorded the CD, *18 Christmas Crackers*. John Berryman conducted and the players taking part were:
Solo cornets: Chris Leonard, Ian Hooper, Mark Leigh, Robert Sandow and Vicki Kellow.
Soprano cornet: Jeremy Squibb. Repiano cornet: Mo Whitehead. Flugel: Andrew Mitchell.
Second cornets: Chris Netherton and Tracey Abbott.
Third cornets: Sharon Hooper and Becky Richards.
Tenor horns: Graham Barker, Wayne Brown and Charlotte McCaffery.
Euphoniums: Robert Jose and Steve Thomas.
Baritones: Rachel Trudgeon and Aldene Button.
Trombones: Nick Abbott, Gareth Cottrell and Chris Wooding (bass).
E flat basses: Tim Joslin and Graham Boag.
B flat basses: Lee Trewhella and Jonathan Bond.
Percussion: Nigel Chadd and Mark Rosewarne.
Guest players: Phil Blake and Eric Thomas (B flat basses), Iain McKnight (E flat bass) and Gareth Lancaster (second cornet).

2004 April – The Junior Band become Junior Champions of Great Britain.

In July 2004 the Band made a special CD – a personal performance for Stefan Schwed who was dying. He had married Rosemary Phillips, a Camborne girl, in the 1940s and later moved to New Zealand with their children. His niece, Juliet Lingham, wrote to ask if the Band had a recording of the *Flora Dance* – a tune which Stefan would love to hear again and to have it played at his funeral. None was available but within a few days a special recording was made at P M Sound and winging its way to New Zealand

2004 October – Graham Barker appointed Musical Director.

2005 – New Bandroom at Tuckingmill Pavilion officially opened.

The Band had occupied the timber building at the rear of the Camborne Community Centre for almost 70 years but it was no longer suitable and needed to be replaced. It was built in 1936 by Olley Ruse and had served them well but the sound of music had been heard there for the last time. In late 2004 the bandroom was vacated and the equipment, regalia and memorabilia transferred to a temporary bandroom in Tuckingmill Pavilion. That simple statement conceals a tremendous amount of work and for Brian Leigh it became a full-time job for a while. Terry King, Roy Nancarrow, Ray Pascoe and Pat Farr all worked tirelessly to achieve the transfer and the Camborne School of Mines donated a set of chairs. On the 19th February 2005 the new (temporary) bandroom was established and Reg Toy had the honour of cutting the ribbon to open it. The building, a former recreational facility for the workforce at Bickford Smith & Company, was occupied on a three-year lease during which time it was hoped to build a new bandroom. Reg Bennett, Chairman said, *" Our existing bandroom does not have toilets, it doesn't comply with the 2004 disability discrimi-*

The Band's temporary home at Tuckingmill Pavilion

2005 – Three stalwarts – Ray Pascoe, Brian Leigh and Roy Nancarrow (Brian joined the Society Committee in 1993, the same time as Bob Mitchell)

nation act and with the Youth Band, the Training Band, the 'B' Band and the Senior Band there is a footfall of about 130 players a week. So we need to look for new facilities."

David Bray died on the 11th March 2005 and a Service of Thanksgiving was held at Kehelland Methodist Church on the 2nd April. Former player Alan Toy conducted a brass band comprising former playing colleagues, players taught by David and members of the current Youth Band. Participating players were: Leonard Adams, Barrie Trevena Andrew Mitchell, Reg Bennett, Jessica Tredrea, Alan Pope, Marcus Dunstan and Desmond Burley (cornets), Simon Kendall (euphonium), Ben King (baritone), Amber Roberts (tenor horn), Dave Roberts and Russell Kellow (basses) Lester Ashton, Derek Johnson and David Nicholas (trombones).

I had met David on two occasions when he'd provided me with information for this book. Quite apart from any other attributes I was struck by how proud he was to have been a playing member of Camborne Town Band.

2005 April – The Junior Band become Junior Champions of Great Britain for the second year in a row.

2005 - Graham Barker resigned as Musical Director.

Following the Youth Band's success in winning the National Junior Brass Band Championship of Great Britain at Manchester in March 2005, Jeremy Taylor (percussion) and Jessica Tredrea (cornet) were promoted to the ranks of the Senior Band. Jessica had been the Principal Cornet with the Youth Band and Jeremy had won the best-player award at the recent National Final. It did not end there as the Mayor of Camborne also presented Jeremy with an award in recognition of his success.

The Band Dinner was held at the Old Shire Inn in February 2005 when the annual awards were made. Chris Leonard (Principal Cornet) was presented with the Best Performance award (2004) for his playing of *All the Flowers of the Mountain* at the National Championship, Ian Hooper (cornet) was the 2004 Bandsman of the Year, Vicky Kellow (repiano) received the 2004 Best Young Player award and Eric Thomas (bass) was the Players' Player of 2004.

The Committee of 2005
John Pope (Mayor), Alan Pope, Michael Weeks (Chairman), Roy Kelynack, Brian Leigh, Mark Leigh, Tony Bunce (in dark spectacles), Roy Nancarrow, Janet Farr, Jeremy Bond (at rear), Angela Netherton (front), Nick Abbott, Ray Pascoe, Marcus Dunstan (at rear), Roy Netherton, Jeff Wilson (dark jacket), Revd Basil Brown (former Band President) and Pat Farr.

The 2005 annual general meeting was held in March when the following officers and committee members were elected to serve for the forthcoming year:

President - David Roberts	Chairman - Reg Bennett
Vice- Chairman - Jeremy Squibb	Treasurer - Marcus Dunstan
Asst Treasurer - Roy Nancarrow	Secretary - Angela Netherton
Asst Secretary - Janet Farr	Musical Director - situation vacant
Band Manager - Jeremy Squibb	Bandmaster - Steve Thomas
Registration Sec - Mark Leigh	Musical Director (Youth Band) Alan Pope

A compact disc, *Cornwall,* featuring Marc Lloyd Ellery and the Camborne Town Band was recorded in 2005. Above & Beyond Promotions were the producers; Steve Sykes arranged the music for the Band and also conducted the performance. Forty per cent of the proceeds were donated to the RNLI and the Cornwall Air Ambulance - another example of the work the Band undertakes for local charities.

2005 - Stephen (Steve) Thomas appointed Musical Director.

Following the resignation of Reg Bennett in 2005, Michael Weeks was elected Chairman of the Camborne Town Band Music Society. Michael was a former player and Vice-Chairman and had done much to keep the band on the straight and narrow in the past.

A new CD, *Music for Macmillan*, was produced and recorded by PM Sound (Paul Martyn 01872 263300) in September 2005 and featured Karen Hurn, St Hilary Primary School Choir and Camborne Town Band. The proceeds were in aid of Macmillan Nurses and the recording included: *Gaudate, Mid All the Traffic, Softly Softly, Evergreen* (tenor horn soloist Mark Letcher), *Battle of Shiloh* and *Morning in Cornwall. Lieutenant Colonel Chris Davis* and Steve Thomas, the resident Musical Director, conducted the Band.

Players who moved on

John Berryman joined Camborne Town Band in 1951, shortly after Mr F J Roberts had taken over as Musical Director; by 1955 he was the Principal Cornet.

While playing at Camborne John was accepted for membership of the National Youth Brass Band of Great Britain, which he described as, *"A great highlight of my young playing career"*. He attended 10 courses, held in various venues in Britain and is extremely proud to have been Principal Cornetist for nine of them. John said, *"I was not the only representative from Camborne Band; Eric Thomas and Adrian King were also there. My last course was something I will never forget as I was asked to perform the second and third movements of Haydn's Trumpet Concerto at the end of course concert. This solo was also featured in a BBC broadcast which was recorded that week. My time with the NYBB was significant for reasons other than musical as it was there that I met my future wife and we are still together after 43 years. It was a rich period as I played under leading figures in the band movement at that time such as Denis Wright, Eric Ball and prominent musicians from outside the brass band sphere, namely Sir Adrian Boult, from the orchestral world and Colonel Jeagar, who was Director of Music for the Irish Guards."*

In 1959 John entered the Solo Championship of Great Britain at Oxford and was heard by an official of Munn & Feltons – two weeks later he had joined as assistant Principal Cornet to James Scott and within a year he was promoted to Principal Cornet, a position he held until he left in November 1969. In that time there were many highlights including three National Final wins, countless broadcasts and television appearances, and tours to Holland, Switzerland, Denmark and, not forgetting, to Cornwall. John said, *"My playing highlight was performing as soloist in the two festival concerts at the Albert Hall which followed the National Final Contest. On another occasion the GUS Footwear Quartet also performed at the festival concert after winning the Quartet Championship three years in succession. All nerve wracking, but unforgettable all the same. I made many recordings with the Band under the Columbia label. It was always an exciting day as they were made at the famous Abbey Road Studios – where the Beatles also recorded. They were long days because we would start at 10.00 am and finish at 5.00pm. Demanding on lips but we always made it."*

John commenced his conducting career with Bodmin Town Band where he remained for almost five years until he was appointed Conductor of the Grimethorpe Colliery Band where he worked closely with Elgar Howarth. Northamptonshire Education Authority was seeking a peripatetic brass teacher and John was appointed and held the position for 22 years during which time he was also the conductor of the very successful County Youth Brass Band. Concurrent with this, he was appointed Musical Director of the William Davies Construction Group Band (now defunct). He said, *"I held this position for 10 wonderful years with the highlight being when it was awarded BBC Band of the Year"*. For the last 30 years or so, he has adjudicated at many brass band contests and music festivals at home and abroad – and in Cornwall, of course, where he has the rare distinction of having played, conducted and adjudicated at the Bugle Band Contest. In 1985, he became conductor of the GUS Footwear Band, an appointment that lasted seven years, albeit in two periods. More latterly he has been Musical Director of the Kibworth Band as well as being busy with freelance work.

Stuart Chappell (Principal Cornet/flugel and Bandmaster) joined in 1985 having previously played in Falmouth Town and Lanner & District Silver. He left in 2001 and is currently the Musical Director of recently promoted Lanner & District Silver which gained a commendable eighth place at the 2005 Area Championship playing Howard Lorriman's arrangement of *Rienzi.*

Stuart recalled Camborne winning the South-West Area Contest in 1990 as particularly memorable when Stephen Sykes conducted the Test Piece *The Beacons* by Ray Steadman-Allen.

Edgar Floyd (tenor horn), and his brothers Jack and Gordon, joined Camborne circa 1928 and he played until the 1950s. During his last few years with the Band he was its Bandmaster and also the Musical Director of St Stythians Band. His sons, Alan (cornet), Dennis (soprano) and Gordon (tenor horn) played under him at St Stythians and Gordon was a member of Camborne Town Band when it took part in the BBC Best of Brass Contest at Derby.

They recalled that their father cycled from Four Lanes to Camborne, stood and played during practice and cycled home again. During the latter stages of Mr Parker's illness, Edgar often took over the conducting role and Gordon says, *"Some of the boys at Camborne certainly liked a pint and Dad tried to curb this by keeping them playing for as long as possible to restrict their drinking time"*. Even after he finished playing at Camborne he returned to help out when the Band was short-handed.

Edgar took St Stythians to Championship status and, for a while in the late 1960s, St Agnes enjoyed some friendly contest rivalry with them.

When I met Edgar's sons, their mother, Edgar's wife, had just died and a number of photographs had come to light, some of which have been included in this book. He won many awards for best horn player and had two pieces of music dedicated to him: the hymn tune *St Stythians* by Donald F Broad and *Just as I am by* Monty Pearce, who was very friendly with him. Edgar died in the early 2000s so I missed my chance to renew my acquaintance with him. I knew him when I played in the Cornwall County Youth Brass Band from the 1959 course to the late 1960s. I remember him as a popular and dedicated tutor who did much to develop that organisation.

James "Jimmy" Gribben became the solo trombone champion of Great Britain in November 1980 and another Camborne player had made his name on the national stage. He later joined the RAF Central Band.

Mike Hocking (percussion) joined in the early 1960s and was a member until 1975 when he was accepted to play for Brighouse and Rastrick, under Derek Broadbent. While he was there, Brighouse was Granada Band of the Year and took both the National Championship at the Royal Albert Hall and the British Open Championship at Belle Vue, Manchester.

He returned to play at Camborne for a year in 1982 and since the late 1980s has been a member of Helston Town. During his long career he also played in the Cornwall Youth Brass Band and in 2004 chalked up his 102nd contest of which he has been in the winning band 41 times.

Norman Johns (cornet) was the Assistant Principal at Camborne and later conducted Redruth Town.

Derek Johnston Jnr (trombone) joined in the early 1970s when his father, Derek Johnston Snr, became Musical Director. He left in 1974 but returned to play again in the late 1990s. He is currently the Musical Director of Hayle and St Stythians Bands.

Adrian King (cornet) commenced playing with Carharrack & St Day in 1949, when he was 10 years old. After a couple of years his parents moved to Illogan and his father took him to meet Joe Trounce who taught the young players at Camborne. Having struggled with the shy, young boy for a while he passed him over to his brother, Jack Trounce, with the comment, *"I can hardly get a word out of him but there's something there worth pursuing"*.

Young Adrian gradually came out of his shell after working with Jack on a one-to-one basis. He began to develop both as a player and as a person. He said, "*I was very nervous but my confidence was growing and I was brought into the Band on third cornet. There were many great players at that time including Joe Trounce, the inspirational Jack Trounce, Telfer Rule, the impressive Jack Berryman and that fine euphonium player, Gerald Fletcher. I remember Sundays when John Berryman and I would be up at 6.00am and heading off to Gwithian on our bicycles. A quick swim and we would be on our way back to the bandroom where we would spend the day playing pieces from the library. A few others often joined us and we would clear the room and practise our marching.*

I played in the Cornwall County Youth Band and in the mid 1950s I was accepted for the National Youth Brass Band of Great Britain. Freddie Roberts had been a great supporter of this and had encouraged many youngsters to join but he began to feel it had become a poaching ground and that Camborne was being used to train players for the big bands. In late 1961 I had an audition with Stanley Boddington of Munn & Feltons (later GUS Footwear) and I remember telling Mr Roberts I had been successful. He took it very calmly and didn't try to talk me out of it, he just said, 'They grow lovely roses up there,' – he loved his roses."

Late 1950s – Adrian King, before he moved to Kettering to play with Munn & Feltons Footwear Band.
(Photo by Henry Parkinson of Camborne)

Adrian remained at GUS Footwear until 1975 and during that time he toured Switzerland, Holland and Canada as well as recording regularly on BBC broadcasts and on 20 or more records. National and World Brass Band Championships were won during that period when he also played with Harry Mortimer's All Star Brass Band of Great Britain.

In 1972, he was appointed Peripatetic Brass Teacher for the Bedfordshire Education Authority and in that same year he formed the Brio Brass Ensemble which built up a strong reputation as a pioneer Brass Chamber Group. Quite apart from its activities in and around Bedfordshire, it has taken part in Cornish festivals and recorded for the BBC. Most of the ensemble's music repertoire is concentrated around the great Venetian School of composers but it also performs a steady number of original compositions written especially for it by a growing company of composers, *Quintet for Brass,* a fanfare *Professional* by Colin E Cowles, two set pieces by John Anthony Ireland and *Quintet for Brass* by Donald Hart. A commissioned suite for brass, *Music for St Ives* by the London-based composer John Blood, and Christopher Brown's *Seascape* were given their first public performance at the 1981 St Ives September Festival. Since 1973 Adrian has studied trumpet - playing with Philip Jones and John Miller – and the art of brass ensemble playing with members of the Philip Jones Brass Ensemble at their summer courses.

Apart from playing with the Brio Brass Ensemble he does a lot of free-lance work. He was Principal Trumpet for the Bedfordshire Symphony Orchestra from 1972 to 1986 and for the Cambridge Symphony Orchestra from 1976 to 1986. He has also played with the Cambridge Sinfonia, the National Sinfonia, various other orchestras, choral, Gilbert & Sullivan and operatic societies.

In 1976, Adrian was faced with a decision; should he continue with GUS Footwear under its new conductor, Geoffrey Brand, or should he change direction and embrace a full-time music career in the orchestral world. An exciting new future seemed to be opening up with GUS Footwear but even Geoffrey Brand agreed with his eventual decision to make the break.

Adrian told me of an occasion when he returned to Cornwall and visited Jack Trounce. He said, *"Jack put his arms around me and recalled when I was a shy, young boy. He couldn't get over how I'd developed as a person and he told me I was his greatest success – Jack was a special person; I have been lucky to have had many great teachers."*

I spent a delightful three hours talking to Adrian when we must have covered every subject under the sun – including how this passionate Cornishman joined the Rebellion Walk from St Keverne to Blackheath – by accident. He'd been walking for a while when he enquired how far the walkers would be going!

W (Billy) E Moyle was born in Camborne in early 1904 and began his brass band career with Camborne Town. In 1922, he moved to Newquay to work and joined Newquay Town Band as solo cornet under George Cave. Shortly after, he went to live in Canada and found himself playing trumpet and piano in a travelling circus – possibly Barnum and Bailey's according to Dudley Currah (formerly of Newquay Town Band).

Illness forced his return to this country in the late 1920s when he attended London Guildhall School of Music and gained his LGSM qualification. He moved back to Newquay where he played piano for the silent films at the Old Pavilion Cinema.

During the Second World War he worked for Kershaw Optical Works making bombsights. He played cornet with Yeadon Old and St Hilda's Bands and later became cornet player and Bandmaster with Brighouse and Rastrick Band - deputising for Eric Ball.

In 1947 he returned to Newquay Town Band as Musical Director. He also led a dance band - *Billy Moyle and his Super Dance Band* – which won the Championship of Cornwall in the 1930s. During the 1950s and 1960s he was the pianist and conductor with the Goonhavern Banjo Band.

He composed a number of pieces including his favourite, *Cornish Cavalier* and when he died in 1988, it was included as a test piece at the following year's Bugle Contest.

Peter Richards (bass) joined Camborne Town Band from Truro City and subsequently played with Yorkshire Imperial, Carlton Main and Hammond Sauce Works.

Sam Roberts was Fred Roberts' younger brother and also played cornet for Camborne Town Band during the 1920s. Like Fred, he moved to Brighouse and Rastrick and they often played together in quartets and other groups. He later became Musical Director of the Rogerstone Band, based near Newport in South Wales. He died in 1969. His son, John, also played for the Band during the 1950s.

Telfer *"Spanner"* Rule (soprano) played from the 1920s and into Freddie Robert's era and his list of achievements are spread throughout this book. He was Bandmaster for some years and during the 1950s he trained the juniors. He is said to have always been in the thick of things, had a sweet tone, but was a hard man. He later became Musical Director at St Austell and Pendeen.

I've been told that Telfer often carried his instrument case in his hand but preferred to carry his soprano under his arm. It seems that this was very useful at tea-treats when the food provided by the chapels was more than enough. The case would then be used to store sustenance for the homeward journey – allegedly!

Shaun Thomas (euphonium) died in March 2005, aged just 35. He had recently been appointed Musical Director of St Keverne and Phillip Hunt's headline, in his *West Briton* column *brass notes,* said "*Brass Band community in mourning*". Shaun's funeral was held at St Michael's Church in Newquay and many former playing colleagues travelled from around the country. Thirteen of them, from Sunlife, Camborne, St Keverne, Mount Charles, Helston and Buy As You View, combined in a brass group conducted by Dr Roy Newsome.

Shaun started his playing career with Falmouth Town, at the age of 12, before transferring to Camborne where he spent his teenage years before studying at the Royal Welsh College of Music and Drama at Cardiff. He'd been principal euphonium of The Sunlife Band, had played with Parc an Dare and several other top bands. It was with Sunlife where he had carved out a name for himself, notably as a soloist. On returning to Cornwall in 1997 he played with St Austell, Mount Charles and Camborne and was a founder member of the South West Tuba Quartet. He played with Camborne when the Band won the West Of England title in 2001 and he made his final appearance on the contest stage in its National Championship performance in October 2004, under the direction of Frank Renton.

David Tonkin played cornet at Camborne before moving to Brighouse & Rastrick.

Alan Toy joined the full Band in 1955, at the age of 12, having been taught by Joe Trounce in the learners' group where it was a case of theory first and then a test before being issued with an instrument. He said, *"It was a tribute to Joe that I made such rapid progress; he was a superb teacher".* Alan recalled his first engagement, *"It was playing carols at Lowenac House when I was about 10 years old and after a while I was asked to attend a practice and sit next to my father when I had to read the music and press imaginary valves – with Freddie Roberts watching. I played second horn during the summer of 1955, when players received fourteen shillings (70p) for an engagement unless, like me, you had not yet played at a contest when the payment was only seven shillings.*

In 1958, I became a reluctant solo euphonium player when I was transferred, at Telfer Rule's (Bandmaster) request. It seemed a crafty move as Telfer immediately took over on tenor horn and I was unable to move back for a while. Because of my studies I left in 1962 but returned again the following year - on tenor horn.

I was invited to join Brighouse and Rastrick in the 1960s - when it was National Champion. I was taking part in a solo contest at Helston and had been awarded first place. The adjudicator, Walter Hargreaves, asked me to play the piece again and then made the invitation. I declined and some time later, when the Band was travelling all the way to Leeds to compete in a contest, I became convinced I'd made the right decision."

Alan finished playing in 1975. Having had a taste of conducting, he decided to make the move in that direction and, in 1977, he took over Hayle Town Band. In 1983 he moved to St Stythians where he was Musical Director until 1987. He re-joined Camborne as a player in the late 1980s, initially under Stephen Sykes and then under Derek Greenwood. He also conducted Redruth (1996) and St Keverne, for a short while, in 1997.

Alan won many honours as a soloist in his band career but has always held the view that he was only part of a great team and wonderful family known as Camborne Town Band. He was the youngest known solo horn player at 13 years old and treasures the memories and friendships he made during his 25 years with the band.

Barry Tresidder (E flat bass) joined in 1952 and was aware that he was continuing a family tradition that stretched back to about 1900 (you will have already read about some of his relations).

He played with the Band until 1957 when he left to attend Kneller Hall, the Army school of music, where he began a 23½ year career playing in the Royal Army Medical Corp Staff Band where he achieved the rank of Band Sergeant Major.

Back in civilian life he played with Camborne for a few months in 1981, when there was a temporary shortage of players but his ambition was to take up the baton and he became conductor of the Penryn Concert Band. After a couple of years he took over St Erth Band and then had periods at Lanner & District, Porthleven and Hayle.

Joe Volante (cornet) played from about 1913 to 1935 before turning to conducting. He took Redruth Town in Class "A" at Bugle Contest in 1949, 1950 and 1951 when it competed against Camborne.

Reg Toy recalled, *"I played with Joe Volante; he composed the hymn tune, 'Margaret,' named after his granddaughter, and all the profits went to the RAF Benevolent Fund".*

Joe also conducted Perranporth and often dragged his grandson, Toni Volante, in to help. Toni said, *"I would try and avoid him so he couldn't ask but he used to wait for me as I went home from work. He was a good player, I remember him playing a duet with Harry Mortimer at the Scala cinema. He liked to play a few tricks on people but he got his come-uppance when playing at one of the summer concerts at Looe or Porthleven. Someone removed his cornet from its case and replaced it with a crab and when he reached down to pick it up he had a bit of a surprise."*

Eddie Williams at Brighouse & Rastrick

Roy Wearne (soprano) moved to Camborne from Helston Band in the late 1950s and was a National Youth Brass Band member at the same time as Desmond Burley. He joined the 5th Inniskillen Dragoon Guards in 1964, trained at Kneller Hall and took part in the trumpet fanfare at a number of major events. He rose through the ranks and conducted various military bands both as Bandmaster and Guest Conductor and on leaving the forces he became Bandmaster of the Metropolitan Police Band before taking up a music post in Dubai.

Eddie Williams (tenor horn and Bandmaster) played for Camborne from about 1939 to 1951 when he moved "up-country" where he lodged with Fred Roberts and family when he first played for Brighouse & Rastrick. His father, Edwin Williams, had once conducted Camborne Band and it was he who wrote a number of solos for Eddie but it seems they were never published.

He played in the All Star Band of Great Britain for a few years and for the Fairey Band before coming "home" to conduct St Dennis in 1958. He was Musical Director there for many years during which time St Dennis was a significant force, competing on the national stage as well as locally. He was made a Cornish Bard for his work with young musicians and received a medal from the Worshipful Company of Musicians of the City of London. Eddie's wife, Lorna, said, *"He never worried about a contest result, win or lose, he was just determined to do better next time".*

Musical Directors and Bandmasters

Mr W J Uren was conductor from 1888, when it was the Military Reserve Band. He successfully conducted at a number of contests including the first Bugle Festival, in 1912.

William Uren (right) Camborne Town conductor for 25 years

1913 - Walter Nettle

Following Mr Uren's death, or possibly just before, **Walter Nuttall** (possibly Nettle) took over as conductor. He had previously been the trainer and seemed the natural successor. The Band took top place when he conducted at the 1913 Bugle Contest but I cannot be sure if his appointment was intended to be temporary or permanent.

Will Layman conducted for a while, probably 1914/1915, but I don't know in what capacity – Musical Director or Guest Conductor.

Edwin Williams then became Musical Director. He conducted the Band at the 1919 Bugle Contest and held the post to 1924. His wife played baritone and euphonium with St Ives Band and took part at the Bugle Festival – the first woman to do so. She was a prize-winning contralto singer and performed at a number of Camborne Town Band concerts when Edwin was conducting.

Edwin Williams (left) when conductor at Carharrack & St Day with a young Eddie Williams who was to become one of Camborne Band's most famous "sons".

George Rosevear took over as Bandmaster but it appears this was intended to be a temporary situation. Indeed, there is little mention of this and it could be that his period with the baton may have been earlier than he appears in my listing.

He is reputed to have been a fine trombone player who not only played in Camborne Town Band but also for the Redruth Picturedrome Orchestra. He appears in a number of early photographs but only rarely is he seen looking directly at the camera.

He reverted to playing when a new conductor was found but it seems he and Mr Parker never got on.

(Photo courtesy of J Arthur Osborne)

Mr A Wathew Parker from Treharris, South Wales, was appointed Musical Director in 1925. He'd been a member of the famous St Hilda's Band and had also played with Besses o' the Barn. He made an immediate impact at Camborne by winning the Championship Section at Bugle Contest.

During the 1930s he took the Band to many local contests and to compete at the Crystal Palace in London. The gradual rise in the standard of playing was rewarded in 1945, when he led the Band to the National Second Section Championship.

Gerald Fletcher remembered him as a marvellous musician and excellent man-manager. *"The Band was not as good technically as it is now but had good players in the key positions. Mr Parker would bring out the best in all players but if, for example, the second or third cornets were struggling, he would re-write the parts so that the repiano or front cornets would cover for them.*

I used to play with the mouthpiece to one side of my mouth and Mr Parker suggested that it might be better if I could position it to the centre of my lips. I tried but found it very difficult. One day I was walking towards the bandroom when I heard someone playing Carnival de Venice; it was beautiful. I walked in and realised it was Mr Parker and I stood and listened for a while. When he finished he noticed I'd been watching where the mouthpiece was placed on his lips – to one side. He smiled at me and said, 'I'm afraid it's a case of do as I say, not do as I do.'"

Gerald recalled the fun he had in the Band but also remembered one occasion when it rebounded. *"Sunday Evening Concerts would take place in Camborne and in the surrounding villages and on this occasion we were visiting Carharrack. Playing started at 7.00pm and finished at 9.00pm which suited those who liked a pint as it left them about half-an-hour. And some of them could drink! One of the pieces on the programme was 'A Sailor's Life', a piece of music in which the percussionist had to ring out six-bells. Alfred John Tresidder had the hammer in hand completely oblivious to the fact that his equipment had been tampered with. Donald Cock and I had stuffed grass up one of the tubes and what should have been a clear dong came out as a dull thud. Alfred John was livid and picked up the bells and threw them over the hedge but Mr Parker said nothing. The concert continued until 9.00pm when the players started putting their instruments away. Mr Parker said, 'I'll think we'll play just one more'. And after that it was 'just one more' and 'just one more' until the clock moved to 9.30pm and departure time. Mr Parker had guessed who had played the trick and by depriving the drinkers of their refreshment knew that the boys would be in trouble from their colleagues.*

As I said, there were a few heavy drinkers, well a lot of them liked their pint but some of them were always the last to tear themselves away from the bar. I'm thinking of Telfer Rule, Fred Skinner (B flat bass) and Sidney Kean (B flat bass) and maybe one or two others. We'd been told what time the coach was leaving but a few would still be finishing their pints. Without saying a word, Mr Parker would walk into the pub and order a drink. He'd look at his watch, drink his beer, look at his watch again and then walk out. I couldn't believe that they'd leave beer on the bar but they followed him out, finished or not."

Fred Waters touchingly recalled, *"I shall never forget his funeral; it was held in Camborne Parish Church. The Band marched from his house in Enys Road, Camborne, to the church and how we managed to keep playing the Dead March from Saul to an acceptable musical standard, I will never know. I remember seeing the side drummer's wrists when we reached the church after he had played a non-stop drum roll with snares off all the way from the house - they were completely white.*

The church was packed with most of the top names in the brass band world including Eric Ball, Harry and Alex Mortimer, Stanley Boddington, Tommy Powell, George Thompson, Harold Moss, Walter Hargreaves, Bill Scholes with Frank Phillips and Frank Gillard representing the BBC.

His death hit me particularly hard as I had been his only pupil for his last three years and, at the age of 13, it was my first close experience of death. His widow gave me the silver furled ebony baton that he used at the Albert Hall Championship and I still have it today; I slept with it by my pillow for about six months after he died which indicates just what an indelible impression he must have made on me at this tender age."

Tom Ruse described him as, *".... quiet and well liked; a man of considerable ability who was well respected. He liked a traditional band sound - louder than would be acceptable today - Camborne Town Band had a big, full tone in those days."*

Mr A W Parker was held in very high esteem by the people of Camborne and, like most of the players, Edgar Floyd had great respect for him. When he died a collection was made to buy a trophy in his memory and it was used at the Camborne Music Festival.

The A W Parker Trophy

Tim Richards, ex Royal Marines, took over for a few months when Mr Parker died but this may have been a temporary arrangement.

Mr F J Roberts was born in Treherbert, South Wales, but the family had strong connections with West Cornwall. In 1913, when he was five years old, he started his playing career with Camborne Salvation Army; his father was the Bandmaster. Fred's first instrument was a bass drum, or a scaled down version of one, made by his father, Sam. The framework was an old cheese tub to which was fitted skins and tensioning cording and, apart from size, it performed just like the real thing. Melba Hale (née Roberts), Fred's daughter, still has it but it's now used as a base for her parrot's cage rather than for making music. When a little older he moved to cornet, an instrument on which he was to excel. I'm not sure when he joined the Band but it was certainly when Edwin Williams was conducting - circa 1920. He became Principal Cornet at the age of 14 and built an impressive reputation be-

The Roberts family - Fred, Sam Snr & Sam Jnr with the drum

fore leaving for a short period to play with St Dennis before the lure of playing for his home town brought him back to Camborne again. His love of music took him in many directions including as a member of a small group who accompanied silent movies at the King's Cinema.

In 1930 he was offered a position with Gresford Colliery Band in North Wales and he and his family made the move north. This turned out to be a stepping-stone and after about a year, he joined Brighouse & Rastrick. During 1933 and 1934 he played with the famous Munn & Feltons (later the GUS Footwear Band) but sometime during mid 1934 Fred and his family made the trek back up north to play with Brighouse and Rastrick again where he was Principal Cornet for many years, including in 1946, when it became National Champions.

He transferred to Manchester C W S (the old "Tobacco Band") in 1947, as Principal Cornet and Bandmaster and during his time there the Band had considerable success including winning the British Open Championship.

Fred Roberts returned to Camborne to work in his father's business. Sam Roberts, his father, made sweets in a garage at the bottom of their garden at No. 9 Vyvyan Street, Camborne, using the front room of their house as a shop. As the business grew he built a factory and store opposite (now Foyco) and opened a shop on the corner of Chapel Street and Cross Street. Fred had worked in the business prior to moving to Wales and was to be involved again. In 1953, however, he commenced working for Holman's where he remained until retirement.

Fred Roberts in his Brighouse & Rastrick uniform

Mr A W Parker had conducted Camborne for a great number of years but was aware his health was failing. He contacted Fred and asked him if he would be prepared to take over the Band and in 1951, Mr F J Roberts became the Camborne Town Band Musical Director, a position he held for about 20 years.

During this period he had considerable success. The contests results are set out later in the book and these, together with the stories behind them, will indicate what a successful and stable period this was.

David Reed remembered Fred Roberts as a hard trainer but, *"He treated everyone alike; he had no favourites"*. Tom Ruse said, *"Fred preferred a softer, more orchestral sound in line with how brass bands were developing at that time"*. Eric Thomas remembered him as a hard man who gave little praise. His reasoning seemed to be that he shouldn't praise the players too much or it would go to their heads.

In 1971 Fred Roberts began conducting St Austell Town Band as well but this caused some friction and he resigned his position at Camborne. He stayed at St Austell for five years and had considerable success but his health was failing and he could no longer

F J Roberts (Photo by Eric Parsons)

meet the demands of being Musical Director of a Championship Section band. Fred's reluctance to be far from the conductor's position however lured him back - as Musical Director of Redruth Town Band when Philip James left. He was one of 10 applicants from many parts of the country and was unanimously appointed. He was there until his health made it impossible for him to continue and during the latter stages of his illness he lost the power of speech and could only give written instructions. Reluctantly he had to give up doing what he loved most.

Fred Roberts died in October 1978, of motor neurone disease, a progressive, muscle wasting illness. He had battled against it for a few years and his conducting spell at Redruth was only accomplished because of advancing technology when his hand-written instructions were displayed on a screen on the wall. A huge funeral procession marched solemnly down Trelowarren Street led by Edward Ashton and a massed band of 40 players drawn from the eight Cornish bands with which he had had some association. A large number of former players were also in the procession. Eddie Ashton recalled that Mr Roberts had written down exactly what he wanted; the music to be played, the cortege route and the choice of bands to be represented. Eddie was asked by the family to select the players and to lead them. He said, *"I had to contact the various bands and ask the players if they would take part and then organise a rehearsal. It was a lot of work but I felt honoured to be asked to do it".* The funeral was a fitting tribute for this Cambornian who became famous as a brass bandsman, teacher, conductor and adjudicator.

At the funeral, Salvation Army Captain Pam Saunders read this eulogy by Eric Ball.

"To all assembled at The Salvation Army, Camborne, Cornwall. I am grateful for this opportunity of paying tribute to Fred Roberts, friend and musician. Personally I have a great deal to thank him for, especially in regard to the days when I began working in the brass band contesting movement. His invitation to me to conduct the great Brighouse and Rastrick Band, and his sharing with me the vast and valuable experience he had gained was invaluable to one coming from another and different field of activity. I shall be ever grateful for those exciting and well-remembered days.

But I would write also on behalf of Fred's many friends and acquaintances in the world of brass bands. His valuable work as a cornet soloist, and especially as the leader of his section, was first class. On the most testing of occasions we could be sure that his playing and attitude were firm as a rock.

He had firmly held opinions about bands and band music, and a tenacity of character not easily moved. His work as a conductor was thorough and the results effective, and often reached a very high artistic level.

Fred was a shining example of the great company of resident conductors who week after week work hard at the art they love – music through the brass band. One wonders if they are sufficiently appreciated – we guest conductors often receive all the applause!

Already we write of Fred in the past tense – buy why? Somewhere in one of our Lord's many resting-places Fred will be looking, not for rest, but the opportunity to exercise his talents!

To Mrs Roberts, Melba and the family I send greetings and assurance of our prayers. Their support of Fred in good days and bad is worthy of deep appreciation. God bless you all."

Fred Roberts was a perfectionist and all his efforts were channelled towards his ultimate goal of making perfect music. Many players have said he was not the easiest man to play under but he had his standards and, as one former player has said, *"His imposing presence engendered teamwork and made us the formidable force that we were".*

During his life he was involved with a number of bands, helped many others and was one of the leading figures in setting up the Cornwall County Youth Brass Band; he was its first conductor. But surely nothing could have given him more pleasure than leading Camborne Town Band to victory on so many occasions.

Alan Toy was principal tenor horn and Bandmaster at the time Fred Roberts left and he conducted for about a year while the search went on for a new Musical Director.

Derek Johnston was born in Carlisle and started playing when only four years old. His father, John Johnston, played in the Salvation Army Band at Carlisle, so brass bands were a part of family life. On his demobilisation from National Service he played principal trombone with Carlisle St Stephens and later played solo horn for Grimethorpe Colliery Band.

He commenced conducting at the of age 16 and went on to become the Musical Director at Liddisdale Temperance Band in Newcastleton, Scotland, taking them from fourth to top section in consecutive years. During the early 1960s he moved to Rossington Colliery in Yorkshire, then to Dimington Colliery and, prior to moving to Cornwall, he was Musical Director of Creswell Colliery. While at Rossington he took them to Holland (1965) and to Germany (1969), where he won the World Band Championship. He also conducted Carlisle City Band, Diddington Band, Thurcroft Band and a number of male voice choirs.

In March 1971 he was appointed Musical Director of Camborne Town Band and his period of leadership included a great number of superb events and impressive contests results.

Following a dispute with the committee over "*irreconcilable differences*," he left in September 1974 but continued to be involved in the local brass band scene.

Leonard Adams - The position of Musical Director was advertised immediately and in the meantime, 20 year-old Leonard Adams (Bandmaster) took over the role until a replacement could be found.

Bernard Bygrave - The identity of the next Musical Director was revealed at a Christmas concert in 1974 but it was dependent on his finding a suitable, local job. Bernard had returned from a six-year period in Australia and was keen to commence at Camborne.

Both his father and grandfather were bandsmen and Bernard started with Staveley Works Band before playing Principal Cornet with Dannemora Steel Works Band and then joining Brighouse and Rastrick. He was Principal Cornet with Black Dyke and then played with Crossley Carpets Band. His stay at Camborne was short and in late 1975 he resigned as Musical Director and returned to Australia with his family.

Leonard Adams (Bandmaster) again took over the role of conductor until a new Musical Director could be appointed.

Derek Greenwood started his banding career at Earby Silver Band in his home county of Yorkshire and in 1965, joined the Grenadier Guards where he became solo euphonium. He was there for 10 years and played at the Wembley World Cup Final in 1966. Peter Parkes was the Musical Director for some of that time and he was amenable to players conducting civilian bands and Derek began his conducting career with the Crystal Palace Band.

When he left the Guards he applied for the vacant Musical Director's position at Camborne and was appointed immediately (1976) following his audition. For the first three months he commuted to Cornwall but then moved to live in Camborne. Derek said, *"I was aware that I was joining a band with a great tradition, not least by the reminder I received whenever I looked up and saw the photograph of Freddie Roberts staring down at me; his eyes seemed to follow me everywhere.*

Derek Greenwood in action at his audition

I was determined to achieve a good playing standard and nothing pleased me more than to take the Band to a contest and have the same players at a concert the following week; I'm, not a great lover of borrowing players. Contest results are important but they will come when the Band is playing at a consistently high level and I wanted Camborne to regain its reputation of being the band that everyone wanted to be in. I brought my own discipline or perhaps it was more a case of instilling a level of self-discipline. Whatever it was, I felt it an honour to conduct such a splendid group of musicians who were like a family unit.

Leonard Adams was Bandmaster and gave me tremendous support; I knew that it was inevitable that he would eventually leave to start a career in conducting.

In my early days at Camborne I had a very young back row of cornets who had just come up from the Youth Band - David Whear, Nigel Cock, Kevin Goninan, Andrew Kemp and Alan Pope. They were a good group and we enjoyed regular sectional rehearsals and then go off for a game of beach football. At that time, rehearsals were well attended and players needed a good reason to be absent."

Sometime around 1980 Derek Greenwood took a conducting post at Truro School and is still involved there. Frank Moore (The St Agnes Silver Band Musical Director for many years) previously held the post but had recently died.

"After the 1977 National Final, when Camborne was fourth, a group of us went to a nearby pub to celebrate. Harold Stuart led the Cornish singing; I don't think London knew what to make of it.

I remember returning from Bugle Contest one year and standing outside the Camborne Community Centre. A supporter asked the result and on being told that we were placed second she hit one of the players over the head with her umbrella. I'm not sure what she would have done if we were third.

In 1984 we spent a week in Paris accompanying Brenda Wootton. We had to take part with a number of groups and singers and while the audience were appreciative I don't think they were really

The Band under Derek Greenwood (Photo by B Errington)

The Band of the late 1990s under Leonard Adams (Photo by B Errington)

2002 with Frank Renton in front of the Royal Albert Hall

2005 - The Champion Band at Bugle

into brass band music. What surprised us was how big a star Brenda Wootton was over there. We just couldn't believe that this lady from Cornwall was so well known in Paris.

Our hotel was directly opposite a sex shop where live shows also took place and it was all I could do to round up some of the players for the concert but I'm mentioning no names.

I left Camborne in 1985 and conducted St Austell for two years and then St Dennis - which I really enjoyed. In 1991, I was asked to take Camborne on a visit to Holland and by the time we arrived home I had agreed to return as the Camborne Town Band Musical Director."

Apart from the association with the bands already mentioned, Derek has been involved with Bethnal Green Band, Hammersmith Band, Tredegar, Woodfalls, Sunlife, Bideford and, of course, St Keverne where he became Musical Director.

Derek said, *"Robert Tanner was an amazing player but there were a few doubters when I promoted him from third cornet to principal. But my confidence in him was justified and I was sad that his brass band career was curtailed because of his studies. Robert Cook is another player who I rated very highly - Camborne Band has had many fine players but he is up there with the best."*

Michael Weeks recalled Derek Greenwood's time as, *"Very busy, successful and settled,"* and John Phillips said, *"There was something magical about his conducting. With others we would practise and practise and then transfer that standard to the contest or concert stage but with Derek Greenwood, the performance was always better than the rehearsals. It was as if he had a reserve of adrenalin which would help him raise our playing to another level."* In a quote in *The Bandsman* in 1992, Derek said, *"There is always one band you become attached to more than the others and for me it is Camborne. Even when I was away from it, I maintained an emotional attachment."*

Eddie (Whisky) Ashton

Eddie Ashton (trombone) joined in 1958 having played at Helston for 15 years. In 1957, he was asked if he would be interested in transferring but he did not pursue it. About a year later he made the approach and was a bit surprised when four people came down to interview him. Telfer Rule, Dick Tresidder and Gerald Weeks accompanied Fred Roberts and after some concern about his range of interests he promised to give up his involvement in dance bands, cricket and football; he was in.

At first he had no transport so he sold his dance band trombone to put the money towards buying a car. His first contest was at Truro, in 1958, when the test piece was *Coriolanus*.

He was Bandmaster and played regularly until 1969 when he took over as Musical Director at Helston. Even after that, he continued playing occasionally for Camborne. He said, *"It all became a bit much and there was one occasion when I conducted Helston at the Cornwall Brass Band Association contest at Truro and even before the result was known, I was on my way to Leicester to play in the W D & H O Wills Championship".*

During the early 1980s Eddie was not well and he gave up the baton at Helston. After a while, in late 1985, he was approached about the vacant Musical Director's position at Camborne and he agreed to take it on a temporary basis. As it turned out he was there for almost two years. During this period he conducted at some contests and for others he prepared the players for a guest conductor. In 1988, rehearsals were under way for the Area Championship when the test piece was *Ballet for Band*. Eddie telephoned Stephen Sykes to ask if there were any particular instructions regarding the

Eddie Ashton with his son, Lester who also played solo trombone at Camborne.

piece and was told, *"You carry on and do it your way".*

He returned to conduct Helston and continued until September 2002 when John Hitchens took over. He said, *"Having been involved in brass banding for about fifty years I can't remember exactly how many Flora Days I've played at".*

Stephen Sykes has been described as *"one of the finest soloists to emerge from the British brass scene".* A former player with Grimethorpe, he won the title "Granada Television Soloist of the Year" and has conducted bands at the highest level in the contest world.

He was appointed Musical Director of Camborne Town Band in 1987 and enjoyed some splendid contest results and other events. He resigned in September 1991.

John Hitchens, the Bandmaster at that time, was appointed temporary Musical Director while the position was advertised and a new appointment made. To enable him to continue playing occasionally, Derek Greenwood and Leonard Adams took over the baton from time to time.

Derek Greenwood was appointed Musical Director for a second time and took his first practice on the 27th November 1991 and it was clear that the players were pleased to see him back.

In spite of a number of good contest results at Bugle, in the Area Championship and at Yeovil, this was not to be a return to the halcyon days of 1977 and 1982 and in November 1996 the Society was, once again, considering the position of Musical Director following Derek's resignation. At the 1997 AGM, John Hitchens (Bandmaster) referred to Derek as, *"The most successful conductor the Band has ever had,"* and went on to say that he would be difficult to replace. John was right but Derek's departure did not signal the final occasion when he and Camborne Town Band would join forces.

John Hitchens (euphonium) joined Camborne Town Band in 1984 having previously played with the Junior Band, St Stythians Silver and Redruth Town. During his 15 years with the Band he won many awards and details of these are spread throughout the chapter about contesting.

He took part in many solo contests and the following are some of the major events:

1981 - Finalist in the National Junior Solo Championship of Great Britain held in Sheffield when Robert Tanner and John were the two representatives from the South-West of England.
1991 - Fifth in the Final of the British Open Solo Championship.
1993 - Sixth in the Final of the British Open Solo Championship.
1994 - Won the title *British Open Euphonium Champion.*
1996 - Gold Award Winner in the National Festival of Festivals at Warwick University.
1998 - Won the title *British Open Euphonium Champion* for the second time.

In addition to playing in the Band, John received a number of invitations to perform as a soloist:

1986 - Guest soloist in Germany.
1989 - Guest player in Switzerland (10 day tour with the Leyland Band).
1990 - Guest Soloist in the world famous Pump Rooms, Bath.

John Hitchens - May 2000
(Photo by Joyce Hitchens)

1994 - Guest Soloist in the Netherlands with the Excelsior Ferwerd Band.
1996 - Guest Soloist in the British Federation Festival of Festivals Gala Concert at the Queen Elizabeth Hall, London, hosted by Sir Donald Sinden to an invited audience including Sir Andrew Davis and Maureen Lipman.
2000 - Guest Soloist in the International Gala Concert in Inverness.
2000 - Guest Soloist at Leeds Town Hall.
2002 - Guest Soloist in Gala Concert in Maesteg, Wales.

Following Derek Greenwood's resignation in 1996, it was decided to appoint a Musical Director from within the Band and to engage professional conductors for some, or all, contests. John was unsure if he wanted to commit himself to the permanent role and was appointed Acting Musical Director. By January 1997 he was prepared to give it a go and finally accepted the appointment and became the resident Musical Director. It seems, however, that his reservations had not disappeared and he soon found that he missed playing. In June 1997 he resigned his position of Musical Director and returned to the euphonium rank.

Since leaving Camborne John has worked with two or three bands and in 2002 he was appointed Musical Director of Helston Town.

Leonard Adams first started playing a brass instrument at the age of eight when his grandfather, Ben Oliver, who had played in Four Lanes Band, taught him. He had private lessons with Edgar Floyd before joining the Cornwall Youth Brass Band and then Redruth Town under Otto Rihlman.

After a couple of years he moved to Carharrack & St Day Band playing under Clifford Bolitho before moving to Camborne - in December 1969. His father, Donald Adams, became a stalwart worker and his brother, John Adams (B flat bass), also played and became a member of the "B" Band.

Leonard took over as Principal Cornet from Monty Ray in 1976 and when he left, in 1981, Robert Tanner replaced him – three outstanding cornet players.

His interest turned to conducting and even before passing over his position to Robert he was wielding the baton at Redruth Town. He had considerable success there and under his guidance the Band moved up into the Championship Section. He opened a shop, Trevada Music, in 1984 and this was taking up more of his time and he found it necessary to relinquish his position at Redruth It was a similar story at Bodmin and then at St Austell where he took them into the top section and enjoyed considerable success. Each time though his period with them was curtailed due to increasing business commitments.

The vacant position at Camborne was advertised but it was discovered that Leonard Adams had left St Austell Band and an approach was made and in June 1997, he was appointed Musical Director.

At the annual general meeting on the 13th May 1998, Leonard said, *"This is my first AGM since being appointed Musical Director. A position which I feel honoured to hold, following on from men that have given years of their lives to establish the tradition of Camborne Town Band.*

The Band has made steady progress during the last 11 months with progressively better performances at concerts and contests culminating in qualifying for the Nationals at the Royal Albert Hall in October. We are very fortunate to have the quality of players that give up a tremendous amount of time to be part of Camborne Town Band. I would hope that more local support could be given to what must be the area's biggest asset, representing Camborne and Cornwall at National level. For us to compete at National events, with quality equipment, looking and sounding good not only requires the dedication of the players but also money. I urge local business people to get involved, so that this Band is not held back by lack of funds. We need to be mixing with the very best.

I hope I can keep the enthusiasm, enjoyment and momentum going and can write more notable successes in the history of Camborne Town Band."

Following some extremely good contest results, Leonard resigned in 2000. Trevada Music had grown from a one-man business to a limited company with shops in Camborne and Ammanford, near Swansea. He started by selling to the brass band world but soon offered a full range of musical instruments.

Leonard still has a treasured silver and ebony baton which belonged to A W Parker and a cornet mouthpiece given to him by Fred Roberts. He is still involved in the brass band movement and is currently Chairman of the Cornwall County Youth Band and one of the Trustees of the Camborne Town Band Music Society.

Chris and Frank Renton with the Band at Bugle (Photo by Marcus Dunstan)

Chris North became Musical Director for about six months in 2000. He came from a military background, had played with the GUS Footwear Band (later Travelsphere) and conducted St Austell.

Graham Boag *(The Colonel)* played with the RAF Central Band for 12 years before moving to Cornwall. He had also played with and conducted a number of bands in the London area including the famous Hanwell Band. He became Musical Director at Camborne in 2001 and held the post for just under a year during which time he collaborated with Goff Richards who was writing music to celebrate the bi-centenary of Richard Trevithick's first road vehicle.

Within a couple of months of relinquishing his position as Musical Director he returned to play bass. He left in October 2004, after about three years, and later became a player and Bandmaster at Lanner & District.

Derek Greenwood returned again in late 2002 but illness limited his involvement to just a few months.

Graham Barker had previously played for Indian Queens, St Austell and Mount Charles when he moved to Camborne in 1999. Initially he played cornet but soon transferred to tenor horn where he won many special awards.

He started his conducting career at Indian Queens and when he was appointed Bandmaster at Camborne he managed to combine the role with that of solo horn. He decided to concentrate on conducting and was appointed Musical Director in October 2004 - his last playing engagement as solo horn was at Goff Richard's 60th celebration concert on the 6th Nov 2004.

In early March 2005, Graham decided to step down and the Band was, once again, looking for a new Musical Director.

Stephen (Steve) Thomas moved from Hayle Town to Bodmin Band in 1987 where he played solo euphonium and was featured on *Calling Cornwall*, the music used to introduce Radio Cornwall's daily programmes. This was included in the Goff Richards' Celebration Concert at the Hall for Cornwall in 2004 when Stephen and Aaron Harvey (cornet) took the lead in recognition of the fact that they were the original soloists. In 1994, Steve moved to Redruth Town Band and then, in 1996, to the resurgent Penzance Silver which he also conducted.

He joined Camborne Town in 2002 and within a couple of years he was appointed Bandmaster. He became the resident Musical Director in June 2005 and said, *"...This is a great opportunity for me, and one which I intend to grab with both hands. My aim is to bring a regular stream of top flight professional conductors to Cornwall to work with the Band..."*

He is currently studying under Ray Farr at Durham University, one of the Band's Guest Conductors in 2005. Steve is a highly respected euphonium player and musician; he has arranged many pieces of music including three hymn tunes for brass band; *Margaret* by Joe Volante (grandfather of Toni Volante), *Copperhouse* by Joseph Ivan Gill and *Camborne* by Joseph Henry Thomas (his great grandfather).

Musical Director Steve Thomas
(Photo by David Barnes who occasionally guests for Camborne and is a member of Celtic Brass Ensemble)

Guest Conductors:

John Berryman worked with the Band in 2002, the first time for many years, when it recorded *18 Christmas Crackers.* He returned again in 2003, 2004 and 2005 as Guest Conductor and intends to spend more time in his beloved Cornwall.

Mike Cotter (ex Flowers) conducted for about 18 months before Stephen Sykes became MD. He had previously played for Manchester C W S and wanted to move to Cornwall. He conducted at a number of contests and had shown some interest in becoming the resident Musical Director but as things turned out Stephen Sykes took over and Mike went to St Austell.

Captain Pete Curtis BMus (Hons) LRSM AMusTCL RM was born into a Salvationist family and learnt to play the piano and the cornet. Preferring the latter, he joined the local Salvation Army Brass Band and by the age of 12 was their Principal Cornet player.

Having watched the Royal Marines Band perform in his hometown of Bath, he applied to join and in January 1986 he entered the Royal Marines Band Service as a solo cornet player. On completion of training at Deal he was drafted to the C in C Fleet Band, London, and travelled the world extensively for two years. For the next seven years he was the Principal Cornet of both the Royal Marines Bands in Dartmouth and Scotland and it was during this period that he made contact with the Brass Band world, firstly playing, and then conducting both Totnes Band and Tullis Russell Mills Band.

In 1997 he was appointed Solo Cornet Instructor at the Royal Marines School of Music, Portsmouth, during which time he successfully completed the M1 Course, with a distinguished pass, and was promoted to Sergeant. He was then offered a place on the Warrant Officer Bandmasters' Course, which he successfully completed with another distinguished pass. He was also awarded two civilian diplomas - an Associate (Music) with Trinity College London, for Theory and a Licentiate with the Royal Schools of Music, for Conducting, along with a prestigious Silver Medal from the Worshipful Company of Musicians, London.

Following a brief spell in the Portsmouth Band, he was promoted to Colour Sergeant and appointed Bandmaster of the Royal Naval Volunteer Band at HMS Collingwood. During his two-year tenure, they won many prizes including "RN Concert Band Champions" (2001 & 2002) and "RN Best Overall Band" (2002). During this time, he studied for his Batchelor of Music Degree, graduating with First Class Honours. He resumed his connection with the brass band world, as resident Conductor of South West Trains Woodfalls Band and the Musical Director of Southampton-based Ocean Brass Band.

A return to the Royal Marines School of Music followed, in order to be an Academic Instructor and the Band Service University Liaison Officer. Following promotion to Warrant Officer 2, he was appointed as the Chief Instructor of the Higher Training Department. It was during this time that he was awarded a place on the Admiralty Interview Board from which he was selected for a commission.

He was promoted Lieutenant RM in April 2004 and attended the Staff Officer Course at Lympstone. On completion, he was promoted to Captain RM and began studying for a Masters Degree, specialising in Conducting, at the University of Salford, Manchester, working under Professor

David King. He has also been working with the famous Besses o' th' Barn Brass Band in Manchester and has appeared as Guest Conductor with Camborne Town Band.

He was appointed as the Director of Music of the Band of Her Majesty's Royal Marines Commando Training Centre in May 2005.

He is married to Rachel and they live in Lympstone with their mad Devon Rex cat, Mollie.

Lieutenant Colonel Chris Davis BA (Hons) MMus LRAM, Royal Marines Commandant Royal Marines School of Music and Principal Director of Music, was born in Hampshire in 1959. He played in various ensembles before joining the Royal Marines Band Service in September 1975.

On completion of three years training at the Royal Marines School of Music, he joined the Band of Her Majesty's Royal Yacht Britannia and spent the next eight years performing for the Royal family all over the world including two circumnavigations, two Royal honeymoon cruises and trips to the Americas, Australasia and the Far East.

He completed the Bandmasters' Class of 1988, received the Worshipful Company of Musician's Silver Medal as the top student and successfully gained his Licentiate from the Royal Academy of Music, after which he was promoted to Band Sergeant.

In 1992 he was successful on the Admiralty Interview Board and was commissioned on the 1st January 1993 to the rank of Lieutenant, Director of Music. Two years of study at University College Salford followed where he gained a First Class Honours Degree in Band Musicianship, studying conducting with David King and composition under Ray Steadmen-Allen and Peter Graham. His first appointment as a Director of Music was to the Band of Her Majesty's Royal Marines Scotland, based at HMS Caledonia in Rosyth.

In 2000 he was promoted to Major and took over the Portsmouth Band where he spent two happy years performing with the principal Band of the Royal Marines throughout the UK and on many foreign tours including Australia and New Zealand.

In 2002 he was promoted to Lieutenant Colonel and assumed command of the Band Service, a role he continues in today. He is the senior Director of Music of Her Majesty's Armed Forces and is responsible for all major ceremonial music making.

Brass bands have played a major role in his life, beginning in the early days with the Hampshire Youth Concert Band. It was with the City of Winchester Brass that he began life as a conductor, staying for the next three years until his Royal Marines career took him away. Whilst at Salford he conducted at Marple and then was fortunate in taking several Championship bands in Scotland, including Newtongrange, Clackmannan, Kelty and Cowdenbeath. A return south gave him an opportunity to work with SWT Woodfalls and Bournemouth Concert Brass before returning to his roots with the newly named Otterbourne Brass (previously City of Winchester). In 2003 he was asked by the Leyland Band to take them at the Brass in Concert contest at Spennymoore as well as several other high profile concert appearances. He is clearly delighted to be involved with Camborne Town Band and hopes that the fledgling relationship blossoms.

Chris recalled his first evening with Camborne in 2004 when the players were rehearsing for the All England Masters, *"Like all conductors I have to say that I was a little apprehensive before the first rehearsal, how was it going to go? What type of people was I going to be working with? All the little niggling doubts that build up inside you. I needn't have worried, within a short time the music making took over and the friendliness and sense of fun from all the players was so overwhelming, that the evening shot by.*

What I really enjoyed about working with the Band was their sense of integrity, an ability to respond quickly to direction and most of all, their great professionalism. These qualities must not be taken for granted and come at great expense, not only financially but in terms of time and energy. I had to keep reminding myself that these people play for the love of it and many of the professional musicians that I work with could do with experiencing the commitment and many hours of hard work that the Camborne Band put in. They would also do well to achieve the same consistently high standards of performance realised by this top band."

Ray Farr (b.1948) was brought up in a musical family in the small town of Hereford, England. He started playing the cornet at the age of five, and later joined the Hereford Salvation Army Band where his father was Bandmaster. Important early influences were the County Youth Orchestra, the National Music Schools of the Salvation Army and the National Youth Brass Band. When he left school he also played with Birmingham Citadel and Tottenham Citadel Salvation Army bands.

Between 1965 and 1969 he studied at the Birmingham School of Music (with John Lamb) and at the Royal Academy of Music (with William Overton), where he played first trumpet in the academy's orchestra. During this period he was frequently featured as a soloist with different bands and orchestras.

In 1969 Ray was appointed co-principal trumpet with the now defunct BBC Midland Light Orchestra in Birmingham and was often used as extra player in the City of Birmingham Symphony Orchestra. He was also appointed Trumpet Professor at his former conservatory, the Birmingham School of Music. He left Birmingham in 1973 to join the BBC Radio Orchestra in London as co-principal trumpet. In the years that followed he also worked with other top London orchestras for concerts, film sessions, TV and records. This was also the time he started conducting various amateur bands.

In 1979 he accepted a full time position as Resident Conductor with Grimethorpe Colliery Band, which featured in the movie *Brassed Off*. During the five years he was with Grimethorpe the band won many contests and gave hundreds of concert in Britain, France, Austria, Germany, Norway, Sweden, Denmark, Switzerland, Holland, Finland and Belgium. During this time there were many special occasions, notably Leeds Music Festival, Harrogate Contemporary Music Festival, Aldeburgh Festival, Cheltenham

Ray Farr in action with Grimethorpe at the Granada TV Competition.

Festival, Litchfield Festival and the concert tour of Australia, which climaxed in a performance of *Pictures from an Exhibition* in the Sydney Opera House.

While he was with Grimethorpe, Elgar Howarth encouraged him to write music and one of his first arrangements was *Star Wars,* by John Williams, which soon led to a string of successful and popular arrangements. Frank Renton called him: *"Ray of the magic pen",* and now, after hundreds of successes, bands regularly play his pieces which range in style from Stravinsky's *Firebird* to Zappa's *Dog Breath Variations*. Ray has received many accolades and positive reviews for his arranging skills including Joseph Horovitz, *"My first choice band arranger"* and Malcolm Arnold, *"He's a genius!"*

In 1984 the time of the pit closures, he left Grimethorpe to freelance, having developed a reputation as a stylish conductor and a planner of interesting concert programmes ranging from light music to "avant-garde". The Brass Band World writes: *"Ray's conducting was a joy to behold"* and the East Anglian Times says: *"superbly controlled with impeccable timing".* While the British Bandsman states: *"Ray Farr has mastered the programme art".* The critic of Bergen's Tidende says: *"He is an elegant conductor radiating intensity with control who has mastered the art of drawing enormous lines with great dynamic range".*

During this time he appeared as a Guest Conductor all over Europe, most notably with the National Youth Bands of England and Switzerland in several European Gala concerts.

Ray has been much in demand as a band adjudicator, judging at national competitions in England, Wales, Scotland, Ireland, Holland, Belgium, Sweden, Norway, Australia and New Zealand. As a teacher he has given lectures on conducting, arranging and adjudicating at Leeds College of Music, Huddersfield College, Salford College, Newcastle College, Cardiff College and the Music Conservatories of Stavanger, Bergen, Trondheim, Malmø, Gothenburg and Stockholm.

In 1988 Ray won a special Arts Council Award to study contemporary music with Edward Gregson and Jorma Panula, Professor of Orchestral Conducting at Helsinki's Sibelius Academy. In 1990 he moved, with his family, to Stavanger, Norway, to accept a conducting position with the Music School Youth Orchestra where he was able to combine regular conducting jobs with guest conducting invitations, some of which were particularly exciting. The most notable were the National Youth Bands of Norway and Eikanger Bjørsvik Musikklag who flew him to Bergen twice a week for rehearsals and concerts. There were still frequent invitations abroad and Ray visited many European cities. Something new, though, were two invitations to conduct in America and a concert tour of Australia.

It was during this time that he became involved with wind bands and was appointed Chief Conductor with the Trondheim Military Band and conductor of the National Youth Wind Band of Norway. Other wind band conducting invitations soon followed.

The Sandnes Symphony Orchestra (a semi-professional orchestra) appointed Ray as Chief Conductor. This gave him many opportunities to develop in the fields of opera, ballet and oratorio, all of which he loved. It also opened the doors to some exciting possibilities in the bigger orchestral world. He has since conducted Norway's Radio Orchestra on five occasions including a European broadcast, the Stavanger Symphony Orchestra on a World Wide TV program and the Kristiansand Symphony Orchestra in an exciting concert of French music.

In 1995 his affection for Eikanger Bjørsvik Musikklag caused him to move, once again, this time to Bergen where he was appointed Musical Director. With them he has given many innovative performances of a wide variety of music on stage, TV, radio, and CD. There are now two CDs with all Ray Farr arrangements called *Best by Farr.*

In 2003 Ray joined the teaching staff at the University of Durham, England as Conductor In Residence.

Brian Grant conducted at the National Championship in London in 2001.

Brian Howard conducted at Pontins' Final in 1981. He was a cornet player and resident Musical Director for the Stanshawe Band when Walter Hargeaves was its professional conductor.

Stan Lippeat conducted at the 2000 Pontins' Final at Prestatyn. A former Grimethorpe Colliery player, he has also been involved with the Camborne Youth Band.

Major Paul Murrell - Psm CAMus is currently Director of Music of the Band of The Royal Corps of Signals, an Armed Forces Band based in the West Country. He joined the Army at the age of 15 and was made principal clarinet of the Royal Artillery in 1974. He has extensive touring experience including the USA, Canada, Middle East and Europe. He was selected for Bandmaster training in 1984 and graduated from the Royal Military School of Music, Kneller Hall, in 1987 as Bandmaster of The Worcestershire and Sherwood Foresters Regiment. He remained there for seven years and was then selected for promotion to Staff Bandmaster of Kneller Hall, being responsible for the training and development of musicians in British Army bands. In 1996 he was selected for commission to the rank of Captain when he assumed the position of Armed Forces Music Bursary Officer, a post responsible to the Ministry of Defence, looking at methods of training musicians for the Army, Navy and Air Force. In 1998 Captain Murrell was selected to become the Director of Music of the Band of The Prince of Wales's Division where he remained for two years prior to his current position with the Royal Signals Band. Major Murrell has also worked extensively with Civilian Youth Bands and Brass Bands as conductor. He is a Diploma Examiner for the London College of Music and has twice adjudicated for the UK Regional Wind Band Festival. He became involved with Camborne in 2002 and has developed a very strong relationship with the Band.

Thomas Wyss was appointed conductor for the Area Championship in 1997. He was also asked to conduct at Bugle Contest that year but it was later decided not to attend.

Frank Renton - Musical Advisor. *"It's odd that I should have become so involved in brass bands because when I started to play, nothing was farther from my mind, and virtually the whole of my professional career as a player and conductor has been with orchestras and wind bands.*

My dad's uncle, Harold Webster, was a professional trumpet player and after a successful career in London he returned to Yorkshire and semi-retirement. On my tenth birthday I arrived home from school to find great uncle Harold ensconced in the sitting room (not normally used on week days) with a second hand Higham cornet ready to give me my first lesson. From what I can remember, progress was quick; I could already read music as I had been playing the piano for three years and it was just a matter of puckering up the lips and getting on with it. I think by the end of the first lesson I could successfully negotiate one octave of the scale of B flat Concert. Two years later I made my first trip to London to play the Hadyn Trumpet Concerto at the Wigmore Hall at a concert organised by the Music Teachers' Association and my career path was set.

On return to Yorkshire I auditioned for Alex Mortimer at the Black Dyke Mills Band. He was very complimentary but felt that at 12 year-old, I was a bit young for Black Dyke so I was consigned to the Junior Band and the gentle musical leadership of Hubert Hepworth. He insisted that I start at the bottom so I played one rehearsal on third cornet, one on second then was promoted to repiano where, in every important performance, a piece of manuscript music would appear and I finished up playing most of the solos for cornet or soprano - hard work but good training. That lasted for two years until, aged fourteen, I was judged to be old enough for the big band but instructed to dispense with my short trousers and to wear long trousers only in future.

Four years with Black Dyke was a great privilege and a steep learning curve for a teenager but at the same time, I became a member of the trumpet section in the National Youth Orchestra of Great Britain and was building a solo career in the north. Aged 18, all that came to an end when I decided that I was going to be a professional musician and went off to study at the Royal Manchester College of Music.

Two years later, I realised that I was never going to be a good enough player to earn my living at the highest level and I had met and worked with Sir John Barbirolli. He was simply inspiring and is to this day, the strongest influence on my musical life. So a change of direction was called for and I set about working towards a career as a conductor. First however, there was a small matter of completing my National Service, so I joined the Band of The Royal Horse Guards conducted by another quite brilliant musician - Major Tommy Thirtle. He was very supportive, encouraging even, and in no time I was a newly promoted Corporal teaching brass at the Guards' School of Music at Pirbright, and soon invited to conduct the local band - The Guildford Silver Band, a Fourth Section outfit.

Guildford was soon in the Championship Section and I was reporting to Kneller Hall as a Student Bandmaster. In 1969, ten years after joining the Army for three years conscription, I was on my way to Germany to be Bandmaster of the Gordon Highlanders. Ten years in the Army and they'd taught me how to ride and play a cornet on horseback (albeit badly) and now I was expected to wear a kilt every day of my working life; nobody could say that life was dull.

I spent seven terrific years with the Gordons when I lived in Germany, Cyprus, Scotland and Singapore. I taught at all sorts of universities, conducted bands and orchestras all over the place and laid the foundation for a career. When in Scotland I conducted the Broxburn Band, had a lot of fun and not a little success. After seven years with the Gordons and with an Army career which seemed to be coming to an end, the Army asked me to take command of a Music School in York, recruiting and training young musicians for the Bands of The King's Division. It was a great job, working with talented young people and good teachers. Additionally, the Army Golf Club in Strensall was a great course to hone the skills of my other passion.

I hadn't been in York long when the Wingates Band was on the phone, so I was soon travelling across the Pennines twice a week to rehearsals and conducting at all the major contests as well as some good quality concerts. Then I was asked to work with the James Shepherd Versatile Brass with whom I had three years of outrageous fun and enjoyed being with brass players of great quality. Out of the blue, I was asked to do some concerts with Grimethorpe. They were a great success, we all got on very well and I could see a new career path opening up for me as I was due to leave the Army at any time. Then it was suggested that the Army might commission me as a Captain and make me Director of Music for The Parachute Regiment - another change of pace and a job in the south of England. It meant breaking all my commitments in the north for the time being so after a wonderful concert tour of Australia in 1978, I said goodbye to the James Shepherd Versatile Brass, Wingates and Grimethorpe and set about organising the bands of my new Regiment.

Working in the southeast brought me back into contact with the professional musical world in London and all sorts of opportunities presented themselves to guest conduct with orchestras, all of which was great fun. Then I took on the job of Music Director at CWS Manchester but sadly the great days for this band were diminishing. The Company was pulling back enormously on its sponsorship and the band had difficulty attracting and keeping good players but we did some very innovative things together.

My four years with the 'Paras' passed in a flash. They were and are a totally professional group of soldiers and quite wonderful to work with but I didn't have to jump out of aeroplanes! In 1982, I was sent to be Director of the Royal Artillery Mounted Band, in truth I had been sent to bring the long history of the band to a close as Army cuts meant less bands. They were a terrific bunch however and I had two and a half great years before disbanding them and sending everyone off to a new life. Some came with me to Germany where I went to re-organise the Royal Artillery Alanbrooke Band for six months and many went to Woolwich, to The Royal Artillery Orchestra and Band and I joined them there in January 1985. There followed three of the most fulfilling and enjoyable years of my life.

The Royal Artillery Orchestra remains the oldest established orchestra in Great Britain, and from its very beginnings, in 1762, all the musicians in the Royal Artillery Band had to be competent on at least two instruments. Many were firstly string players and secondly wind players and that allowed the Director of Music to create a full symphonic ensemble. I guess that over the years many conductors had failed to see the significance of this and to utilise the musical forces to their full potential. With my orchestral background and early work with Sir John Barbirolli in Manchester, the job was a dream and I immersed myself totally in the band and orchestra. We were constantly on the road giving concerts all over the country, devouring a vast amount of repertoire and working with some of the finest soloists in the business.

In 1989, The Kitkintilloch Band in Scotland were looking for someone to bring back the success they had enjoyed when the 'wee professor,' Walter Hargreaves, was working with them, so I agreed to become their Music Advisor and Principal Conductor and 15 years on, whilst I don't conduct them very much now, I'm still involved with the band and its future, indeed we are recording a new CD together this month. It's a great satisfaction to see the band firmly listed amongst the best 20 in the world and a reflection of the tremendous amount of hard work and dedication by all.

In 1988 I left the Royal Artillery Band to become Principal Director of Music for the whole Army and Director of the Royal Military School of Music at Kneller Hall, some thirty years after I'd joined the Army as a young musician. I was responsible for the total musical output and training for all the bands. I was also working regularly with the BBC Staff Orchestras and had become Principal Conductor of the British Concert Orchestra. By 1992 I was being asked to do so many things that something had to give, so I resigned my commission and became a free-lance conductor, writer and broadcaster and started another exciting period of my life.

In 1995, I became the regular writer and presenter of 'Listen To The Band' on BBC Radio 2, and that brought me into contact with bands from all over the world. In 1999, the BBC organised a brass extravaganza in the Hall for Cornwall with the grand finale being a concert by the four top Cornish bands with me conducting and presenting. A year later I was asked if I would visit, advise, and perhaps conduct, and the rest, as they say, is history.

Five or six years ago, without the hard work and vision, the Camborne Town Band might have slid out of existence. It had lost several key players and it was difficult to keep the whole thing turning over. The miracle is that five years on the Band can look back on one of the most successful periods in its history, it's on a sound financial footing, there is a thriving 'B' Band and Junior ensemble where many young people are learning to play and adding a new dimension to their lives.

When I look back on our first South-West Area Competition, when the test piece was 'Jazz' and we somehow managed to stitch a winning performance together, I look at the Band and the whole structure in Camborne and am full of admiration for both the musicians, committee, and supporters who have worked hard to create a consistent and capable level of performance. It's not a miracle - it's just hard work - but it's close to being one!"

Trevithick Day and All That

Trevithick Day 2005 (photos by Clive Letcher)

Richard Trevithick was born in Illogan in 1771 and became one of the greatest engineers of his time and yet, he continually fails to receive the credit he deserves and most people will tell you that it was George Stevenson who invented the steam locomotive.

Trevithick was a mining engineer and the inventor of the high-pressure steam engine used in powering mining equipment and transport. He built and drove the world's first road engine at Camborne on Christmas Eve in 1801 and three years later, in 1804, he ran the first track locomotive at Penydarren

in Wales. This was 25 years before Stevenson invented *The Rocket*. He has been described as the "*Cornish Giant*" – both intellectually and physically. He died penniless but took pleasure in his achievements as indicated by a statement he wrote shortly before his death: *"I shall be satisfied by the great secret pleasure and pride that I feel in my own breast from having been the instrument of bringing forward and maturing new principles and new arrangements of boundless value to my country. However much I may be straitened in pecuniary circumstances, the great honour of being a useful subject can never be taken from me, which to me far exceeds riches."*

His statue stands outside the Public Library in Camborne; a testimony of the enduring affection he holds in Cornish hearts.

The first Trevithick Day was held in 1983, on the last Saturday in April, and each year since, the aficionados of steam, and the public in general, pay homage to his memory. In 2004 the organisers were told that the presence of moving traction engines in the town's streets posed an unacceptable risk to the public. The engine drivers were so incensed that they marched in silent protest along the route usually taken by the engines. But after an absence of just one year the traction engines again took pride of place at the Trevithick Day celebrations on the 30th April 2005. The whole of Camborne rejoiced at getting their event back on track when the steam procession was reinstated. After a great deal of negotiation, and a bit of compromise, a revised route was agreed and the engines travelled "Up Camborne Hill".

The steam parade is the main focus but the one-day festival celebrates Camborne's industrial heritage with street stalls, music and dancing. Children and adults dress in Cornish colours of black and gold and parade behind Camborne Town Band. Actually, two bands are provided for this prestigious event – the Junior Band are also present. On one occasion the Senior Band was absent at a contest but conscious of the commitment, an arrangement was made for Redruth Band to step in and cover.

It's a day of great fun and hard work but I'll let you read it from a bandsman's point of view.

Trevithick Day - Saturday 30th April - Steam, Steam and More Steam

"With excitement in the air the day gets off to a grinding halt – just like many of those failed attempts to design a steam powered road car. Steve (Thomas) has very kindly transcribed and laminated 'Camborne Worthies' for us.

Squibby (Jeremy Squibb) notices that his part starts on an 'a'. 'I normally start on second valve and the rest just follows,' he remonstrates as everyone starts to look a little perplexed. After a little investigation it appears that Steve had been handed the original parts which he duly copied and laminated. Alan (Pope) had distributed them to the Youth Band to practise in time for the big day.

Now then, when Trevithick Day started back in 1983, Geoffrey Self composed 'Camborne Worthies' and after a couple of years of complaining from the cornet players about the pitch and range of the tune it was decided to re-write it in a lower key. By dropping a 'third' the cornets did not spend most of the march playing top 'a' and the soprano part could be a little more flamboyant. So, for about 20 years, the cornets have had a 'comfortable' blow through the town and the soprano could start on a middle valve.

Today however, we are back to the old days, with the cornet players' lips drained of all feelings. The bass section seem delighted with the new key, however there does seem to be an absence of those searing soprano bars from both Squibby and Samuel – what a delight for the crowd in the afternoon dance when they get together!

Aside from having to learn the new key, we have the huge frustration of following the mini traction engines; normally, one or two chug along happily in front of us but this year there are about 15 leading the dance. Nice to watch but frustrating when they keep stopping and starting as they try to get around the corners of the town and less than pleasant to inhale their steam and smoke for 45 minutes as you struggle up the hill at the end of Trelowarren Street.

None too soon we reach the Vyvyan Arms car park and we can listen to the second band enduring what we have all just experienced. Soon enough they trudge up the hill, finish the dance (which is Squibby's annual attempt at conducting and we can all see why) and head off to prepare for the lunchtime concert.

Down in the square we discover that Pete's microphone fails to work. Roy Netherton dashes off to 'mend' it with Chris shouting from the back row 'he can't even turn the telly on never mind mend a microphone'. Back it comes but still in several pieces so Pete (Curtis) has to shout and address the audience in two halves giving him the opportunity to voice his cheesy gags twice.

With Steve and Josey unavailable due to work, Peter Harvey, from the Youth Band, is our euphonium section with Ben on first baritone. Both did an absolutely fabulous job as did young Rory back on percussion and, of course, our two, now well established, new players Jeremy and Jessica.

As we finish with the rousing 'Farandole' followed by 'The Battle Of Shiloh', the square erupts with cheers with calls for more encores. Unfortunately, the timings for Trevithick Day are very precise and we have to leave the stage in order to allow the next act to start on time.

As we filter back from our break we hear the bad news from Pete (Curtis) that he has to return to Portsmouth for the rest of the week due to family illness. Regretfully, he bids us farewell and leaves us all in a bit of a panic – what do we do about Blackpool Contest? Who will conduct us? Do we go? – Only time will tell.

Back in Bassett Street for the 2.30 pm dance the 52 strong band forms up with whispers of our bad news spreading quicker that a pound of butter on a hot sunny day. Off we set, this time with three sopranos all bidding for the most flamboyant bar award; this, as you would expect, wore off quite quickly as the lips started to drain.

With the mist in the air and the smoke from the engines, the afternoon dance seems more like a trip back in time to Olde London Town. As we reach the end of Trelowarren Street the dancers spin into their customary circle and Trevithick Day is over for another year as far as we are concerned.

Further down the road the massed ranks of the steam engines are under way but we are off home to rest our lips and try to figure out how are we going to cope with the conducting situation."

Of course, Trevithick Day is just one entry in the Band's busy calendar. Engagements are the life-blood of any band and although the type of events have changed over the years it is still about entertaining the public and hopefully, earning a pound or two at the same time. It costs a lot of money to run a brass band and without the income from fetes and carnivals, bands would not be there for concerts and contests.

Camborne Town Band has been amongst Cornwall's finest since the day it was founded and that, in itself, is sufficient justification for event organisers to seek its services. The standard of play on the contest stage is transferred to even the smallest engagement, a claim which could not fairly be made by every band in Cornwall. So, value for money is what is offered and that has been the case right through its long history.

Of course not all functions are booked by outside organisations and the Band is active in arranging its own events, often in conjunction with local choirs or individuals and occasionally involving names from the bigger stage like George Chisholm, Don Lusher, Jethro, Alan Opie, Fern Britton and, of course, Cornwall's Mr Brass Band – Phillip Hunt.

Whit Monday was once a big day in Camborne, when most of the chapels held their tea-treats. It was a busy day for the Band playing at Lowennac and finishing up at Trevu.

A rugby match usually ensures a large crowd although the players are realistic in appreciating that most of the spectators are not there for the music. Often this involved marching from Commercial Square down to the Recreation Ground, playing before the match and again at half-time. It was a good opportunity to make some money which was always welcome. It's often the role of military bands to play at major sporting events but in Cornwall we can do without the woodwind; Camborne Town Band attended the rugby semi-final between Cornwall and Yorkshire and made a "proper job" of it.

Hospital Sundays were annual events in many communities when funds would be raised for the Royal Cornwall Infirmary and district Nursing Associations. The Royal Cornwall Gazette in August 1905 reported, *"At one time it looked like nothing would be done this year and the financial result, although less than last year, must be considered satisfactory when all circumstances are taken into consideration. Headed by Camborne Voluntary Band, members of the Philanthropic, Oddfellows and Rechabite Societies walked in procession through the streets (of St Agnes) and a collection was made along the route. There was then a service in the Wesleyan Chapel and at the conclusion the Band, assisted by several vocalists, gave a sacred concert in the Odd Fellows Hall to a large and appreciative audience."*

1905 Hospital Sunday at St Agnes with Camborne Town Band in attendance.

The Band was there again the following year when the recipient organisations received £5.6.0 each. Dr Whitworth thanked Bandmaster Uren and the players for giving their services free.

The Marazion & St Michael's Mount Annual Regatta was held on Saturday the 1st August 1925. It appears to have been a prestigious event and the Band, under A W Parker, provided an afternoon concert, led the Furry Dance and played at an evening concert in the Rookery Grounds. It's not clear if it also supplied the music for the concluding dance which featured the popular Waltz, One-Step, Grand March Lancers and Foxtrot, all performed with the assistance of a Master of Ceremonies.

1907 – Tea-treat at Mithian with the village's favourite band. An item in the *Royal Cornwall Gazette* of the 6th June 1907 reports, *"Large numbers went to Mithian on Saturday to hear the Camborne Town Band, and to witness the sports, held in connection with the Mithian School tea."*

An extract from my book, *St Agnes and its Band* said, *"On the 13th June 1936 Camborne Band played at Mithian Sunday School tea-treat when the weather was described as 'nice'. The musical entertainment at Mithian was always provided by a brass band and the popular recollection is that it was always Camborne Town Band. It was certainly the premier brass band in Cornwall and organisers Franklyn Ennor and his cousin, Stanley, would always insist it was booked. Tea-treats continued for many years and, whilst I can recall playing there with St Agnes Band in the 1960s, more often than not, it did feature that famous band from Camborne."*

The Band played at many tea-treats over the years at venues too numerous to list. These events provided a good opportunity for playing music and for raising much needed income. Every religious group in each village held their own so you can imagine the potential for engagements. St Agnes, St Dennis, Foxhole, Blackwater and a host of other bands played at Mithian but the Ennor family held sway for a lot of years and Franklyn Ennor would have Camborne Band or he would not attend. He considered it to be the best in the county and that it made, *"Some ansum sound"*.

1910 to 1920 judging by the uniforms

Tea-treats have been largely confined to history and it may be that many people will not appreciate their significance to the church and the community in general. Everything stopped for the occasion and in some of the smaller communities it was the biggest event on the calendar. The majority of people attending were local but visitors were always made welcome. The venue may have been in someone's large garden or in a suitable field. The grass would have been cut, decorations erected and a number of tables placed in position to act as stalls or for the preparation of the food. The schoolroom forms would be placed in the formation required and I can testify these became harder and harder as the day progressed. In the early 1900s bands would probably have played standing up and that may have been preferable to the hard seating used later.

The event commenced with a procession led by the banner carriers. Each chapel or church had its own banner and it was proudly carried at the front of the procession as a testament to the members' faith. Immediately behind them would be the band, followed by the children and the adults. The route always seemed endless and for most of its length there were very few houses and the band played to the hedgerows and the cows. Eventually the procession returned to the tea-treat field and the players took their place on the wooden forms in readiness for the official opening.

A local dignitary usually opened the day and the band then started their afternoon programme. Much of the time there were very few listening but the occasional burst of applause made it all seem worthwhile. To this background music, various competitions and sports took place for the children and often, for the grown-ups as well.

Every so often the players took a break and had a chance to take part in a competition or buy some fruit from one of the stalls. Adrian King recalled the cherries which were always on sale. This struck a chord with me and I still associate tea-treats with large saffron buns and cherries. As young bandsmen, we used to compete in cherry-stone spitting contests – to see who could spit them the furthest. It doesn't make us sound like public performers but I suppose we could justify it by saying it helped our tonguing technique.

At some convenient point the children were given their tea-treat bun, a huge saffron bun - surely larger than the ones in the shops today. Whatever else people remember about these events, the buns are always mentioned. Tea was a high spot and when the children had finished, it was the turn of the bandsmen and no matter how hungry (or greedy) they were, the food just kept on coming. No committee worth its salt was going to send a band home hungry and the acceptance of an engagement was often based on the players' memory of the tea.

Most tea-treats included an evening concert and if the weather remained fine then it was also held in the field with the players perched on those infamous wooden forms. This was an opportunity to play some music that could be described as, *"a bit more substantial"*. By now, the fun and games were over and the audience were much more attentive. The event was usually concluded with the traditional *Serpentine Walk* when everyone danced around the field behind the band.

Playing at a tea-treat during the 1940s the players decided to take a break. Alfred Tresidder (bass drum) pushed his stick under the diagonal tensioning cords of the drum and went off to get a cup of tea. A man of habit, he always re-started by taking the stick in his right hand, passing it to his left and licking his right hand. It was only then that he realised that one of his colleagues had rolled the handle in a cowpat.

Idris Stone from St Erth was keen for Camborne Band to attend his local tea-treat and was eagerly awaiting the arrival of the players' coach. Before it reached the field, half of the players got off and the coach arrived with the depleted Band. They told Idris there was a lot of sickness in Camborne and the remainder would not be coming. He must have been very relieved to see the others walk around the corner.

J Carah Roberts was the Chairman for a concert at Holman's Canteen on Sunday the 16th June 1946; the proceeds were for Wheal Gerry and District Welcome Home Fund. A W Parker conducted Camborne Town Band, which was joined by Gladys Harris – contralto (Dame Clara Butts prodigy), Frederick Harvey – baritone (BBC performer) and Oswald Mitchell – accompanist. Another artist was making his debut – the four year-old boy soprano, Kingsley Hitchens, sang *Christopher Robin* and *Mighty Like a Rose* – (yes, the very same Kingsley Hitchens who was to serve the Band so well). The Band played the march *Copenhagen, Poet and Peasant, Jamie's Patrol*, the mighty *Lorenzo* and finished with Handel's chorus, *And the Glory.*

Sometime during the late 1940s the Band played a concert in a marquee on Plymouth Hoe and to finish the first half the players walked off one-by-one until just Alfred John Tresidder was left there beating the drum and reading his newspaper. The audience loved it; they hadn't seen it done before. The concert finished with A Sailor's Life and Alfred John Tresidder was given free rein to replicate the sound of thunder. It finished to a standing ovation and Mr Parker called on Alfred to stand up for special acclaim. He'd never experienced that before and the tears were running down his face.

In 1950 Gerald and Betty Fletcher went on holiday to Plymouth with Clifford Harris and his wife. Gerald said, *"We'd got the dates a bit mixed up and Clifford and myself had to come home for a day to play at Camborne Show – we were really popular!"*

Sometime around 1960 the Band was invited to take part in a concert in Crewkerne and, while there, to play in a church service. To get to their position above the organ the players had to make their way up a narrow spiral staircase and for the basses, this was not easy. Peter Richards (bass) managed to hit his instrument against the stone walls all the way up and each prang was accompanied by a curse or a swear word. It didn't stop until he reached the top where he came face to face with the vicar.

Paul Bourdeaux kindly took Eric Thomas and Tony Volante to an engagement in his car which was nicknamed the *Silver Bullet.* They knew where they were going but, unfortunately, it was not the same place as the rest of the Band. The confusion was over two places with similar sounding names – so prevalent in Cornwall. Having realised their mistake they set off to join the others and arrived red-faced and late. Alan Toy said, *"Freddie Roberts wasn't very pleased".*

On another occasion Paul was travelling down Paul Hill in Newlyn with Alec Oliver in the car and when he pressed the brake pedal, nothing happened. After that his colleagues must have gone

1957 - on the march

off the idea of riding with him - the coach must have seemed a lot more attractive. Alec Oliver (euphonium) was Stanley's son and played for about three years in the mid 1950s.

Recalling his time at Camborne, Barry Tresidder said, *"They were good times and we always had a lot of fun like when we were giving some concerts at St Ives. Toni Volante, another player and I decided to hire a rowing boat during the break period between the concerts. It was okay going out but when we turned to come in, we found that we couldn't row against the tide. There we were, three bandsmen in uniform, waving for help. A passing motorboat towed us in and we could see our colleagues on the quay - cheering. I don't think Freddie Roberts was too impressed."*

Another such story involved Ashley Bennetts and, once again, Toni Volante. Playing on Plymouth Hoe they found they had some spare time between the afternoon and evening concert. According to Toni, it was Ashley Bennetts' idea to hire a motorboat. *"Well, we were a long way out and Ashley was holding the tiller when he suddenly did a sharp turn and we almost capsized. I'm not sure*

1957 - Townshend tea-treat
Back row: Adrian King and Jack Pascoe.
Front row: John Berryman, Jack Trounce, Alec Oliver and Idris Stone.

we could have swum back wearing those thick uniforms. As it was I had to play the evening concert with one side of my tunic soaking wet." Ashley Bennetts (cornet) later joined the Metropolitan Police Band.

I mentioned earlier about the players exiting the stage one-by-one to leave only one person to finish the piece. *Jamie's Patrol* lends itself to this and most bands have played it from time to time. Reg Bennett recalled Camborne playing it in the 1960s when the departure started with Freddie Roberts throwing his stick down in disgust. One by one the other players followed him off the stage until the percussionists, Mervyn Charleston and Dick Tresidder, were left on their own. They rolled up their trousers and sat back reading the *Reveille* as they finished beating out the end of the music. It seems the last bit was unscripted and not really appreciated by Mr Roberts. (For younger readers I ought to add that the *Reveille* was a weekly newspaper for the men of the family – and you thought the Sun invented page three!)

Late 1950s/early 1060s - rehearsing in the open air - maybe for Bugle

Reg Bennett recalled an occasion when Camborne was playing at Frogpool tea-treat in 1960 or 1961. *"We had a long march which took us past the home of Mr and Mrs Thomas of E Thomas Construction. Mrs Thomas must have thought that we were thirsty as she came out with a wicker basket of Britvic drinks. I think these must have been a new drink as Freddie Roberts stepped forward and told us all to get back. He then examined the label until he had assured himself that the drink contained no alcohol and only then were we allowed to drink them."*

The Scala Cinema, Camborne, was the venue for a concert in March 1964 when Eric Ball was conducting and Derek Garside of Manchester C W S was guest soloist; Derek had previously played under Freddie Roberts. *Alan Toy recalled, "The programme included the famous 1812 Overture by Tchaikovsky and there was a lot of discussion regarding how the sound of the cannon could be replicated. A local farmer with a shot-gun was enlisted - firing blanks I suppose. He took his cue from Freddie Roberts and fired the gun into a dustbin at the appropriate time. It certainly made the audience jump and there was a hell of a lot of smoke."*

A celebrity concert at the Scala Cinema, Camborne, on the 19th December 1966 featured Camborne Town Band and guest soloist, Ian Richards, who was the principal trombonist for Manchester C. W. S. The programme included the overture, *Le Domino Nor*, the concert march *Trelawny* by W E Moyle who conducted it, *Triumphant Rhapsody* by Gilbert Vinter and a number of trombone solos. *Triumphant Rhapsody* had been the test piece for the 1965 National Championship in which Camborne had been placed sixth.

Mishap at Mabe - the Band travelled to Mabe for a concert in the late 1960s and found a smart bandstand erected in the field. It was built of scaffold tubes and really looked the part. "*Trouble was,"* said David Reed, *"when we walked on it the whole thing sank into the ground; they hadn't used any base plates at the bottom of the poles. The start of the concert had to be delayed while it was dismantled and re-built – this time with base-plates."* George Ansell was playing bass and recalled the bass section being bigger and heavier than their colleagues on cornet. He said, *"We slowly settled into the ground while the cornets side of the stage remained where it was. It was hilarious."*

Perranwell's "Hey Day" was held on Bank Holiday Monday the 30th August 1971 when Camborne Town Band led the carnival parade and played throughout the event.

During the early 1970s St Dennis and Camborne Bands combined to perform a series of concerts. The programmes included some lighter stuff as well as major pieces and must have provided a feast of entertainment. The first concert was held on Sunday the 26th September 1971 and billed as *Massed Brass Bands in Harmony in a Concert of Polished Brass.* It was held at Retallack, St Columb, and was chaired by Joe Pengelly of BBC Radio and Television. The programme included the marches *Bandology* and *B.B.& C.F., Mill on the Cliff, Rhapsody in Brass* and *Slavonic Rhapsody No. 2.*

Barrie Trevena recalled the rivalry between the bands – no doubt friendly! *"It was the custom for the band whose conductor was taking that particular piece, to play the solos. During one piece conducted by Eddie Williams there was a rather difficult cornet solo and I remember Peter Menear of St Dennis was playing. He had hoped, no doubt, that Monty Ray would join in to help out but alas, Monty was 'having trouble' with one of his valves and had taken it out just at that moment, leaving Peter to struggle on."*

The "return" concert took place at the Flamingo Hall, Pool, (or was this changed to the Regal Cinema, Redruth?) in December 1971 and included *Zampa, Les Preludes, The Best of the Seekers* (remember them?) and the *New World Symphony.*

The third concert was on September 1972 at Retallack Farm, St Columb. The first half included *Tancredi, Capriccio Italien* and *Symphony of Marches* and the second half was topped and tailed by *Lorenzo* and the *Hallelujah Chorus.*

The programme for the fourth concert, on Sunday the 10th December 1972, included the *Introduction to Act III Lohengrin, The Explorers* and *Finlandia.*

The Morrab Gardens, Penzance, was a popular venue for concerts where there were always plenty of holidaymakers to fill the collection boxes. One such concert was held on the 22nd June 1969 when Monty Ray played a piece called *The Warrior Solo*. It was an excellent performance but Freddie

Roberts liked to show the strength in depth and called on Barrie Trevena to play *The Holy City* as an encore. Barrie said, *"I received 10 shillings from my grandfather so I was quite pleased".*

Townshend tea-treat took place shortly after and Barrie's diary notes of the time said, *"There were two girls there and Peter (James) and John (Morrissey) 'went after them!' Not sure if they caught them! The only thing I managed was to pinch some wild strawberries growing nearby. This strawberry picking became an annual event at the tea-treat, as did the girls."*

The Hoe Theatre concerts at Plymouth were popular. On one occasion, during rehearsals, Dougie Piper appeared on stage dressed as a fluffy bird; he'd found the costume in the make-up room. Roderick Facey recalled that everyone found it hilarious - except Mr Roberts. Roderick (euphonium) joined from Carharrack & St Day and was a member from the late 1958 to the 1970s.

Barrie Trevena recalled a trip to Exmouth in August 1970 as, *"Very eventful".* He said, *"On the way up we had to stop the coach for Neil Peters to be sick (it was a rough journey) and then a second time when he'd passed out altogether. He was unconscious for nearly 10 minutes, much to everyone's consternation. Then on the way back we stopped twice for food and drink – the second time Mr Roberts got very annoyed and said that if the older ones didn't leave the pub quickly it would be the last we would see of him. I think it was the start of the upset with him, as he was also taking St Austell by then. The following Tuesday he wasn't at band practice. A delegation went to his home and didn't get back until 10.00pm to tell the rest of us what was going on. Then he missed our Harvest Festival in September 1970 and eventually handed in his notice on Friday the 13th November. I was a little amused when it was announced that he'd won £1.00 on the 50/50 draw that night."*

Straw bales topped with boards make a fine bandstand but at Frogpool tea-treat, in the 1970s, things didn't turn out as planned. David Reed recalled, *"Everything was alright to begin with but the bales turned out to be full of insects and it wasn't long before everyone was more involved in scratching than playing. We finished the concert but were certainly pleased to get away from the stage."*

Carnivals are still popular and provide regular work for brass bands; after all, what is a carnival without a band. Someone told me that Camborne once took part in carnivals on nine consecutive Saturdays (that must have been fun! Whoops, has my mantle of impartiality slipped there?).

There was a time when it would have been unthinkable to hold a community event without having a brass band but, of course, times have changed and there is now a much greater reliance on canned music. Even so, the bookings can range from garden fetes and gymkhanas and from band Sundays to weddings.

In April 1971 the first public concert by Camborne Town Band under their new Musical Director, Derek Johnston, was a resounding success. Nearly 700 people crowded into Holman's Canteen, Camborne, to see the new conductor in action. It was announced that for the first time in seven years the Band would be competing at the West of England Bandsmen's Festival at Bugle and everyone was delighted to hear this news. The concert included solos by Alan Toy and Monty Ray and an outstanding item by five young cornetists - Leon Johnston, Peter Goldsworthy, Barrie Trevena, Jonathan Morrissey and Paul Wicks.

In June 1971, the day after a successful performance at Bugle Contest, the Band led the Civic Parade from the Community Centre to St Martin's Church for the annual service. David Mudd, the Member of Parliament for Falmouth & Camborne, attended as one of the official guests.

A rather unusual event took place in November 1971 when the Camborne-Redruth Urban District Council held a Road Safety Service. It was a religious service of hymns, prayers and lessons in which the Band accompanied the singing.

The Band's Gala Day/Garden Fete was held on the 14th August 1971 with the proceeds going to the new instrument fund. Ken Bowden, Chairman of the Camborne-Redruth Urban District Council, opened the event with a brief history of the Band since 1896. He said, *"In those days the Band would march through the main street on every Friday night. Memories of this were carried to all parts of the world by local people when several of the early members served in the Boer War."*

The concerts seem to be thick and fast around this time and on Sunday the 3rd of October 1971 the Band was in action again – at Redruth Ambulance Hall. *The Contestor* was followed by *The*

Mill on the Cliff, a few lighter items and the majestic *Lorenzo* to finish the first half. *Knight Templar* and *The Explorers* started the second half and *Slavonic Rhapsody No. 2* concluded the concert.

Sounding Brass and Voices was the title for a concert by Camborne Town Band and Mousehole Male Voice Choir at St John's Hall, Penzance, on Sunday the 28th November 1971. It commenced with the *Cossack* by Wm Rimmer and included the overture *Poet and Peasant* and the tone poem *Lorenzo*. Monty Ray was the soloist and played *High on a Hill.*

Perran-ar-Worthal Village Memorial Hall was the venue for a concert in February 1972. Derek Johnston conducted a very full programme which included *Prelude for an occasion,* the march *Whitehall, Date with a Square, Seventy-six Trombones, Padstow Lifeboat, Coppelia* and *From the New World Symphony.*

Camborne Town Band and Four Lanes Male Voice Choir combined for a concert at Holman's Canteen on Sunday the 23rd April 1972. The programme included the overture *Zampa*, *Padstow Lifeboat,* Derek Johnston Jnr played the trombone solo, *Recitative and Romance* and Barrie Trevena played the cornet solo, *The Holy City.*

My own village of Mithian prided itself on producing first-class concerts and Camborne Town Band was always its number one choice. On Monday the 19th June 1972 an open air concert *"in a field near the Chapel"* provided the community with a real treat. The full programme was *Whispering Brass,* W E Moyle's *Cornish Cavalier, Rhapsody for Soprano* - soloist Peter Goldsworthy, *The Best of the Seekers, Blackfriers, Penlan, Padstow Lifeboat, Rhythmic Danube, Recitative and Romance* – soloist Derek Johnston Jnr, *Date with a Square* – Derek Johnston, Douglas Piper and Barry Clift, *My Prayer* and *Slavonic Rhapsody No. 2.* The Band did not disappoint.

At the Band Gala Day in 1972, eighteen year-old Teresa Johnston won the Miss Camborne Town Band title and three year-old Colin Weeks won first prize in the fancy dress competition.

The players travelled to Lostwithiel in August 1972 and gave a concert for the Lostwithiel Band Gala Day held in the King George's Field. Opening with the *Cossack* march, the programme included *Poet and Peasant, Morganblatter, Slavonic Rhapsody* and the *Hallelujah Chorus.* The programme notes refer to Camborne as the Champion Band of the West of England. It said, *"Since 1945 they have won the West of England Championship more times than all the other bands added together. This year so far, they have won the West of England Championship, the Cornish Brass Band Association Contest, Bugle Band Contest and numerous best-player awards. Their list of successes over the years is tremendous and under their new Musical Director (Mr D Johnston) they seem destined for even greater things."*

A pre-London Albert Hall Concert was held at Holman's Canteen on the 8th October 1972 when Mrs Sally Roberts was the guest soprano. Accompanied by Miss Betty Gluyas she sang four solos. The main items on the programme by the Band were *Colonel Bogey, Tancredi, Capriccio Italien* and the *Hallelujah Chorus.*

The football fans amongst the players had a treat in October 1972 when the Band played at a match between Plymouth Argyle and The Arsenal.

A combined concert with Chacewater & District Male Voice Choir for the Royal British Legion at Wadebridge, on the 29th October 1972, provided the audience with a feast of music. In the first half the Band played *Sousa on Parade, Light Cavalry, Gold & Silver, Cornet Roundabout, Trumpet Voluntary* and *Slavonic Rhapsody No. 2.* After the interval they continued with *Bugle Call Blues, Till, The Acrobat, From the New World Symphony* and they joined with the choir to finish with *The Long Day Closes* and the *Hallelujah Chorus.* (Something there to suit all tastes).

One of the services to the community is to take part in the annual Remembrance Day and in November 1972 a young Barrie Trevena had the honour of playing the "Last Post".

The Band travelled to Kingswood on the 8th December 1972 for a combined concert with Shaftsbury Crusade (Bristol) Band. Billed as *Friday Night is Music Night,* the concert had been arranged to coincide with a BBC Television recording by Camborne and both bands had waived their fees so all of the profits could be donated to the new-instrument fund of The Bristol East Temperance Band.

Camborne Town Band has given many concerts with local choirs and on Sunday the 21st January 1973, they combined with Praze Male Voice Choir at Wall Methodist Church. Mrs Honor Collins was the guest soloist and the Revd John Elford was the Chairman. The marches chosen were the *Hungarian March* and Army *of the Nile. The Pirates of Penzance, Tituana Holiday, Simon called Peter* and *Robert Farnon* were also included as well as a number of items played with the choir.

Kimberley Park in Falmouth was a good place to find the visitors and made an excellent venue for a series of concerts in the summer of 1973.

On the 14th October 1973 the Plaza Cinema at Truro was full to appreciate the music of the West of England Champions, Camborne Town Band, and the singing of Treverva Male Voice Choir. More than 1100 people were there to hear a tremendous performance when brass joined forces with the choir under its Musical Director, Edgar Kessell. Stuart Hutchinson of Westward Television chaired the evening and proceeds went to the Cornwall Ambulance Service Benevolent Fund. The Bands contribution included *Washington Grays, Rhapsody in Brass* and *Morning Noon and Night* and the soloists were Neil Peters and Monty Ray.

George Chisholm joined the Band and the Goff Richards Trio for a concert at the Regal Cinema on the 9th December 1973. He was a well-known trombonist having played in nightclubs and recorded with Fats Waller and Louis Armstrong. He also appeared on television with the Black and White Minstrels Show, Val Doonican, the Billy Cotton Band Show and many other such programmes - he was a big celebrity at that time. Goff Richards, one of Cornwall's famous sons, appeared with fellow Cornishman Vic Thomas (bass), Jimmy French (drums), Ian Wheeler (jazz clarinettist) and Rod Mason (trumpet). Derek Johnston conducted and produced a quality concert. Unfortunately George Chisholm arrived too late to rehearse a Goff Richards composition for trombone and it was played by Monty Ray on cornet.

Four Lanes Gala Association held its event in July 1974 when Camborne Town Band led the parade and played an evening concert.

The Band took part in a Brass and Voices occasion in October 1974 when it was joined by Treverva Male Voice Choir under Edgar Kessell, Treviscoe Male Voice Choir under Kenneth Yelland and Devon and Cornwall Police Choir, also conducted by Edgar Kessell. Leonard Adams conducted and Stuart Hutchison of Westward TV was the Chairman. The programme included *Ruy Blas* by

Don Lusher joined the Viv Rodd Trio, the John Austin Big Band and Camborne Town Band in a Brass Extravaganza at the Regal Cinema, Redruth, in April 1976. (Photo by Eric Parsons)

Mendelssohn, the march *BB and CF* and *Slavonic Rhapsody* and the "B" Band led the Community Hymn Singing.

Sunday the 16th February 1975 and another concert at Holman's Canteen. This time the programme included *The Magic Flute, Panis Angelicus, West Side Story*, a cornet solo by Monty Ray called *Sparkling Eyes*, *Three Cornish Miniatures* by Goff Richards, *Symphony of Marches* and *The Contestor*.

Bernard Bygrave was conducting in a concert at Four Lanes Gala on Saturday the 26th July 1975. The marches *Colonel Bogey* and *Padstow Lifeboat* topped and tailed the programme which included the overtures *Barber of Seville* and *Black Domino*. Monty Ray (cornet) and Neil Peters (euphonium) were the soloists.

Redruth born Alan Opie (baritone) and his wife, Kathleen Smales (mezzo-soprano), joined Camborne Town Band and the Camborne Circuit Wives Choir at the Regal Cinema, Redruth, in October 1975. Bernard Bygrave was conducting and presented a varied programme including Trevor Sharpe's *Fanfare and Soliloquy*, the humorous *Little Liza*, the hymn *Great Soul* by Cornish composer Kenneth Pelmear and Elgar's *Nimrod*. Richard Sharpe, former Cornwall and England rugby player, was the Chairman and Bill Cheshire from St Agnes led the community hymn singing which was accompanied by the Camborne "B" Band under Keith Rowe. Camborne Town Band concluded the evening with *Les Preludes*.

On the 30th October 1977 a concert of Brass and Voices at the Plaza Cinema, Truro, was held in aid of the Royal National Lifeboat Institution. Richard Radcliffe was the Chairman.

Another concert with the Camborne Circuit Wives' Choir but this time with John Keay House Ladies Choir, Four Lanes Male Voice Choir and Treviscoe Male Voice Choir. It included a programme of Cornish music composed or arranged by Carharrack born Kenneth Pelmear.

John Briggs, a pianist of national repute, joined Camborne Town Band for a concert at St Ives Guildhall in November 1979. It was an outstanding event but, with only about 100 people in the audience, it was a financial disaster. The Band and pianist joined to play the first movement of *Grieg's Piano Concerto* and finished in fine style with *Rule Britannia*. A return visit was arranged at St George's Hall, Bradford, when the players were hosted by members of Barnoldswick Brass Band.

A booking at the Bath and West Show in 1981 turned out to be on a very wet and blustery day but the Band played on and the players were not sorry when the event was over.

In July 1982 Bodmin, St Austell and Camborne bands took part in an open-air, massed band event. It was held at Trelissick Gardens and conducted by Vilem Tausky. This was repeated in July 1985 and the afternoon performance went well. Unfortunately the evening concert had to be abandoned half way through due to heavy rain. Phillip Hunt has cause to remember the weather – he was the compère.

During an engagement on St Ives Sea front Tim Joslin had failed to secure his music and a gust of wind blew it away. Unfortunately it was during a long duet, Tim on baritone and the flugel player. He had to play his part from memory and understandably, he became a little less confident. Derek Greenwood, who was completely unaware there was anything amiss, was desperately trying to get him to play it more boldly.

Darren Hendy - Principal Cornet

The Gala Day of the 29th August 1987 provided an unusual attraction when about 30 former players gathered to take a share of the playing. Leonard Adams, Edward Ashton, Allen Knight and Alan Toy brought the veterans together for rehearsals and a crowd-pleasing performance. The march, *Old Comrades* and *Memory* were appropriate choices in a programme which also included the Camborne favourite, *The Cossack*. Carharrack & St Day and Hayle Town bands also took part in the procession and the concert. The eight hours of events was opened by Guy Slatter of Radio Cornwall and concluded with thanks by Chairman, Allen Knight.

In August 1988 the annual summer celebrations again included a band of former players and this time Gordon Nicholas, a cornet player from the 1920s, was among them. The event was held at Treswithian Fairfield and opened by Daphne Skinnard of Radio Cornwall. Arthur Goodman organised the event which included bands from St Stythians, Helston and St Dennis as well as the Camborne Senior and "B" Band. Kenneth Pelmear, the composer, conducted some of his own music and Brenda Wootton sang. Band Chairman, Group Captain Brian Ashall, undertook the introduction and former committee member, Jimmy Chapple, compèred.

During the late 1990s there was a joint concert with Bodmin Town at the Hall for Cornwall. The first half was conventional but Camborne opened their second half with *Cry of the Celts*. Leonard Adams was conducting and he adjusted the players to a flat layout rather than a horseshoe. The soloists stood in front and played with no music - the playing and its affect was staggering.

Thick mist didn't stop a brass concert from taking place at the Minack Theatre in May 1991. Camborne Town Band and Mousehole Male Choir combined to provide an outstanding evening at the magical setting and Musical Director Stephen Sykes brought the event to a close just as the weather worsened.

The role of Engagement Secretary is extremely important and Karen Pritchard (née Triggs) (cornet) was kept busy arranging the bookings in the early 1990s. Gary Lannie (horn/baritone) took over the role for a few years when he joined from St Austell. He later conducted Launceston Band.

It was Cornwall verses Yorkshire at the Recreation Ground, Redruth, on the 20th February 1993 and the Band was there to provide the pre-match entertainment. There were no specific musical requests apart from, *"Play something light and make sure you round it off with Trelawny"*.

During the early 1990s the Band played at the Royal Cornwall Show and in September 1995 took part in a joint concert with St Dennis at Truro Cathedral.

The Band was due to play at the Minack again in 1995 but the weather was so bad that the concert was transferred to St Buryan Church. Playing *The Pines Of Rome* it wasn't long before the noise and vibration caused the plaster to start falling from the ceiling of this very old church.

The Tall Ships Race in mid 1998 was the occasion for a spectacular concert at Pendennis Castle. The Glastonbury Festival stage was set up – complete with mud residue – and the Band shared it with a number of choirs and groups. It was a Cornish evening which finished with Trelawny and a huge firework display. A truly Celtic celebration.

In April 2001, the Band joined with the Holman Climax Choir in the *Last Night of the Proms* for Rotary International at the Bournemouth International Conference Centre. It was conducted by Frank Renton and performed in front of 5000 Rotarians.

Playing for the holidaymakers in the summer is a must and regular concerts are given at Victoria Park in Truro, St Ives, Penzance Harbour, Newquay Killacourt and at Padstow when the march *Padstow Lifeboat,* by Malcolm Arnold, just has to be included in the programme.

In January 2003 Camborne Youth Band presented a concert at the Hall for Cornwall featuring Sonar Brass (a five piece ensemble) and Camborne Town Band. Major Paul Murrell conducted the Band in *Be a Clown, Deep Inside the Sacred Temple* by Bizet (euphonium duet – Robert Jose and Steve Thomas), *Coming to America, Erin Shore, The Barbarian Horde and Windows of the World* by Peter Graham. Sonar Brass comprised five musicians - Alan Morrison and Richard Marshall (cornets), Nick Hudson (trombone), Owen Farr (tenor horn - then of Faireys) and Shaun Crowther (tuba - Grimethorpe) and the audience certainly had value for money as they played a programme of about 20 pieces. The following day the five top musicians held a workshop for young players. The CD, *Live,* was made in 2003 with pieces from this concert and Frank Renton conducting the test pieces, *Jazz* and *Whitsun Wakes*.

The CD, *Fanfare,* was released in 2004 and featured the Camborne Town Band and the Royal Corp of Signals. It was a recording at the Hall for Cornwall in April 2004 when Major Paul Murrell psm CA Mus. conducted the individual and combined bands. The programme included the *Grand March from Aida, In the Miller Mood, Evocations, Eve of War, Gethsemane* (soprano soloist

Jeremy Squibb), Copeland's *Fanfare for the Common Man, Cornish Through and Through by* Goff Richards, and the *Finale from The Enigma Variations.*

The September Promenade concerts at St Ives have become an annual event and in 2004 it was a huge success with its Union Jack flags, hats and hooters. Frank Renton was conducting and Karen Hurn was the guest soloist. A very full programme commenced with *Liberty Fanfare,* followed by *Zauberflaute, Music of the Elizabethan Court, King's Hunting Jig, Somewhere* and *Tonight* sung by the guest soloist and *Farandole.* The second half featured some stunning war theme music; *War on the Big Screen, 633 Squadron, Bridge over the River Kwai, The Great Escape* and *Band of Brothers* before the really big one - the *1812 Overture* - complete with cannons. The event was all wrapped up with the traditional Promenade Concert items *British Sea Songs* with its hornpipe, *Rule Britannia, Jerusalem* and *Pomp and Circumstances No. 1.* Value for money? I should say so!

The Band playing in Queen's Pit in 2004 with the Union Jack and St Piran's flag flying proud. Graham Barker is conducting but before the trombone section makes a complaint, it wasn't me that cut you out of the picture. The players were surprised to learn from Eric Thomas that this was not the first concert the Band had given there; he'd been a playing member at a concert in 1954. (Photo by Roy Netherton)

A charity concert celebrating Goff Richard's 60th birthday was held at the Hall for Cornwall on the 7th November 2004. It was a memorable evening and featured Camborne Town Band (Leonard Adams), St Austell Town Band (David Loukes), Four Lanes Male Voice Choir (Alastair Taylor) and a number of singers and guest conductors including Geoffrey Whitham. The event was compèred by Phillip Hunt and raised £10,000 for local charities and earned many plaudits for its musical and entertainment value. A CD, *Celebration,* was made of items from the programme which were all written or arranged by Goff.

Andrew Tellam was playing bass drum in a concert which included the *1812 Overture.* The sound of the cannons was to be played on the drum but it needed a bit of a hefty whack. Andrew was equal to the task but, unfortunately, the drum wasn't and he managed to split the skin. With quickness of mind he swung the drum over and carried on playing but the three weetabix for breakfast had taken their toll and he split that side as well. Not satisfied with that, he managed to do it again at Trevithick Day in 2005.

On the 3rd April 2005 Camborne Town Band gave the first concert in a series entitled *Cornish Champion Brass.* St Austell, Mount Charles and Camborne bands collaborated in producing the events held at the Burrell Theatre, Truro School. Phillip Hunt compèred a varied and technically demanding concert delivered with a high level of excitement. The *Battle of Shiloh* was breathtaking and superb, Mark Letcher with *Evergreen* was exquisite and *Dundonnell* from *Hymn of the Highlands* brought the first half to a stunning conclusion. Andrew Mitchell gave a superb performance of *I know why,* one of the many arrangements undertaken by his colleague Steve Thomas (euphonium) and the concert concluded with an exciting performance of the Overture *Rienzi t*aken at a slightly quicker pace than at the recent Area Championship. A disappointingly small audience appreciated the superb playing, not least by the splendid percussion players and if you feel there are a few too many superlatives in my writing then you were obviously not at the concert!

Constantine Silver Band's "Brass on Grass" concert in 2005 was a splendid event when the sun shone and the music was played in ideal conditions. Four bands attended: Camborne, Helston, St Keverne and the hosts, Constantine, and each performed its individual programme before combining for the last three pieces conducted by Keith Anderson. The playing was superb and each band played its part in producing a very entertaining programme which was appreciated by the audience. Jessica Powell joined Camborne for the summer and played principal cornet at this concert. There were a number of other guest players to cover for absences: Ben Martin of Helston Town Band (percussion), Mark Rosewarne (percussion), Barry Buist of Lanner & District (second trombone) and Stuart Tregembo of the "B" Band (baritone)

Camborne began with the evocative *Agincourt Song*, followed by *49th Parallel, Softly Softly,* a moving rendition of *Goodbye to Love* played by horn soloist Mark Letcher, a scintillating performance of *Toccata in D* – which required an encore – and the popular melody *One Voice* with its atmospheric lead-in by euphonium player Robert Jose. Ray Farr conducted Camborne and, with the exception of 49th Parallel, he had arranged all of the music.

The Victoria Gardens at Truro make a superb setting for a concert but, with so much percussion, bands now seem to have ougrown the band- stand. Camborne pro- vided an excellent peformance but as they gathered for a photograph, my digital camera failed to work and I'm indebted to Clive Letcher who was on hand to save the day.

The Contest Stage

Competition is natural and it should not be surprising that rivalry between the early bands led to challenges being issued for head-to-head contests. This added a bit of excitement and it was not long before these "duels" grew into organised contests involving a number of bands. Grading was introduced; initially based on the number of players but then on standard of play. There were "own-choice" or set test pieces and entertainment contests where bands were required to play a short programme of music. Each band sought to improve its standard so that it would have a better chance of winning and this must have done more than anything to raise the level of playing. Contesting was a simple process of comparing your music making with others and although the rules and the standard of play have changed over the years, this remains the primary objective.

In the early days, the adjudicator's notes and comments accompanied the results in the local papers; such was the wide appeal of the brass band movement and its competitions.

One of the first band contests in the country took place in 1845, at Burton Constable, near Hull. Only five bands competed, each playing an "own-choice" test piece and having a maximum of 12 players. These events grew in popularity and it wasn't long before national contests were being held. The first Crystal Palace contest was held in 1860 and did much to spread the appeal of brass banding to the south of the country.

The National Band Festival at Crystal Palace under John Henry Iles was held in 1900 and continued to 1938; the start of the Second World War. In 1945, the Daily Herald took over the National Band Festival introducing Area Championships with qualification to the National Finals.

I cannot say when contesting first started in Cornwall but, influenced by other parts of the country and by the creation of a number of brass bands during the latter part of the 1800s, it was certainly no later than circa 1880.

Prize money won at contests has always been secondary to the prestige of winning and being able to display the silverware. No matter what the status of the contest there is nothing to match the excitement of taking part and waiting for the results; sometimes it means disappointment and sometimes glory.

Frank Moore, from St Agnes Band, always held the view that success should not only be measured on the contest stage. A band should be judged by its public every time it takes part in a musical activity and the only way to achieve real, long-term success is for every performance to reflect the standard achieved in competition. But contesting does provide an opportunity to compare your standard against other bands and to compete in an atmosphere of friendly rivalry. Most bands experience the highs and lows and it is a never-ending battle to maintain standards and retain players. My banding experience was enhanced by participation on the contest stage and while I would agree with those who say it is not the be-all and end-all, it is the part I recall with most pleasure.

Many contests have been included in this chapter but I am aware that the early days of banding included a host of others including a Second and Third Section contest at St Agnes in 1914. There have been contests at Nanpean, Redruth, Truro, Lelant and many other places but the records seem to have slipped into obscurity. Perhaps, one day, someone will research and catalogue them but I don't envy them the considerable task.

As I sat in the Cornish Studies Library combing through the microfilm records of local newspapers (I must get out more) I came across an item in March 1912 where the *Royal Cornwall Gazette* was lamenting the difference between the top bands in the country and the Cornish championship bands. Under a heading entitled *Our Point of View* it was advocating the bringing together of the best-players in Cornwall under one baton to form a band to compete with the country's best. It bemoaned the fact that local bands are, *"Currently under the guidance of conductors who have only a rudimentary knowledge of the brass instrument"*. Well, that may have been the case in those days but not any longer, as I hope the following will show.

This chapter is about the results achieved by Camborne Town Band. I do not claim that it is comprehensive but it is the result of more hours of research than I wish to count. References to many other bands appear; the band names may not be accurate but are as stated in newspaper reports and contest programmes.

Considering Camborne Town's long pedigree and extensive involvement in contesting, this section is extensive and full of statistics. To many, it will be a chance to reflect on the considerable success enjoyed by Camborne Town Band but to others, the more casual supporter, it may be a chapter that gives too much detail. I hope, however, that everyone will agree that it is an essential part of the Band and no book on its history would be complete without it.

Trevenson Park Contest (Pool) was held for a number of years in the 1890s and maybe before and after. You may recall that this was the contest which caused the dismissal of the Volunteer Band with the happy result that Camborne Town Band was formed as an independent organisation. The Band took first prize in 1896 but, of course, this was before the split and while it was still a military band.

The August 1898 event was advertised as *A Band Contest and Sports* and according to the newspaper report it attracted 8,000 spectators (I checked it twice!). Seven bands entered but only four turned up; Camborne took the "premier honours" with Troon and St Erth taking the next two places.

The County Contest in August 1897 was reported in the *West Briton* and included the following report which confirms that Camborne Town Band has been successful almost from the day it was formed.

"Quite a number of people took what at present and from Camborne the tedious journey to Newquay. The reason is to be found in the fact that Camborne Town was competing in the county contest, and Cambornians have still their pride in their Band, and went up confident that they would find them able to hold their own against all competition. Had they not thought so, it is more than probable they would not have gone. Nor were they disappointed, Camborne not only coming first, but Bandmaster Uren distinguished himself as cornet soloist. The spectators returned quite as jubilant as were the members of the Band themselves."

This was the seventeenth contest so, unless any years had been missed, it had started in 1881. Many contests took place on weekdays and in this case it was a Monday when the bands paraded in the square and then marched to the contest ground.

Eight bands had entered but only five turned up. The newspaper report said, *"The judge regarded the Camborne Band as far and away the best and Mr Uren won the cornet soloist prize".* Penzance Silver was placed second, Stenalees third and St Erth fourth. Camborne took first place again in 1898 and the win was by a country mile as this report shows.

"General ensemble particularly good; attack very good; solo playing fair on the whole; marks of expression well observed; tempo generally well observed.

Marks deducted: For errors in execution - 6; for errors in respiration - 6; slight fault in the rendering of cadenzas - 6;
Total deducted 18.
Number of marks 82."

The Band of the 1890s (Photo by courtesy of David Thomas)

Troon was second with 50 marks and St Erth was third with 43 marks.

Playing the test piece *Le Domino Noir* Camborne won the day **St Austell Contest** (date unknown) and, according to adjudicator J Brier from Bradford, played *"By far the best performance ..."* Its players also took home medals for cornet, baritone, horn, trombone and euphonium. In second place was St Dennis with Queen's Band third with the remarks, *"I presume you have no sop......your numbers are rather small, I should think"*. Saltash Band was unplaced and an interesting comment in the adjudicator's remarks is *"clarinet good"*. The inclusion of woodwind suggests that the contest was very early – probably in the 1890s – either that or woodwind was permitted to a later date than is thought.

Fraddon Contest was held on the 16th September but I wish I knew which year. The test piece was *Song Echoes* and the adjudicator was W Halstead from Queensbury. Camborne Town was in first place and its players took the medals for cornet, euphonium and trombone. St Dennis Temperance (W Juleff), was second and were said to have played, *"A good performance generally"*. Liskeard Temperance (R J Honey) was third and J Tanner took Lelant to fourth place.

Pencoys, Four Lanes Contest commenced in 1909 and claimed to be *"The Largest Musical Event in the West."* Unfortunately I do not have any results but it is likely that Camborne would have attended. The First Section was for bands not exceeding 24 performers and the second was for smaller groups of not exceeding 16. Like most local contests at that time there was no grading based on standard of play. The top prize in the First Section was *"£15 and a Class A (B flat) Prototype Silver-plated and Engraved Cornet (value £11.11s) specially made for this contest by Messrs Besson and Co Ltd., London, sole makers of the famous Prototype and Harmonic Vale Instruments as used by the famous Foden's Band, and other leading bands in the Country"*.

There were lesser prizes for the second section and numerous medals for soloists including a special award for the best baritone. The event included a March Contest, with a prize of one pound, and was judged as bands paraded the village.

The event was wound up with a *"Grand Slow Melody Solo Contest"* when the President provided a medal for the best Bombardon solo. The adjudicator was Mr Wm Short, LRAM (The King's Trumpeter).

In 1912 Redruth Town was conducted by Monica Orchard's great uncle, Richard Wills, when they beat Camborne and it's said the Camborne players were not very happy and walked home across the fields kicking the turnips out of the ground as they went.

At the fifth annual contest, on the 9th August 1913, the Revd L C Carpenter was the President and Thos Valentine the adjudicator. Playing the test piece *Maritana* Camborne Town (Wm Wren - probably Uren) was in first place with a special prize for the best soloist (cornet) and medals for cornet and trombone. In second place was Redruth Town (R Wills) with a medal for the neatest and best dressed bandsmen. St Dennis Temperance (W Juleff) was third and Foxhole Temperance (J Morcom) fourth.

The second annual **Wadebridge Contest** took place on Monday the 10th March 1913; it was a fine day and approximately 3,000 people turned up to hear the 10 bands play in a field at *Gonvena.*

There were two sections with five bands in each. The First Section test piece was *The Bohemian Girl* and was for bands of 24 performers, while the test piece for the Second Section was *Village Bride* and was restricted to bands of 16. Adjudicator J Brier was impressed with the playing and considered the bands in the Second Section to compare favourably with those from Lancashire and Yorkshire. Camborne (W Uren) came out on top and also collected soloist medals for euphonium and cornet. Redruth (R Wills) was second, St Austell Territorials (T Morgan) third, St Dennis Temperance (J G Jubb) fourth leaving Barry Dockers' Prize Band from South Wales, out of the placings.

Foxhole Temperance, St Agnes and Liskeard Temperance took the first three places in the Second Section leaving Indian Queens and Bugle unplaced. There were 26 entries in the solo contest but the Camborne players were not in the prizes.

I'm not sure for how long the **Lelant Contest** was held and I'm afraid I don't know to which year this result relates; Wm Uren was conducting Camborne so it must be pre 1914. The test piece was *Emilia* and the adjudicator was Mr J Manley. Camborne won the First Section with medals for best euphonium, trombone and soprano. St Dennis Temperance (W H Juleff) was second with a medal for best cornet and Redruth Town (R Wills) was third.

Camborne also won the March Contest but was said to be, *"Slightly on the rough side"* but, "*decidedly the best today*". St Ives Town was second and St Agnes third. St Agnes Band was described as *"a very good band"* and *"the best all round performance up to now,"* presumably that was before St Ives and Camborne had played.

Penzance Contest was held in St John's Hall and Camborne competed there in 1928. Having taken first prize, the players looked around for 14 year-old Edgar Floyd who was needed on stage to receive the best solo horn of the day award. They eventually found him outside, playing football. The adjudicator was, "*Amazed to find someone so young playing with such superb quality"*.

The first annual **Falmouth Bandsmen's Festival** was held on Saturday the 1st July 1939. I don't know how many years it ran or if Camborne ever attended but they were certainly not competing in 1939. It was held at the Recreation Ground and Section "A" comprised four bands – Falmouth, Indian Queens, Redruth Town and St Dennis. The commentary on the programme described the curious feature of *"fastening up the judge"* so there would be no suspicion of cheating.

The 1927 **St Ives Contest** took place in perfect weather and drew a crowd of nearly 3,000 people. This annual event was popular and on this occasion the open section attracted five bands. Camborne took first prize for the test piece *Operatic Beauties* with Bugle in second place followed by Hayle, Falmouth Town and Penzance Independent. For the hymn tune, Camborne had to be satisfied with second place behind Bugle. Telfer Rule (soprano), Fred Roberts (cornet) and S Roberts (euphonium) won soloist medals with the President's Cup for the best soloist going to Fred Roberts.

Camborne Band Contest and Cycle Races was held on Thursday the 25th August 1898 at the New Recreation Ground; it seems to have been an annual event. The bands had to play an "own-choice" piece in addition to the test piece *Maritana* and in this particular year there was a major upset as Pen-

Early 1930s - Camborne Town Band attempting to win the deportment prize at ***Dorchester Contest.*** *A Band Sergeant was used and Olley Ruse was given the role. For appearances sake Ernie Yeoman swapped his trombone for Olley's tenor horn and pressed the occasional valve to make it look as though he was playing.*

zance Independent pushed the host band into second place. It's interesting to note that the third and fourth placed bands, Illogan and Porthleven, were brass and reed bands.

The *Royal Cornwall Gazette* commented, *"............ there was a band contest, which resulted in the Camborne Band being beaten by the Penzance Band, this was very galling to the Camborne boys, for they had freely boasted of being certain of the first prize. However I have no doubt this will do them some good by letting them see that there are others capable of beating even them. Conceit is a deadly foe. It is pleasing to know that the judge's decision is considered fair, even by the disappointed ones.*

Can it be true that Penzance engaged outsiders to play for them in order to beat Camborne? I should think not, although rumour has it to the contrary."

During the 1930s the **Camborne Junior Contest** was run for lower section bands; St Agnes attended in 1934 and won first prize under the nomadic conductor Mr G W Cave.

The **Camborne Town Band March, Hymn Tune and Deportment Contest** was for Second and Third Section bands, similar to the more famous contest at Stenalees.

Fred Roberts was the adjudicator at the first contest, held in the open-air at Rosewarne, Camborne, on the 11th September 1954. Playing in the Second Section, St Agnes took first prize for the march and second for the hymn. The hand written results are a little unclear but it appears it was also first for both pieces in the Third Section.

The Second Section competitors were Bodmin Town (W D Lawton), Helston (C L Hender), Penzance Silver (J Grand) (may have withdrawn), Perranporth (J Eustace), Porthleven Silver (E Bawden), St Agnes (F E Moore) and Mount Charles (T A Cooper).

In the Third Section were Helston (C L Hender), Penzance Silver (J Grand) (may have withdrawn), Perranporth (J Eustace), Porthleven Silver (E Bawden), Mount Charles (T A Cooper), St Agnes (F E Moore) and Newlyn East Silver (N Halls).

St Agnes was definitely second in the deportment section held at the Recreation Ground and judged by Lt. Col. G. J. Miller, M.V.O., M.B.E. Frank Moore had talked the players into entering, *"Because no one else ever bothered"*. Apparently there was some good prize money offered and, as luck would have it, Frank was correct and only two bands took part. Helston had clearly been well drilled and performed like a military unit so there was no chance that St Agnes was going to take the top prize. But equally, there was no doubt that it was going to pick up the second prize and, of course, some prize money. It seems they set off in an orderly fashion but at some stage the instruction was given to halt. Unfortunately, only about half of the players heard it and the rear section piled into the backs of their colleagues. A bit embarrassing but they did take home some money.

Rivalry between bands is always friendly - well almost always. I guess there is as much gamesmanship and rule bending as in any other competition and there are those who are always looking for reasons to appeal or, at least, to explain away their defeat. One such occasion was when St Agnes won the top prize at Camborne's Recreation Ground when a close contest was expected with Helston. Frank Moore had a habit of tapping his music stand twice to bring the band to order and he did it on this occasion. It was suggested this had been a signal to the adjudicator and the fact that St Agnes won seemed to prove it in some people's judgement.

A note in the programme congratulated Mr F E Moore and the St Agnes Band on their great success at the Stenalees contest. It went on to say, *"Their steady rise in quality of performance has been noticed by all*". St Agnes won the march and the hymn in both sections and must have returned home very pleased.

In 1955 the adjudicator was A V Creasy and one of the prizes was the A W Parker Trophy. St Agnes (F E Moore) was first overall in the Second Section with Truro (Alwyn Teasdale) second and Mount Charles in third place. The test pieces were *Rigoletto* by Verdi and *March of the Peers* by Sullivan. In the contest programme notes, L A Fletcher Hon. Gen. Sec. said, *"We would like to thank those bands that cannot be with us owing to the harvest but sent us their good wishes"*.

The **Cornwall Brass Band Association Contest** commenced in 1956 and has been held at Bodmin, Truro (City Hall and The Hall for Cornwall) and St Austell. It became established in the Hall for Cornwall and was often referred to as *Truro Contest*. However in 2005 there were concerns that support was insufficient to warrant the cost of hiring this large hall and it remains to be seen if there will be a change in venue for the 2006 event.

The Association was formed in November 1955 with the competition restricted to member bands. Quite a few joined but the number taking part in the early contests was poor. Despite that, the *West Briton* headline was,

"First Band Festival at Truro was Great Success"

The first event was held in March 1956 and took place at the City Hall, Truro. It is difficult to find too many superlatives about the old hall; the toilets and changing rooms were in a terrible state and the new Hall for Cornwall is superior in every way. And yet, when I think of this contest, my mind goes back to the City Hall, a venue of happy memories and associations.

There were only two bands in the Championship Section and Camborne was declared the winner, just ahead of Truro City. Camborne's "own-choice" test piece was *Mendelssohn's Music*, the same piece that was used at Bugle Contest that year. A 16 year-old cornet player won the best-player award; it was the start of John Berryman's hat-trick of wins at this particular contest.

The conducting for the evening concert was shared by, W D Lawton of Bodmin Town - a former member of Foden's Band, Alwyn Teasdale of Truro City - a former member of the London Symphony Orchestra and the St Hilda's Brass Band and Fred Roberts of Camborne Town Band. The Cornwall County Youth Brass Band also took part and 12 year-old Monica Orchard played a cornet solo.

Alan Toy was playing first horn and had a particularly difficult part which was littered with accidentals. He said, *"I felt that Freddie Roberts was ready to pounce the moment I played a wrong note"*.

Only six bands competed the following year which must have been a great disappointment for the organisers and for the public. It was felt that petrol rationing had affected practice sessions but there must have been serious misgivings in the minds of the committee members. It was Camborne verses Truro City again in the top section and in the test piece, *Themes from Beethoven's Ninth Symphony*; the result was the same as in the previous year with Camborne receiving 98 points for an *"outstanding performance"*. The surprise came when the result for the Open March Section was declared. Truro City took first place and Camborne was not in the first three. As you will have gathered, John Berryman won the best soloist award.

Normal service was resumed in 1958 when Camborne took first place for the test piece and the march. The *West Briton* declared, "*Camborne Supreme at Festival*" and the adjudicator, Bert Sullivan - Bandmaster of Munn & Felton's Works Band - had these remarks for Camborne's performance of *Coriolanus*. *"Thank you very much for a wonderful performance. It was exceptional all through – really first class playing. I could tell without a doubt that there was a musician at the helm."* John Berryman completed his hat trick, winning the Roberts Trophy.

Camborne Town Band did not attend during the period 1959 – 1971 inclusive but I know the fair minded people of Camborne will not mind me mentioning 1967, when St Agnes won the Concert Contest and 1969, when it won the Championship Section from St Dennis, Bodmin Town and Indian Queens.

For the first time for many years Camborne Town competed in the 1972 contest and took first place over Mount Charles with their playing of *Blackfriers* by E Cundell. The adjudicator, John Harrison, once the Musical Director at St Dennis and Falmouth, used such comments as *"brilliant and dynamic*" and "*out of this world*". The Band also won first prize in the concert contest and Neil Peters (euphonium) won the best soloist award. Some excellent comments were received from the adjudicator who said, "*What can I say but praise for the execution"*.

In 1973 the test piece was "own-choice" and Camborne chose to play *Triumphant Rhapsody* and took first prize in a section of five bands with Jack Pascoe (flugel) winning the best soloist award. With the complaint that they had played with a little too much show-band forcefulness in the Concert

Contest the Camborne players had to be content with second place behind a superb St Dennis Youth Band. The Camborne "B" was placed third. There was a word of warning from adjudicator Wesley Johnstone to the female players, *"You should not cross your legs, no matter how nice they are. It is not only distracting for the men but it also affects your breathing".*

The following year, playing the test piece *Corsair* and conducted by Derek Johnston, Camborne was placed first, well ahead of St Dennis (E J Williams) and Mount Charles (A Jenkin). It was also placed first in the Grand Evening Concert. The award for the outstanding soloist of the day went to Camborne's soprano player, Peter Goldsworthy.

Still reeling from the affects of losing its Musical Director and four key players, Camborne entered the 1975 contest under new leader, Bernard Bygrave. The test piece was *Symphony of Marches* by Gilbert Vinter and St Austell (F J Roberts) took first prize with Camborne second, St Dennis third, Mount Charles fourth and Bodmin fifth. St Austell also took first prize in the Grand Evening Concert. Tom Chainey, former conductor of Falmouth, Gweek and Pendeen, was presented with a long-service certificate.

In 1977 the test piece was *Comedy Overture* by J Ireland and for Camborne Town (Derek Greenwood) it was a walkover as the only other championship entry, Mount Charles, had withdrawn. Camborne's Leonard Adams (Principal Cornet) received the Silver Cup for the outstanding soloist of the day. With no other top section band taking part in the Grand Evening Concert, Camborne was the clear winner.

Eric Ball's *Journey into Freedom* was chosen as the test piece in 1978 and Bodmin Town came out on top. Camborne (Derek Greenwood) was second, St Austell (Derek Johnston) third and Mount Charles fourth.

John Berryman was the adjudicator in 1981 but Camborne did not attend again until 1983 when it competed against Bodmin Town, Redruth Town and St Dennis. Camborne was awarded first prize for the test piece *The Wayfarer.* This was Jason Smith's first contest with the Band and he describes his first rehearsal when he was, *"Astounded at the awesome sound that was being created".*

In 1984 Camborne (Derek Greenwood) was competing against St Dennis (J Brush) and ran out winners by 11 points with the playing of *Judges of the Secret Court.* The best instrumentalist award was presented to Michael Weeks (E flat bass) of Camborne. A new trophy was added to the collection this year, in memory of Eddie Williams, a former President of the Association and conductor of St Dennis.

The Band next appeared in 1988 when Stephen Sykes was conducting; it took first prize over Bodmin Town (Leonard Adams) and St Dennis (S Appleton). Playing the test piece, *Beatrice and Benedict* by Berlioz, the adjudicator described its performance as sizzling. Camborne players receiving awards for the best instrumentalist in section were: best cornet player - Stuart Chappell, best euphonium player – John Hitchens and best cornet section – Darren Hendy, Chris Parkin, Norman Johns and Stuart Chappell.

Another break in attendance and in 1992 Camborne (Derek Greenwood) was the only band in the top section and so, took first place. Players receiving awards for the best instrumentalist in section were: Paul Bilkey (soprano) and John Hitchens (euphonium) who was also the best player in the contest. Paul had previously played in Helston and Redruth Bands and in 1993 he resigned for work reasons.

A two year break saw the Band there again in 1995 when there was an unusually large section of six; Bodmin were the winners over second place Camborne (Derek Greenwood). The test piece was "own-choice" but both bands chose to play *Paganini Variations.*

In 1996 the CBBA Contest was held at the Cornwall Coliseum, St Austell, once again the test piece was "own-choice" and Camborne (Derek Greenwood), chose to play *Essence of Time.* It was placed second behind Bodmin who played *Year of the Dragon.*

Absent in 1997, the Band returned to take part at the 1998 contest held at the Hall for Cornwall. Bodmin was placed first with *On Alderley Edge* ahead of Camborne (Leonard Adams) playing *Paganini Variations.* The Roger Moyle Memorial Trophy for the best euphonium player went to

Camborne. Goff Richards and John Berryman had both been involved in Camborne's preparation by helping out with rehearsals.

Leonard Adams was conducting Camborne in 1999 when the Band took first prize from Mount Charles. The test piece was "own-choice" and Terry Sleeman (baritone) won the best instrumentalist award.

There was a gap of five years before Camborne returned to compete again – in 2005. Having played *Rienzi* at the Area Championship in March 2005, it was decided to use it again for the "own-choice" contest at the Hall for Cornwall on the 9th April. The only challenge came from Lanner & District (ex Camborne player Stuart Chappell) playing the *Land of the Long White Cloud.* Camborne (Lt Col C Davies) was on top form and a very measured and exciting performance brought the Band the title of Cornish Champions. Robert Jose (euphonium) was outstanding and took the titles of Best Instrumentalist in the Championship Section, the Roger Moyle Memorial Trophy for the Best Euphonium Player at the Contest and the Ivan Kessell Memorial Trophy for the best-player at the Contest (I just hope his sideboard is big enough). The Peter Bailey Memorial Cup for the Best Set of Basses at the Contest went to Camborne - Eric Thomas, Tim Joslin, Kevyn Caddy and Jason Smith - and the E C C Revue Society Shield for the Best Cornet Section to Chris Leonard, Ian Hooper, Mark Leigh and Robert Sandow.

A young lady, Kayleigh Rowe, of St Dennis Youth made an outstanding contribution to her band's pole position in the Youth Section and its second place in the Open Entertainment Section when it was only headed by Camborne. She also collected the Brian Richards Memorial Cup for the Best Cornet Player at the contest and the Cecil E Brewer Memorial Shield for the Best Soloist in the Youth Section.

Led by the inspiring Lt Col Chris Davies, Camborne's performance in the Entertainment Section was outstanding and included a feast of entertainment and superb playing.

Steve Thomas (euphonium) still had one more thing to celebrate; he also conducted Newquay Band as it collected the title of Cornish Third Section Champions.

The **Cornwall Brass Band Association "own-choice" Band Contest** ran for a few years but I have found no record of Camborne ever attending. Wesley Chapel, Redruth, hosted the event on 6th December 1969 when William Scholes was the adjudicator. The result for the hymn tune and march was: St Dennis first, followed by St Stythians Silver and Mount Charles Silver. For the test piece St Dennis was again placed first, ahead of Mount Charles Silver and St Stythians Silver. The following year the event was held at St Ives when Geoffrey Brand was the adjudicator.

The South West Brass Band Association Contest commenced in 1947 with the first contest held on the 22nd November at the Civic Hall in Exeter. George Cave was the adjudicator, a man well known in Cornwall for conducting a number of local bands. In the early years the contest moved around and was held in a number of locations from Bodmin to Barnstaple. Camborne registered in 1948/49 but it seems it was not until 1971 that it made its first appearance.

In November 1971 St Austell Silver (F J Roberts) took first prize for the test piece, *Lorenzo* with Camborne, (Derek Johnston) second and Bodmin third. Peter Goldsworthy (soprano) won the best-player award. In the "own-choice" march section, St Austell was first; Camborne played *Contestor* but I don't have the result.

The 33rd Annual Championship in 1979 was held at the Festival Theatre, Paignton, when Derek Greenwood conducted Camborne Town to a convincing win over St Dennis (second) and Mount Charles (third) playing the test piece *Freedom* by H Bath.

Playing *Salute to Youth*, Bodmin Town won the top section in 1995 with Camborne Town in second place playing *Variations on a theme by Paganini.*

In 1996 *Kings Messenger* by George Lloyd was the test piece and Bodmin Town was placed first with Camborne Town (Derek Greenwood) second. *Padstow Lifeboat* by Malcolm Arnold was the other test piece and this time Camborne was in first place.

Not a good result for Camborne (Leonard Adams) in 1997 when it was unplaced in a section of four. *Salute to Youth* was the "own-choice" test piece but the Band failed to impress the adjudicators and Bodmin, playing the same piece, was in first place.

In 1998, there were only two bands in the top section. The test piece was *Le Carnival Romain* by Hector Berlioz and Leonard Adams conducted Camborne to first place ahead of St Austell.

In November 1976 Derek Greenwood recorded his first win with Camborne Town Band - at **Reading Contest**. Playing the test piece *Freedom* the Band took first place over the William Davies Band conducted by John Berryman. Principal Cornetist Leonard Adams received the best-player award and, according to Bob Seymour, Neil Peters received a new pair of braces. It seems he'd forgotten or broken his own and Bob was despatched to find a replacement.

At the 61st Reading Festival on Saturday the 15th November 1997, Leonard Adams was conducting *Isaiah 40* by R Redhead when the Band was placed third. The day was also memorable for another reason. As the players were relaxing in the bar after their performance the call to leave came and they jumped on the coach. It was only when they'd reached Swindon that a phone call told them they'd left Graham Barker behind. He'd been running after the coach but no one spotted him; he was not best pleased at having to return by train on his own.

Reading Contest 20th November 1976

Derek Greenwood's first win with Camborne Town Band - the look on his face says it all. Playing a supporting role are David Reed, David Parsons and Donald Cock

The **Penwith Band Festival**, organised by Penwith District Council and sponsored by Unigate Foods Ltd, was held in Penzance.

At the first contest, in September 1977, the test piece was *Symphony of Marches* and Camborne Town Band (Derek Greenwood) took first place over St Austell and Mount Charles. Leonard Adams was the best solo cornet and Robert Cook the best solo horn.

Variations on a Ninth by Gilbert Vinter was selected for 1979 and this time Camborne (Derek Greenwood) had to be satisfied with second place behind Bodmin Town. Camborne's Principal Cornet player won The Hawkes Challenge Cup for the best solo cornet.

Yeovil Entertainment Contest started in 1978 when the Cory Band took first place. Conducted by Derek Greenwood, Camborne was placed fifth with their 25-minute, "own-choice" concert.

Camborne was placed fourth in 1979 behind Cory, City of Coventry and Sun Assurance Stanshawe.

In 1980 the Cory Band was again to the fore but Camborne Town was up there in second place ahead of the City of Coventry.

The following year, Camborne (Derek Greenwood) had to be satisfied with sixth place as St Austell (Albert Chappell) picked up the first prize .

Many players dislike being first to play at a contest and I suppose the only thing worse is to follow one of the favourites. Kingsley Hitchens often made the draw at Yeovil and with only two positions left to fill, one and eleven; he chose the dreaded first spot. The following year he was asked if he minded being relieved of his duty and John Phillips went to make the draw. When he returned he was only able to say, "*Sorry lads, we're playing at number one again*".

Eddie Ashton was conducting in 1986 when Foden's won the day and Camborne was placed seventh. On arrival at Yeovil, Wayne Brown discovered he'd forgotten his flugel. Not only that, his music was in the instrument case and as it was an "own-choice" contest he couldn't borrow the music from another band. Conductor Eddie Ashton must have been a bit down in the mouth as someone asked him why he was looking so miserable. He said, *"Well I had to get up early to catch the coach at 5.00am, it's pissing down with rain, the coach driver got lost, we're drawn number one and now I've got no flugel player"*. Things were not quite so bad as Wayne borrowed a flugel from another band and managed to play the concert from memory.

There was a good result in 1987 when Camborne (Stephen Sykes) was placed third behind Britannia Building Society Foden's and Hanwell.

There was a large field in 1988 when Camborne (Stephen Sykes) was placed second behind the winners Desford Colliery Dowty, the reigning National Champions. St Austell (Derek Greenwood) was in sixth place. The Band's "own-choice" programme was *Scarecrow and Mrs King, Carnival Cocktail, Firedance, By the Cool Waters, Hawaiian War Chant* and *Third Symphony.*

In 1989 Foden's took the top prize with Camborne (Stephen Sykes) back in sixth place.

There was yet another sixth place for Camborne (Stephen Sykes) in 1991.

Camborne Town (Derek Greenwood) was placed well down, in eleventh place, in 1992 with Bodmin Town and Mount Charles in fifth and sixth place respectively.

The British Bandsman of 13th February 1993 reported, *"SWEB Camborne Town Band under the baton of Derek Greenwood scored an impressive victory at the South Somerset Entertainment Contest last Saturday with euphonium player John Hitchens taking the prize for the best soloist"*.

The chosen programme was Curnow's *Fanfare and Flourishes*, a part of Tchaikovsky's *Little Russian* symphony, *Carnival Cocktail, Jasper's Dance from Pineapple Poll, Rag Time Robin* - a xylophone solo and *Toccata* by Boellmann. The *West Briton* reported one supporter as saying, *"It's like Cornwall RFC winning the Pilkington Cup. Camborne beat the other bands into the ground, despite being drawn early and having to set off for Yeovil at 5.00am"*. John Hitchens described the result as, *"One of the Band's greatest achievements – our best result for a long, long time"*.

It was down with a bump in 1994 as Camborne (Derek Greenwood) was placed back in seventh place.

Geoffrey Whitham was the adjudicator in 1995 and placed the SWEB Camborne Town Band (Derek Greenwood) back in ninth place; the winning band was Tredegar Town followed by Yorkshire Imperial and the Cory Band.

A better year in 1996 as Derek Greenwood took them to second place with Tredegar Town in pole position again. Yorkshire Imperial was third and The Cory Band fourth. Darren Hendy won the soloist's award and the adjudicator also had some praise for John Hitchens who had just missed out.

Stephen Sykes adjudicated in 1998 when Camborne (Leonard Adams) was placed ninth. Leonard said, "I was *fairly pleased with the way the Band performed. John Hitchens had played exceptionally well and on the whole the Band played well together".*

Bodmin Town was victorious in 1999 but Camborne (Leonard Adams) was in the frame with a very good third place.

Camborne was unplaced in 2000 but it was twice in a row for Bodmin as they picked up first prize once again. John Hitchens, now of Bodmin, was the winning soloist for the second time and the first player to win it twice – albeit with two different bands.

Camborne (Major Paul Murrell) was in sixth place in 2004 with Bodmin taking third.

Chris Davies was conducting in 2005 when the Band collected sixth place again.

Pontins' National Championship commenced in 1974 and soon became one of the most popular brass band contests in the country. Although I never intended to produce a comprehensive list of results, I am particularly disappointed regarding this contest about which information has been difficult to find and in many cases I do not have Camborne's placing nor am I certain that they even attended. No doubt more information will turn up after the book has been published.

1974 Final Test piece – "own-choice".
1975 Final Test piece – "own-choice".
1976 Final Test piece - *Les Preludes.*
1977 Final Test piece - *Symphony of Marches*.
1978 Final Test piece – *Les Franc Juges* (St Dennis was in third place and St Austell, fifth.)

Tam O'Shanter's Ride was the test piece at the Area qualifying contest in 1979 when Camborne (Derek Greenwood) was third out of the 18 competing bands. This meant qualification to the Championship Final at Prestatyn where the test piece was *Festival Music* by Eric Ball. Derek Greenwood conducted the Band to an excellent second place behind The Cory Band. David Whear had a busy day as he had to play the piece a second time when he stepped in for Webb Ivory Band whose soprano had been taken ill.

1980 Final Test piece – *Carnival Overture.* (William Davies Construction (John Berryman) was in first place.)

At the 1981 Final the test piece was *James Cook, Circumnavigator* and a Cornish band won first prize but it was St Austell (Albert Chappell) with Camborne (Brian Howard) some way back in eighth place.

Camborne was on top again at the Area Contest in 1982 as they qualified for the Final at Prestatyn. Eighty-three bands took part in the 1982 Championship of which 15 competed in the Championship Section playing *The Festive City*. Following their success from the previous year St Austell (Albert Chappell) was placed third with Camborne (Derek Greenwood) fifth and Bodmin tenth. Tim Joslin recalled the nine-hour coach journey to Prestatyn and the holiday camp which he said, "*Was cold, wet and miserable".*

Camborne Town, (Derek Greenwood) took first prize again at the 1983 Area qualifying contest with their performance of *The Accursed Huntsman* by Cesar Franck. Yorkley Onward was second and St Austell (Albert Chappell), third; the best soloist award went to Simon Williams (euphonium). Lester Ashton had arrived at Camborne at 5.00am to help load the instruments and other equipment on to the coach before setting off for the contest. As they travelled up the motorway he suddenly had doubts about whether he'd transferred his uniform from his car – he hadn't. Playing solo trombone he was positioned nearest the audience and the lack of uniform would be obvious to everyone – including Derek Greenwood! A plan was hatched and very soon he had borrowed a jacket from Helston Band which was only slightly different from his own, a pair of black trousers came from another person – a somewhat shorter person - and a white shirt from yet another source. Unfortunately two other people had already worn the shirt; David Pascoe of Helston had also forgotten his and had borrowed it before passing it on to Lester. Taking great care to avoid Derek Greenwood, Lester took the stage with the rest of the Band. After the performance he walked outside, turned a corner and came face to

1984 Pontins' Championship at Prestatyn
Back row: Steve Weeks, Michael Smith, Marcus Dunstan, Robert Tanner, John Hitchens, Robert Cook, Shaun Thomas, Jason Smith, Lester Ashton, Jonathan Bond, Michael Weeks, Kevin Goninan, Andrew James, Neil Rutter and Wayne Brown.
Front row: Eric Trerise, Michael Long, Stuart Chappell, Michael Pritchard, Michael Couch (cornet - commenced playing with St Ives and joined Camborne in 1983), Terry Tonkin, Derek Greenwood (Musical Director), Mark Medlyn (soprano - played in the mid 1980s before leaving and playing for St Austell. He returned to play with Camborne for short period in the 1990s), Chris Parkin (joined at end of 1973 and played into the Sykes era), Norman Johns, Tim Joslin and Andrew "Sidney" Kemp (baritone/ E flat bass- who left and re-joined in December 1998). The first thing window cleaner Michael Smith did on arrival was to clean the windows of his chalet.
(photo by Donald Williams)

face with Derek Greenwood who said to his companion, Steve Walkley, *"I don't think you know our new solo trombone player do you?"* He turned back to Lester and said, *"Pillock,"* and walked on. In the Final the test piece was *Le Carnival Romain* and Camborne was placed fourth and received a cheque for £150.

Camborne (Derek Greenwood) again qualified in first place in 1984 when the test piece was *Le Roi D'Ys* by E Lalo. Bodmin (A C Jenkin) was placed second and Solent Concert, third. Barrie Trevena gave a lot of credit for the win to soloists Ian Hughes (flugel player who had previously played solo cornet with St Ives Band) and John Hitchins (euphonium). He said, *" Just before we had to play the test piece, literally a couple of minutes before, a valve stuck on John's euphonium! We tried everything to move it, but failed. So he had to borrow someone else's instrument, one he wasn't used to."* The test piece for the Final at Prestatyn was *Diadem of Gold* by G Bailey and Camborne (Derek Greenwood) was placed second.

Jason Smith recalled Ian Hughes moving from St Ives, where he played solo cornet, to Camborne - as a third cornet player. *"It was not until that moment that we realised the enormity of the gap between us and the top flight."*

Terry Tonkin (E flat bass) sounds like a larger-than-life character who did much to raise morale among the players. His escapades at the Pontins' Contest at Prestatyn are remembered with a smile, particularly the occasion when he got out of bed but had forgotten that he'd been sleeping in the top bunk!

1986 - Mike Cotter conducting (Photo by Donald Williams)

Oceans, by Goff Richards, was the 1985 qualifying test piece when Derek Greenwood led the Band to another first place; Robert Tanner was the best soloist. The magnificent tone poem, *Life Divine,* was chosen as the test piece for the Final and Camborne Town (Derek Greenwood) took seventh place. Leonard Adams conducted Redruth Town to thirteenth place.

In the 1986 qualifying contest at Brean Sands Holiday Centre in Somerset, the 20 top section bands played the tone poem *Lorenzo* by Thomas Keighley. Camborne (Mike Cotter) was in first place, some way ahead of Tredegar and Woodfalls who were second and third. The result at Brean sands qualified the Band to compete in the final at Prestatyn when Mike Cotter conducted *Epic Symphony* and the Band was placed third.

Lester Ashton remembered Mike Cotter as an immaculate dresser epitomised by his choice of dress for this contest. He described it as a white suit, white shirt, red tie, red socks and with a red handkerchief in his top pocket. It seems that Mike then sought opinions as to whether he should wear white shoes, red shoes or one of each. The Band took the conservative line and suggested he wore the white ones.

While attending the Pontins' Championship a concert was arranged at the Dobcross Band Club. I suppose the thinking was that it would help pay for the contest expenses. Having finished the concert they set out on the return journey only to find that the coach was faulty and could only travel very slowly. They eventually arrived back at 2.00am on Sunday and it was some very tired players that climbed on to the contest stage later that day.

Variations on a Ninth by Gilbert Vinter was the test piece for the qualifying contest in 1987 and CamborneTown (Stephen Sykes) was placed second behind Aldbourne. John Hitchens won the award for the best soloist. In the Final at Prestatyn the test piece was *Rhapsody on the Cornish Coast* by Henry Geehl but, despite the title, it did not herald a Cornish win. Camborne (Stephen Sykes) was ninth but they did have the consolation of being ahead of Aldbourne.

In 1988, the Area Contest test piece was *Ballet for Band* and Stephen Sykes led the Band to fifth place.

1989 Final Test piece – *Sovereign Heritage.*
1990 Final Test piece – *Festival Music.*
1991 Final Did not attend.

In the 1992 qualifying contest Derek Greenwood conducted Camborne and led them to second place behind Flowers Gloucester. The test piece was *Symphony of Marches* by Gilbert Vinter and Sovereign Brass was placed third and Bodmin Town (Leonard Adams) fourth. The test piece for the Final was *Life Divine* and the amateur adjudicator who wrote on my copy of the programme clearly thought Camborne had played well as he has marked it in first place. The official adjudicators thought otherwise and it was back in sixth place.

1993 Final Did not attend.

1994 Final Test piece – *Les Franc Juges.*

1995 Final Did not attend.

1996 Final Test piece – *Diversions for Brass Band.*

1997 & 1998 Finals Did not attend.

In 1999, Camborne (Leonard Adams) was back in thirteenth place with *Cloudcatcher Fells* by John McCabe when Mount Charles romped home in first place.

Stan Lippeatt was conducting in 2000 when the Band was placed tenth for *Paganini Variations* by Philip Wilby.

2001 to 2004 Finals Did not attend.

Although it has achieved some good results in this competition the Band are still without a win in the Final. Its record at the regional qualifying contest is superb and in Derek Greenwood's words, *"Camborne is the Black Dyke of Brean Sands – nobody goes for a pee when it's playing."*

At the first **Kerrier's Brass in Concert** contest in 1980 Camborne Town was the only entrant in the Championship Section and was awarded 194 points. I'm not sure how many were competing the following year but Camborne returned with first prize again.

The **British Open Championship** is the oldest brass band championship in the world having started on the 5th September 1853 when eight bands took part. Up to 1982 it was held at Belle Vue, Manchester, moving then to two other local venues until 1997 when it transferred to the Symphony Hall in Birmingham. Participation is by invitation but automatic qualification is given to two bands by virtue of their performance in the Grand Shield Contest.

As far as I can see Camborne have never taken part, in fact, three attendances by St Dennis in the 1960s seem to be the only Cornish representation at this contest.

The **Spring Festival - Grand Shield** is often referred to as the Spring Belle Vue. It was instituted in 1921 as the qualifying contest for the British Open Brass Band Championship held later in the year. Originally at Belle Vue, Manchester, it has been held at various concert halls in the north of England and currently takes place at the Winter Gardens in Blackpool.

Having ploughed through the results for the eighty years or so I have come across the names of Mount Charles, St Austell and Bodmin on a number of occasion but, as far as I can see, Camborne have only attended on one occasion. In May 1988 Stephen Sykes took them in the test piece *Un Vie De Matelot (A Sailor's Life)* and was placed eighth; St Austell was in sixth place.

The **Spring Festival - Senior Cup** was initially held in 1952 but discontinued in 1982. In 2001 it was resurrected and held at Blackpool where the top four bands are invited to compete at the following year's Grand Shield Contest which is, itself, a qualifying contest for the British Open Championship.

Although having previously competed in the Grand Shield, the Band's absence of a few years meant that it had to enter the Senior Cup as a starting point in 2003. Camborne was conducted by Paul Murrell and was placed sixteenth playing *Pagannini Variations* by Philip Wilby.

Spring Festival - Senior Trophy could be described as the Third Section but the 2003 result in the Senior Cup coupled with a non-attendance in 2004 meant that Camborne had to climb up through the various sections before gaining their ultimate ambition – a place in the British Open. Many had predicted a Camborne victory in the May 2005 competition or, if not first then surely, a top four placing with promotion to the Senior Cup for the following year but after two full days travelling Camborne Town Band returned home empty handed as their bid to win the Senior Trophy ended in disappointment. Unfortunately, events conspired against Camborne for this contest and with lady luck firmly against it the Band had to settle for seventh place. Due to family illness, Captain Pete Curtis had to return to Portsmouth after only one session and newly appointed Bandmaster, Steve Thomas, stepped in to direct the contest rehearsals.

In May 1978 Camborne entered the **Granada *Band of the Year*** contest at Belle Vue, Manchester, when Barnoldswick Brass Band hosted the players. The layout of the hall was impressive with a row of large, decorative flowerpots on each side of the walkway to the stage. Donald Cock was probably preoccupied with thoughts of the test piece when he managed to swing his trombone sideways and take out one of the pots, flowers and all.

Up against considerable opposition in the traditional home of brass band, Camborne was placed ninth out of the eleven bands taking part. Having said that, every band present was a household name. The three adjudicators' score sheets make interesting reading (well it does to me!) The winner, Carlton Main, was given two third places and a second whilst second place Cory received two fourths and a second. So none of the adjudicators considered either of them to have played the best performance. The third placed band was Sun Alliance (Stanshawe) and they received two firsts and a ninth! Brighouse who was fourth, received a first, a fourth and a tenth. Funny old game this contesting.

Often referred to as the youngest "major" contest, the **All England Masters** commenced in 1989 and is open to invited bands from England only. It is held at the Corn Exchange in Cambridge and attracts most of the best bands in England.

Camborne was invited to the first three contests, each time being conducted by Stephen Sykes. It was placed 13th with *Cloudcatcher Fells* by John McCabe in 1989, 10th with *Blitz* by Derek Bourgeois the following year and 10th playing *Harmony Music* by Philip Sparke in 1991.

2004 – The Band in front of King's College, Cambridge, after competing in the All England Masters when it was conducted by Lieutenant Colonel Chris Davis (H M Director of Music Royal Marines)
Back row: Jo Ryder-Pollard, Wayne Brown, Graham Barker, Rachel Trudgeon, Stephen Thomas, Tim Joslin, Eric Thomas, Graham Boag, Shaun Thomas, Robert Jose, Gavin Knowles, Chris Wooding, Neil Murley and Nick Abbott.
Front row: Tracey Abbott, Sharon Hooper, Chris Netherton, Mo Whitehead, Vicki Kellow, Rob Sandow (cornet), Mark Leigh, Andrew Mitchell, Ian Hooper, Chris Leonard, Jeremy Squibb and Lieutenant Colonel Chris Davis (Conductor)
Percussion not in photo - Mark Rosewarne and Phil Trudgeon. (photo by Marcus Dunstan)

Finances were quite tight in 1992 and it was decided to decline the invitation to compete. An invitation was received for the May 1994 contest and also for the Swiss Open Contest in 1994 but with the recent purchase of new instruments, finance was again a problem and the invitations were declined.

It was not until 1999 that it next attended when Leonard Adams led the players to 20th place with *Tristan Encounters* by Martin Ellerby. Another gap of a few years and in 2004 Lieutenant Colonel Chris Davis was conducting when it was placed 16th for the test piece *Harrison's Dream* by Peter Graham.

Camborne was invited to take part in the radio contest **BBC Challenging Brass** involving 16 bands and in the first round, competed against the City of Coventry Band. The live broadcast was performed at the Perranporth Memorial Hall in February 1965 when W E Moyle's *Cornish Cavalier* was chosen as the signature tune. Having successfully negotiated the first round Camborne then won through against Cresswell Colliery and then Hanwell. The reward, a place in the final at Leeds in April and although beaten by Rushden Temperance, second place in such illustrious company was an excellent result. The programme was completed with a massed band concert featuring Rushden and Camborne.

Freddie Roberts was delighted and asked the players back to his daughter's place for tea – near where he had played with Brighouse & Rastrick. Fred was a strong character and they knew that it was an invitation they couldn't refuse. No doubt they regretted it when they discovered they'd missed their train home and had to hang around until the morning. Frank Woods had gone to see his family in Manchester and had expected to join the other members on the railway station. He travelled back to Camborne on his own – in the carriage reserved for the Band.

Derby City Council and BBC Television originated the **Best of Brass** contest in 1978 when Fairey Aviation Works Band became the first winner. The format was eight bands competing in pairs in the first round with four going through to the semi-finals and two to the finals. The programme I have does not mention the year but I think it's 1978 when the contestants were: Fairey Engineering Works Band (Professor W B Hargreaves), Hanwell Band (Barbara Stone), Great Universal Band (Geoffrey Brand), Dalmellington Band (Richard Evans), Carlton Main Colliery Band (Denzil S Stephens), Ever Ready Band (R J Childs), Parc and Dare Band (Leuan Morgan) and Camborne Town Band (Derek Greenwood).

Sunlife Stanshawe Band won the following year and the GUS Footwear Band took first prize in 1980 and 1981.

In August 1982, Cambourne Band (their spelling, not mine) was invited to take part and compete with Cory Band, Carlton Main Frickley Colliery Band, Clapton on Sea Co-operative Band, Whitburn Burgh Band, Leyland Vehicles Band, Ever Ready Band and Desford Colliery Dowty Band. Camborne won through the first round against Carlton Main when it played *Carnival Day*, *High on a Hill* (soloist Robert Tanner), *Voo Dance* and *The Finale from Faust* but was narrowly defeated in the semi-finals by the eventual winners, Desford Colliery.

Tim Goslin said, *"We were represented by West Country Television's young, beautiful and very slim Fern Britton. I'm convinced she was the reason we played so well and progressed so far in the competition. That's taking nothing away from our Musical Director, Derek Greenwood, and the many members of the band whose appearance is more suited to radio."*

Robert Tanner said, *"Whilst at Camborne, my most memorable achievements were as an ensemble player as opposed to soloist. Nonetheless, I won the BBC Best of Brass soloist award in 1982 playing High on a Hill at the Assembly Rooms in Derby. A moment I shan't forget."*

I have already mentioned the trip to Kerkrade to compete in the Brass Championship of the **World Music Festival.** Neil Peters was taken ill with a bad bout of hay fever and was in such a state that he couldn't take part in the marching contest. Courtney Berryman took his place and remembered the judges walking beside the Band and taking account of any little imperfections in either the marching or the playing. He said, "*It took place in a Dutch football stadium and we played 'The Standard of St*

George'. We were placed second behind a German band which pleased us as we never considered ourselves to be a top class marching band."

Neil recovered for the test piece contest when each band had to play two pieces. The set test piece was played by all the bands but two other pieces had to be brought to the contest and it wasn't until the players were on stage and ready to start, that they knew which piece they would have to play. Camborne's two pieces were *Triumphant Rhapsody* and *Le Roi d'Ys* and with Neil Peters still feeling off colour the players were relieved to hear it was the former. Competing against a number of good bands, including the William Davies Construction under John Berryman, Camborne came out on top.

Mike Hocking recalled the final stages of the journey home when car drivers were acknowledging the win from Indian Queens all the way back to Camborne. After a brief stop at the Crossroads Motel, to change into their uniforms, the players assembled at the top end of the town. Band Queen Margaret Ellis led the march down through Trelowarren Street to *The Cossack* – what else? Mike said, "*It was evening time and the reception laid on in Commercial Square was something really special*". One particular banner in the jubilant crowd seemed to sum up the feelings of the town, it simply said, "*We are proud*". Cornet player David Reed was waiting at the bandroom to greet them; he'd missed the trip due to his father's illness and was presented with a silver tankard brought back by the players.

Derek Johnston was apt to romance about Camborne winning the World Championship. A few players were dismissive of the claim that Camborne Town Band was the true World Champion and the Cornish Packet of the 5th May 1976 quotes Monty Ray in what could be described as a modest or a realistic statement regarding this achievement. *"This world championship thing just isn't on. We won this competition in Holland two years ago, but entry to it was purely on a voluntary basis and I'm sure that not all the world's best bands were there. We just happened to be the winners, that's all."*

But it was good for marketing purposes and a programme for *It's a Knockout* at Vogue Playing Field made capital from it as it advertised:

IN ATTENDANCE
THE WORLD CHAMPIONS
Camborne (CompAir Holman) Band

The Guildhall in Plymouth was crowded for the first South-West area contest for the new **W D & H O Wills Brass Band Championship** in 1969. Camborne Town took first prize ahead of St Dennis with St Austell third. The test piece was *The Frogs of Aristophanes* by Granville Bantock and the top two bands were invited to compete in the Grand Final at Leicester in March the following year. There were two innovations at this contest; the use of percussion and the adjudicator sitting in the open rather than in an enclosed box.

In the final at Leicester the test piece was the *Embassy Suite.* Camborne was placed eleventh and Mr Roberts was not pleased at the adjudicator's comment that he'd taken it too fast. Harry Mortimer conducted the massed band concert which included Camborne.

In the 1970 Regional Contest Fred Roberts was due to conduct both Camborne Town and St Austell but, following his resignation, Camborne withdrew and he successfully steered his new band to first place.

In 1971 the qualifying contest was included in the Mayflower Brass Band Festival and Camborne competed under its new Musical Director, Derek Johnston. St Austell Silver was placed first for the march and Woodfalls won the test piece, *Lorenzo*, with St Austell second and Camborne third. In the Festival Concert Camborne played *Knight Templar, The Mill on the Cliff,* a cornet solo and *Lorenzo.*

The West of England Bandsmen's Festival, better known as Bugle Contest, is famous throughout the brass band world. Its host village takes on a different complexion on the day of the event as the typical clay mining community is transformed into a festival location and becomes a Mecca for bandsmen from Cornwall and beyond. But just as Cornwall at Twickenham is not restricted to rugby fanatics, Bugle has a general appeal; the event is truly a Cornish gathering. Despite the carnival atmosphere, the music produced by the competing bands is of the highest order and no one doubts the importance of this contest. As one supporter so succinctly put it, *"Never mind the Nationals, who won at Bugle".*

Held in the open air, it has to be experienced first hand and although I played there on many occasions I could not adequately describe its unique atmosphere. It is the only outdoor contest remaining from the early days of brass banding, a fact that does great credit to the organisers across the years.

The first contest was advertised as: *"Monster Band Contest at Bugle, Sept 14th 1912. £45 in cash and specials. One and all, come!"*

It followed a decision by Bugle Brass Band and the Committee of the Working Men's Institute, *"..... to co-operate for the purpose of holding a county band contest".* It was not the first such contest to be held in Cornwall but it has witnessed all the others fall by the wayside as it has grown in size and reputation.

There were two sections in 1912 and entry was determined by the size of the band. Class "B" was for bands of 16 or less players and Class "A" for the larger bands. The event was a resounding success and the *Bodmin Guardian* wrote, *"There have been other band contests in the county before Saturday but the important festival which took place at Bugle was, by a long way, the most ambitious and triumphantly successful the Delectable Duchy has known".* And so it has continued over the years: the march down to the contest field with expectations high, the thrill of competition, the tension as the results are announced and the march back up through the village with trophies held high has changed very little over the years. The crowds still gather to cheer on their favourites for there are few impartial spectators along the route.

An advertisement in the *Bodmin Guardian* stated that provision had been made for horses, carriages and traps. The test piece in Class "A" was *Maritana* and Camborne chose *Sandon* as the "own-choice" hymn. Adjudicator G H Mercer placed Camborne Town (W Uren) first with second placed Redruth Town (R Wills) eleven points behind. The reward was £15 plus a cornet. Special awards were made to E C Wills (cornet), W J Uren (soprano), W Tregellas (baritone), G Rosevear (trombone) and Redruth Town player J Sanders (euphonium). St Dennis Temperance (J G Jubb) was third with St Austell Territorials (also J G Jubb) and Tiverton Town (W B Loosemore) joint fourth.

The event was rounded off with a solo contest (slow melodies) in the United Methodist Schoolroom in which 21 players took part. It was won by E J Williams (euphonium and conductor of St Ives Band) with Ford Knight (trombone) second and J Williams (cornet) third. At a subsequent meeting the committee decided that the event had lasted too long and the solo contest was excluded in future years.

Buoyed with success from the first event the committee approached the Duchy Office for support. The result was the presentation of a magnificent cup by the Duke of Windsor, then Duke of Cornwall, which became known as The Royal Trophy - officially the H R H The Prince of Wales Challenge Cup.

Entries were accepted from the West of England for the 1913 contest and there were prizes for both test pieces. With constant rain during the day, Camborne Town (W Nuttall) was placed first for *Emilia* by Donizetti and for *Sandon,* the "own-choice" hymn. The prize was £20 and the newly presented Royal Trophy for the highest combined points. Medals were awarded to every member of the Band with specials going to E C Wills (cornet) and W J Uren (soprano). In the test piece St Dennis Temperance (J E Fidler) was second, St Austell Territorials (Tom Eastwood) was third, Kingswood Evangel (Angus Holden) and Mogg's Military Band (H Mogg) joint fourth and Redruth (R Wills) back in sixth place.

In 1919 Camborne (E J Williams) won two firsts again and retained the Royal Trophy. St Dennis Temperance was second and Redruth Town third. Special awards went to W J Uren (soprano) and H Uren (cornet) who was also the best-player.

Camborne's Certificate of Merit in 1912

In 1921 it was decided to bring the event forward to August – presumably in the hope of better weather. The Bodmin Guardian wrote a glowing report of the silverware being offered and reflected that contest prizes had once taken the form of meat – either alive or dead.

Class "C" was introduced in 1922 for bands of any section – referred to as an Open Class it was mainly won by a top section band but afforded the opportunity of a lower section band pulling off an upset.

Set in an area dependent on metaliferous mining, Camborne was hit hard by the fluctuations in the price of tin. A loss of players through emigration was accompanied by a general downturn in the economy of the area and the Band was not able to attend again until 1924 when Kingswood Evangel Band won first prize for the main test prize and took the Royal Trophy out of Cornwall for the first time. St Dennis, who had won for the previous four years, was second, Camborne Town third and Newquay fourth. Falmouth Town and Penzance Independent were also competing in the top section.

In 1925 the contest was thrown open to any band in the country and this attracted some of the big names but the Royal Trophy was reserved for bands from the West Country. This was the first year of the A W Parker era and it caused a sensation when Camborne swept the board.

Two adjudicators were used for a while in the 1920s and Herbert Bennett and J Jennings were clearly impressed with the playing of Camborne Town awarding them three first places. Ten bands competed in Class "A" and Camborne Town was successful in holding off the challenge of Oakdale Colliery, Carlton Main Frickley Colliery, St Dennis Silver and Kingswood Evangel Silver. Mount Charles, Newquay (G W Cave) Plymouth Corporation Tramways, St Austell Town and Truro Town (Tom Hubbard) were unplaced. Specials awards went to Fred Roberts (cornet) and James Pollard (horn).

C H Baker was conducting St Dennis for the first time in 1926 and celebrated by taking the top honours. He had joined them from Rushden Temperance and over the next few years he was to make his mark on the Cornish contest scene. David Reed recalled his father saying the two adjudicators were split in their views regarding the playing of the test piece, *Oberon*. One had awarded first place to St Dennis and the other to Camborne; the impasse was only broken when one of them gave way.

Four bands from across the Tamar competed in the Championship Section in 1927 but it was Camborne Town that prevailed. It rained all day, the ground became a mud bath and the players had to perform in appalling conditions. The Cornish Guardian referred to the contest as the *"Amateur Band Championship of the West and Open Section*". The adjudicators were T J Rees and David Aspinall whose remarks for Camborne began, "*Big, fine toned band ....* " and went on to say *"A very good performance indeed*". Specials were awarded to F J Roberts (cornet) and J Thomas (trombone). Yeovil Town (third), Cory's Silver (fourth) and Hanwell Silver were all competing for the first time.

Taken at shortly after the 1925 contest. On the back was written:
"Dear Will,
This is Camborne Town Band with all their prizes they won at Bugle last month August 1925. They have a good master and thought you would like to see them. All the town is very proud to have such a splendid band, great credit to them all."
Back row: Telfer Rule, Fred Roberts, Ernest Boase, Cecil Reed, Howard Phillips, Wilson Eustace, Harry Jory, Albert Harris and Martin Oates,
Middle row: Alfred Tresidder, G Floyd, Harry Rosevear, Charlie Dower (cornet - commenced circa 1921 and continued for a few years into the Freddie Roberts era), James Pollard, Leslie Hocking, Fred Uren, Sydney Roberts and J Hocking.
Front row: Sydney Keen, James Tresidder, Percy Truran, George Roseveare, A W Parker (Musical Director), James Carter, John Collins, James Opie and James Penaluna.

A person with the initials E O H was so moved by the 1927 event that they put pen to paper.

How sweet the name of music sounds
In a musician's ear.
Our band's a credit to the town
And worth your while to hear.
It makes the wounded spirit whole,
It puts our heart to rest;
'tis manna to the hungry soul,
Because they were the best.
Two years ago they won those cups
At Bugle, so to speak,
And once again their name is up,
In making it complete.
Take Mr Parker, first of all,
Who trains the four-and-twenty;
Although he isn't very tall,
As good – we haven't many.

There's Fred, the cornet soloist,
He takes a lot of beating;
It's very rare he makes a miss,
He never gets the feeling.
With Jimmy Thomas on the slide
The trombone is his hobby
He showed St Dennis how to hide
Away from Bugle Bobby.
The rain kept falling all the day,
Till five there was no ceasing;
We knew our band was on its way,
Those notes of music squeezing.
The judge made reference to the hymn,
How beautiful they played it;
When every man used all his vim,
Their tone and splendour stayed it.

To see the people stand erect
When, in their test selection,
They must have played it quite correct
They gave such good attention.
And then the masses all arose,
They all then started cheering;
'twas quite five minutes, I suppose,
Before there was a hearing.
Our bandsmen too, I'd like to say,
Are men of various sizes;
They are the only band today,
That bring home all the prizes.
From Hocking's drum to double B
Their tone is simply splendid;
And those at Bugle don't you see,
Were sorry when 'twas ended.
The evening came, as time went on
The people were returning;
We had no news to harp upon,
Which kept us all a yearning.
Just after nine good news arrived;
Our band is crowned with glory;
The people then were all alive,
'twas quite another story.
The news soon flashed, the people thronged,
To glance upon the prizes;
While some chewed on banana long,
And some Moncini's ices,
"Praise ye the Lord" by Holman's Clock
Was sung in simple fashion;
A cry went up, they had to stop,
The band is here in action.
No one can say but what we stayed,
And gave a good reception;
The cups they won, for which they played;
Are such a good collection.
They gave us music through the street,
And all that was desired;
And to accomplish such a feat,
Our men were very tired.
Then Sunday on the sporting pitch,
Again some music rendered;
They went right through without a hitch,
Five thousand people tendered.
Some people take it as a joke.
Give medals too for playing!
But Mr Collins when he spoke,
He knew what he was saying.
Yes! Medals we can give of gold,
Encourage to be steady,
Some people here in town I'm told,
Are always ever ready.
Congratulations to the Band,
For all their past successes;
May they through fame be there to stand,
Upright against the Besses.

1928 was the first of six consecutive wins for St Dennis with Camborne always thereabouts but not collecting the top prize. The best-player in the top section went to Telfer Rule and J Thomas (trombone) won a special award. Telfer Rule also won the best-player award in Class "C" - the Open Class.

Around this time the contest committee was fighting to save the event which was being buffeted by the general slump, unemployment and financial losses. But they were not prepared to throw in the towel and arrangements went ahead for the 1929 event. Stenalees Silver and Swindon G W R S & E Union appeared for the first time in the top section but it was St Dennis who won the day with three first places. Camborne was back in third place; behind new boys Stenalees but J Thomas (euphonium) did collect a special award.

Adjudicator William Halliwell was clearly not impressed with Camborne Town's performance of *Nabucco* in 1930 when he placed it fourth behind St Dennis Silver, Stenalees Silver and Park & Dare Workmen's Silver. Greensplat Silver (C H Baker) and Swindon G.W.R. S. & E. Union completed the section.

Another day of bad weather in 1931 was a severe blow to the organisers who were desperate to see some change in fortune. Camborne too had its disappointment and had to be satisfied with second place to St Dennis who seemed invincible.

Park & Dare Workmen's Silver was becoming regular attendees but it was St Dennis, playing *Donizetti,* that pushed Camborne into second place again in 1932. I'm sure it was little consolation to the players as they took first place in the deportment section. The other two bands in the top section were Penzance Independent and St Blazey & District.

The event had recorded a loss for three years in a row and we can only guess the mood in the committee room. Things were so desperate that the contest committee accepted that there was little prospect of a successful event being run in 1933 and, with great reluctance, the contest was suspended.

With great courage, and a touch of optimism, the organisers resurrected the contest in 1934 when it was moved to July. Either by luck or a good deal of persuasion they were rewarded with an appearance by the famous Munn & Feltons Band and the Kitsilano Boys Band from Vancouver, which must have boosted the number of spectators. Although under threat since then, the Festival has never again been suspended for reasons of funding.

Despite the presence of Munn & Feltons, the top prizes stayed in Cornwall as St Dennis took two firsts. Like Munn & Feltons, Camborne received a second and a third. This year saw an important change when the bands where required to sit for their performance rather than stand in a circle around the conductor. It seems that two bands in a Welsh contest resisted this innovation and chose to continue standing but I'm sure this wouldn't happen in Cornwall! Other changes in this year was the removal of the Open Class, top section bands playing two test pieces and the Royal Trophy being declared open to any band in the country.

Munn & Feltons returned in 1935 to sweep the board and halt the run of St Dennis which had compiled six consecutive wins. With two third places, it was not the best set of results for Camborne but Telfer Rule (soprano) did win a special award.

1936 - A triumphant year for Camborne Town Band

The weather in 1936 was described as "*truly atrocious*" but this did not stop the proceedings nor did it stop Camborne Town. The mighty Munn & Felton's Works Band (W Halliwell) was again competing but this was to be Camborne's year when they pushed that famous band back into second place in both the selection, *Roberto Il Diavolo* by Meyerbeer, and *War March of the Priests from Athalie* by Mendolssohn.

The headline in the Western Morning News read:

Camborne Band Triumph
Premier Honours in Bugle Festival
Defeat Champions of World

The contest programme of 1986 reflects, *"Considerable interest was created by the appearance of the then current National Champions, Munn and Felton's Works Band (W Halliwell), but the day was to belong to Camborne. Under the baton of A W Parker they achieved a remarkable victory over their illustrious opponents, winning both the Selection and the March to take the Royal Trophy. Camborne also swept the board in the Specials Awards with G Nicholls (cornet), H Gilbert (euphonium and best-player in section), J Berryman (trombone) and E Floyd (horn)."* G Nicholls seems to have joined circa 1935.

The weather had scuppered any thoughts of an improving financial situation and the fear of closure hung in the air once again. Responding to the seriousness of the situation, some bands gave concerts and donated the proceeds to Festival funds and this action staved off the immediate danger allowing the committee to plan for the future.

Once again there was to be a huge bonus by the appearance of a top name band in 1937 as W Halliwell brought the mighty Black Dyke Mills Band to Cornwall. They shared the spoils of a first and a second with Camborne Town as they played *Wagner's Works* and *Pomp and Circumstance No 1* but Dyke won overall and the Royal Trophy was taken out of Cornwall for only the third occasion.

Hanwell Silver (J C Dyson) took part in 1938 but it was a local band that was beginning to have some impact on Camborne and St Dennis; Falmouth Town (T G Moore) took two first places and the Royal Trophy. They had been successful in other local contests so the result was not a compete surprise. St Austell and Newquay (W E Moyle) made up the complement of six Class "A" bands.

Despite heavy thunderstorms and lightning in 1939 the rain stayed away – more or less – and Camborne Town made the best of the conditions to move back on top again. Mellingriffith (T J Powell) made the long trip down to Cornwall and Indian Queens (F L Knight), having won Class "B" the previous year, moved up to compete with the big boys. The test pieces were *L'Etoile du Nord* by Meyerbeer and the chorus *By Babylon's Wave* by Gounod. Camborne Town's Jack Trounce (cornet) and Jack Berryman (trombone) received special awards.

Britain was at war again and the contest was suspended for the duration - from 1940 to 1946 inclusive and when the next contest took place, in 1947, it was obvious that the conflict had taken its toll with many bands still re-forming and, sadly, many missing bandsmen. There were only two sections and Camborne Town was in top form in Class "A" with their renditions of *Les Preludes and Hymn to Music.* Telfer Rule (soprano) won the best-player in section award. Falmouth Town was conducted by A G Richards and took a second and third place, as did St Austell. This was the first year of the Camborne's back-to-back hat-trick of wins and Tom Ruse was proud to show me his medals commemorating this achievement. To end the 1947 Festival the adjudicator, Frank Wright, conducted massed bands playing *Abide With Me in* memory of the bandsmen who had died in the war.

1947 – Marching down at Bugle Contest led by A W Parker

In 1948 it rained continuously throughout the day and the organisers, once again, cursed their luck. Camborne was placed first in both test pieces, S P Roberts (soprano) won the Class "A" best-player award and the next in order went to Stanley Oliver (euphonium) who with his brother, Billy (cornet), ran a boat yard in Porthleven.

In 1949 there were thundery showers and the organisers must have wondered what they had done to deserve such bad luck. Camborne was flying high with emphatic wins for *Coriolanus* and the *Grand Chorus* over Kingswood Evangel Silver and Falmouth Town. S P Roberts (soprano) won the Class "A" best-player award for the second year in a row and the next in order went to Jack Trounce (cornet).

1950s - The Band marching to the Bugle Contest Field – Freddie Roberts is carrying his Pomeranian dog. Walking alongside is either Cora Trounce or Christine Roberts (daughter of Sam Roberts).

In 1950 there was continuous heavy rain, high winds and a contest venue that was little more than a muddy field. Camborne's playing of *Carmen* and *Le Prophete* gave them the win by a huge margin over Newquay Town (W E Moyle), Redruth Silver (J Volante) and Stenalees (H Heyes). The best-player award in Class "A" went to Jack Trounce (cornet) and the next in order to S P Roberts (soprano) and Stanley Oliver (euphonium).

In an attempt to improve the weather prospect, the 1951 event was moved to June and it has been held in that month ever since. Although St Dennis took first place for the test piece, Camborne was the overall winner and received the Royal Trophy. Truro City (A W Parker) made a welcome return to the top flight. The Class "A" best-player award went to Jack Trounce (cornet).

A first place for *The Valkyre* and a second for the march was enough to take the Royal Trophy back to Camborne in 1952. Newquay Town picked up the other first place but it was an excellent result for Camborne and for Eddie Williams who won the Class "A" best-player award.

John Berryman recalled 1952 being his first contest. *"We had had a great day at the contest and I have vivid memories of marching down Trelowarren Street, from the Centenary Chapel to Commercial Square, with all the trophies and with the streets lined with cheering Cambornians who then assembled in the Square whilst the band played a march and a hymn tune. These were certainly glory days. All very exciting stuff for a young lad."*

Although Camborne won the overture in 1953, a less well-known band headed them to take first prize for *Pomp and Circumstance No 1* - St Just Silver (A G Richards) had been promoted as winners of Class "B" and in only its second year in the top flight had picked up a first prize. St Stythians, under former Camborne player Edgar Floyd, was also in the top section. The Royal Trophy went to Camborne with the Class "A" best-player award won by G Trevarton of Newquay and the next two in order to S Oliver (euphonium) and J Trounce (cornet).

Fred Roberts receiving the cup at Bugle (Photo by George Ellis)

In 1954 Munn & Felton's Works (Stanley Boddington) was first in the test piece and took the Royal Trophy back over the Tamar. Camborne was in on the act however, and picked up first place for *Aida* and second for *Robin Hood.* The best-player award went to Munn & Felton's with the next two in order to Jack Trounce (cornet) and Jack Berryman (trom).

1955 really did belong to Munn & Feltons as it took two firsts and retained the Royal Trophy; Camborne was awarded second place for both test pieces. The Class "A" best-player award went to the Munn and Feltons' cornet player with the next in order to his soprano colleague and Jack Berryman (trom).

John Berryman receiving an award at Bugle. (Photo by George Ellis)

The adjudicator in 1956 was Henry Geehl who certainly didn't endear himself to the Cornish banding fraternity. Not wishing to fiddle around with the odd point or two, his system was clear and unambiguous. In the top section his marking for the four bands for the test piece was 160, 170, 180 and 190. For the march he awarded marks of 150, 160, 165 and 170. St Dennis won the test piece and Camborne the march but the method of awarding the points seem to upset Freddie Roberts who had to be persuaded not to go up and "sort things out!" Alwyn Teasdale was conducting Truro which had bounced back into Class "A" again.

Camborne Band marched relentlessly on and in 1957 picked up two first places. The Class "A" best-player award went to a certain John Berryman (cornet) with the next in order to M Brewer of St Dennis and Telfer Rule (soprano).

Freddie Roberts and Eddie Williams receiving the cups.
Reg Trudgian in the background (Photo by George Ellis)

Truro City (Alwyn Teasdale) hit the headlines in 1958 when placed first for *The Hungarian March* but Camborne was first with *Cavalleria Rusticana* and took the overall award. John Berryman was the Class "A" best-player for the second year in a row and Telfer Rule (soprano) was next in order. Eddie Williams conducted St Dennis Silver; he had played tenor horn at Camborne for many years and had received the best-player award at Bugle in 1952.

In 1959 Camborne had to be content with a first and a third with Newquay Town winning the chorus. St Dennis collected two second places but Camborne's overall points gave it the Royal Trophy again. The Class "A" best-player award went to Adrian King (cornet) with the next in order to Roy Wearne (soprano).

Morris Motors (S H Boddington) was top band in 1960 taking two first places with St Dennis second and Camborne third. Camborne did not enter in 1961, much to the disappointment of its supporters.

1962 was a year when the Band had to share the Royal Trophy with St Dennis, each having won a test piece by four points. The Class "A" best-player award went to V J Willcocks of St Dennis with the next in order to Ken Haynes (horn).

When I think of Camborne and Bugle Contest I also think of *The Cossack* march. Memory does play tricks but the sound of that march seemed to alert everyone that Camborne Town Band was on its way to the Contest Field. Monica Dean (née Orchard) described the atmosphere at Bugle as something special but remembered one year when the rain and wind was so bad that the players were soaked and the music had to be thrown away after the performance. She said, *"There were so many clothes pegs on my stand that you could hardly see the music, we had to hold on to the music stands with our feet, otherwise they would have blown over. Poor Mr Roberts couldn't do that so Dick Tresidder, the drummer, had to sit in the middle holding on to the conductor's stand. And we were trying to make music!"*

St Dennis collected both first prizes in 1963 with Camborne second and St Stythians third. The Class "A" best-player award went to M Brewer of St Dennis with the next in order to Roderick Facey (euphonium). Fred Roberts was particularly disappointed at the result and although the players were keen to continue attending, he was not. He considered conditions were poor and that they had not had a fair crack of the whip in the past few years.

Despite his strong feelings on the matter, Mr Roberts relented and conducted the Band in 1964 but a first and a second was not enough to take the Royal Trophy and St Dennis won the day. An *"unfortunate accident"* in the piece had thrown the players. The test piece was *Resurgam* and the *"unfortunate accident"* related to the isolated chords which, Alan Toy tells me, are meant to represent knocking on the gates of heaven. I would imagine it's every bandsman's worst nightmare to get that particular bit wrong but that's just what happened and I'm told that Freddie Roberts chased the offending player across the field. As things turned out, that was the last time he conducted Camborne at Bugle

It's interesting to note that the four Class "A" bands were conducted by former-Camborne players. St Dennis – E J Williams, Camborne – F J Roberts, St Austell – Telfer Rule and St Stythians – Edgar Floyd. The Class "A" best-player was S H Dunstan of St Dennis and the next in order was his colleague, J Dunstan and Roy Wearne (soprano).

During the 1960s and early 1970s St Dennis had a run of 11 wins, all under the baton of Eddie Williams, and whilst Camborne did not compete from 1965 to 1970 inclusive, the clay country band was clearly a force to be reckoned with. The 1960s belonged to St Dennis but there must have been many Camborne supporters who questioned the non-appearance of their Band for so many years.

In 1966 the event moved from Peniel to Molinnis Park, the home of Bugle Football Club. We all missed the beautiful setting of Peniel with the stage positioned across the top of a hedge; it had been a wonderful venue and had become synonymous with the event but parking problems and lack of facilities made it no longer tenable.

The 1960s and 1970s saw the emergence of some bands which had steadily been building a reputation in Class "B". Indian Queens Silver, St Agnes Silver, Bugle Silver and Mount Charles were making their move but for a variety of reasons they experienced mixed fortunes; such is the way of banding.

After many June festivals when the weather had smiled, the forecast in 1971 was gloomy as heavy rain and gales descended on the area. A marquee was erected and for the first and only time the contest was held under cover but as it happened, the day remained dry. Camborne Town, under its new conductor Derek Johnston, was second to St Dennis in both pieces but had made a welcome return to Bugle. The Class "A" best-player award went to Michael Bunt of Bodmin Town and the next in order to Rodney Richards of St Dennis and Neil Peters (euphonium). The best tenor horn in Festival award went to Alan Toy. Roy Newsome adjudicated and in his remarks for *Spring* he said, *".... a special pat on the back is due to Mr Soprano".* Despite the event being under cover he claimed to have heard everything, *"Whether I was supposed to hear it or not – including some of the vocal conductors".*

In 1972 the event reverted to being held outdoors but one concession was to introduce a canopy to the bandstand – this helped greatly with any rain which happened to be vertical! As it was, the weather was dry and the stand was not put to any test but its introduction was popular and it has been used ever since.

It must have been a good omen as St Dennis' long run of wins came to an end as Camborne swept the board. The oldest players were Willie Horton (E flat bass) and Gerald Weeks, who was 40, but notwithstanding that, the average age of the players was 23. (Bill Horton played euphonium and bass and resigned in 1974 when Derek Johnston left.) The best-player award in Class "A" went to Monty Ray (cornet) and the next in order to Alan Toy (horn). The best-tenor horn in Festival award went to Alan Toy and the best set of basses to Camborne players Michael Weeks, Bill Horton, Gerald Weeks and George Ansell.

1973 was another Royal Trophy year for Camborne when Neil Peters (euphonium) won the Class "A" best-player award and the next in order went to Jack Pascoe (flugel). The best set of basses in Festival award went to the Camborne players. The test piece was *Le Roi d'Ys* and Courtney Berryman recalled having trouble with the triple tonguing. The Band was practising on the grass outside the bandroom and Monty Ray leaned across and said just make sure you hit the first notes. Courtney's response? *"I'm having trouble hitting any of the buggers!"*

1973
George Ansell
Gerald Weeks
Bill Horton
Michael Weeks
line up to take their place on the contest platform

1973 with Derek Johnston

Fred Roberts must have been extremely pleased in 1974 as St Austell took two firsts and won the coveted Royal Trophy. Camborne (CompAir Holman) (Derek Johnston) was second for the overture but only fourth for the Toccata. It must have been little consolation when they collected first prize for deportment. Mount Charles (A G A Chappell), St Dennis and Soundwell (Bristol) were also in Class "A".

1975 and 1976 were not good years for Camborne as St Dennis took the Royal Trophy for both years. In 1975 Robert Cook was awarded the Owen Tamblyn Memorial Cup for the Best Solo Horn in Festival and for the second year in a row Camborne won the deportment prize. In 1976 David Tonkin was awarded one of the A R Trudgian Youth awards nominated by the committee of the Cornwall Youth Band. There were seven bands in Class "A" in 1976 including Yorkley Onward.

St Dennis took the top award again in 1977 with Camborne fourth for *Triumphant Rhapsody* and first for *Pilgrim's Chorus from Tannhauser.*

St Pinnock (J Armstong) was in the top section in 1978 but Camborne did not compete in that year or the following. St Dennis took the top trophy on each occasion.

Circa 1980

Neil Peters

Albert Chappell conducted St Austell to first place in 1980 with St Dennis second and Camborne Town (Derek Greenwood) third in both test pieces.

A much improved performance in 1981 brought the bad run to an end as Camborne collected the Royal Trophy through a win with the test piece *Freedom* and a second place with the march, *Molinnis Park*. St Dennis was second, St Austell third and Mount Charles fourth. Best Player in Festival awards went to David Whear (soprano), Neil Peters (euphonium) and Robert Cook (solo horn). Bob Seymour, Secretary, said, *"They came home with enough silverware to sink the Titanic"*. But it could have been so different. Derek Greenwood sustained a broken ankle a few days before the contest and he rejected a high stool preferring to stand and conduct. He had always said he would never win Bugle because he didn't have any clay on his boots and, according to Eric Trerise, someone presented him with a paper bag of the stuff just before the contest and that did the trick.

The Band entered in 1982 but subsequently withdrew. Simon Williams received the E J Jacobs Memorial Trophy - one of the A R Trudgian Youth Awards.

Leonard Adams conducted Redruth Town to a Royal Trophy win in 1983 with a first place for *Le Carnival Romain* and a second for the other test piece.

In 1984 Kernow Brass (A N Slaughter) collected a first and a second, as did Mount Charles; John Brush was conducting St Dennis.

Up to 1985 the "Royal Trophy" was awarded to the band securing the highest combined points for the two test pieces in Class "A" but a change in the rules meant that from 1986 the long-held practise of aggregating the points was discontinued. Two pieces were still played but the champion band would be the winners of the principal test piece. I'm told the question of overall points was no longer of significance and while that may officially be the case, I'm sure that many people still undertake the necessary arithmetic to determine this.

The weather was atrocious in 1986 but the bands played on and St Austell (Derek Greenwood) took top honours with Camborne (M Cotter) second for both pieces. Flowers, Gloucester was in third place and St Keverne (Derek Johnston) fourth out of the seven bands. A best-player in Festival award went to Mark Medlyn (soprano). There was a disappointment for Redruth Town which had been placed third in the Championship Section March. The following day a phone call advised Leonard Adams that the Band was actually fifth but that the committee would not be seeking the return of the prize money.

Camborne returned to winning ways in 1988 when it took first place for *High Peak* and the march *British Bandsman.* Bodmin (Leonard Adams) was in second place, St Austell third and St Dennis (S Appleton) fourth. A best-player in Festival award went to Joanne Barlow (Telfer Rule Memorial Trophy for best soprano) and Stuart Chappell (Wm Henry and Melville Juleff Memorial Trophy for best solo cornet). Jeremy Squibb, then with St Austell Youth, received one of the A R Trudgian Youth Awards.

The contest programme in 1989 refers to the death of Billy Moyle, a former Camborne player and Newquay Musical Director. As a tribute, one of his compositions, *Cornish Cavalier,* was included as a test piece in Class "B".

Once again, Camborne Town (Stephen Sykes) took two first places in Class "A" with Bodmin Town, (Leonard Adams) collecting the runners up prize for both pieces. Bristol Telecom was in third place and Yorkley Onwards fourth. Best-player in Festival awards went to Shaun Thomas (Gordon Bennetts Memorial Trophy - euphonium) and the Camborne basses (Samuel Roberts Silver Cup). John Mitchell received the E J Jacobs Memorial Trophy Youth Award.

In 1990 the Band took two firsts for *Benvenuto Cellini* and the *Pilgrim's Chorus from Tannhauser.* Stuart Chappell (solo cornet) collected the Class "A" best-player award and the best-player in Festival (solo cornet) award. Also receiving best-player at Festival awards were Joanne Sykes (nee Barlow) (soprano) and Ian Sutton (solo horn).

Reg Trudgian, the organiser of Bugle Contest from 1959 to 1972, died in the early 1990s. He had been very involved in the brass band organisation both as a player and as an administrator of the Cornwall Brass Band Association and the Cornwall County Youth Brass Band.

In 1991 Camborne entered but subsequently withdrew from the contest. Brassband de Bazuin from Oenkerk, Holland, was visiting Cornwall as Camborne's guests and took part. It was placed third for *A Kensington Concerto* and first for *Toccata from Suite Gothique* and narrowly missed winning the Royal Trophy which went to Bodmin under Leonard Adams. Aldbourne, Lydmet Lydney and Tredegar Bands made it four out of seven bands from "overseas". Tracy Farr and Stephen Uren were presented with the Trudgian Youth Award. (Tracy Farr – horn - joined in the early 1990s and later married Jason Smith (bass). She left for a while but returned in October 1998 and played until circa 2002.)

In 1992 the SWEB Camborne Town Band (Derek Greenwood) won the Royal Trophy for its performance of the test piece *Pageantry.* John Hitchens (euphonium) won the Class "A" best-player award and the best-player in Festival award.

In 1993 Camborne Town was equal on points with Bodmin when both bands were awarded a first and second place with one point difference in each case. By virtue of its win in the test piece, *Carnival Overture,* Camborne collected the Royal Trophy and took it westward. Best-player in Festival awards went to Darren Hendy (solo cornet) and the Camborne set of basses.

The 1994 result was very disappointing and a little puzzling as Camborne was back in third place for the test piece, *Journey into Freedom, and* St Dennis collected the coveted Royal Trophy.

Perhaps spurred on by the 1994 result, Camborne (Derek Greenwood) took two first places in 1995 and, with the Royal Trophy for company, the players must have had a happy journey home. Bodmin Town was a close second in both pieces with Mount Charles (Stephen Sykes) collecting two third places. Darren Hendy (cornet) won the Class "A" best-player award and the best-player in Festival award for cornet. Other winners of best-player in Festival awards were Graham Barker (horn) and the Camborne set of basses. Christopher Netherton was awarded the E J Jacobs Memorial Trophy Youth Award.

Bodmin Town (H Taylor) took the Royal Trophy in 1996 with the winning performance for *Variations on a Ninth.* Camborne, however, won first place for the chorus and gained the highest combined points (oh, I forgot, that no longer matters!) Best-player in Festival awards went to John Hitchens (euphonium) and the Camborne set of basses.

Camborne did not attend in 1997 and Bodmin took the title again. Rachel Retallick received the E J Jacobs Memorial Trophy - one of the A R Trudgian Youth Awards.

Camborne and Bodmin were joint winners in 1998 but the Royal Trophy travelled west once again because of the Band's first place in the main test piece. Stuart Chappell (flugel) won the Class "A" best-player award and the Camborne set of basses was judged to be the best in the Festival.

Bugle Band Contest celebrated its 75th anniversary in 1999 and the committee reflected on the success of the event. It claimed to be the oldest contest in existence after the National Championships and Belle Vue and, *"the only surviving outdoor contest from those early years of banding"*. The programme stated, *"Three bands competing today appeared at our first contest – Camborne, St Agnes and St Breward"*. Disappointingly for such an occasion, only two bands entered the Championship Section. Camborne Town took two first places over Lucketts Travel and John Hitchens was the Class "A" best-player and the best euphonium player in Festival. Other winners of best-player in Festival awards were Jeremy Squibb (soprano), Darren Hendy (solo cornet) and Graham Barker (solo horn).

Following the march back through the village, Camborne, as Royal Trophy winners, played a mini-concert in the square and brought the day to a close with *Treskerby* by Monty Pearce.

Camborne (F Renton) and Bodmin (N Childs) were equal on points again in 2000 but the Royal Trophy went to Camborne because of their first place in the test piece, *The Land of the Long White Cloud;* Mount Charles took the third place. There was a hatful of prizes for Camborne players as best-player in Festival awards went to Jeremy Squibb (soprano), Darren Hendy (solo cornet), Graham Barker (solo horn) and the Camborne set of basses. John Hitchens won the Class "A" best-player award and Christopher Leonard was presented with the E J Jacob Memorial Trophy – one of the A R Trudgian Youth Awards.

In 2001 Camborne (Derek Greenwood) took a year off but returned in 2002 to find it had no competition and took the Royal Trophy by default. Just for good measure the Band picked up second prize for deportment and Robert Jose (euphonium) was adjudged the Class "A" best-player. Best-player in Festival awards went to Robert Jose (euphonium), Graham Barker (horn) and the Camborne set of basses – Tim Joslin, Graham Boag, Lee Trewhella and Jonathan Bond.

In 2003 there was some competition but Camborne (F Renton) picked up another two first places and the Royal Trophy. JAG Mount Charles (R Gay) was second, Bodmin Town (I McElligott) third and St Austell (M White) fourth. The Class "A" best-player award and best-player in Festival (soprano) went to Jeremy Squibb. Other winners of best-player in Festival awards were Chris Leonard (cornet), Robert Jose (euphonium) and the Camborne set of basses – Tim Joslin, Graham Boag, Lee Trewhella and Eric Thomas.

Another hat-trick of wins was completed in 2004 but on this occasion the players did not receive individual medals. Up to the year 2000 any band winning the Royal Trophy for three consecutive years were presented with a set of medals to commemorate the feat. The Duchy of Cornwall had presented them but, after 90 years, it was felt to be an, *"Appropriate time to review this arrangement"* (I think that's a nice way of saying they were going to stop awarding them!). Camborne Town Band was in first place with a superb performance of *The Essence of Time* and the hymn tune *Praise My Soul* with St Austell (D Loukes) in second place. Chris Leonard won the Class "A" best-player and best-player in Festival award for solo cornet. Best-player in Festival awards also went to Jeremy Squibb (soprano), Robert Jose (euphonium), Graham Barker (solo horn) and the Camborne set of basses – Shaun Thomas, Tim Joslin, Lee Trewhella and Eric Thomas.

Contest Music by Wilfred Heaton would not feature in a list of easy-listening music but a test it certainly is and in 2005, Frank Renton led Camborne to first place over Bodmin Town (K Mackenzie) and St Austell Town (D Loukes). Camborne had to be satisfied with second place for the march *Roll Away Bet* as Bodmin picked up first place. The Class "A" best-player award went to Nick Abbott (trombone) and Jeremy Squibb (soprano) picked up yet another best-player in Festival Award as did the Camborne set of basses: Tim Joslin, Kevyn Caddy, Lee Trewhella and Eric Thomas. The day finished with the traditional march back through Bugle with the winning Royal Trophy band be-

2005 - Marching to the contest field and on the stage

Bugle 2005

ing last up and playing in the square. Camborne duly took its place and provided the perfect conclusion to an excellent day by playing three traditional brass band pieces before launching into a crowd-pleasing *Is this the way to Amarillo?*

2005 – Camborne, the Royal Trophy Band, under Bandmaster Steve Thomas, playing in the square at the conclusion of Bugle Contest.

Camborne Town Band's results at The West of England Bandsmen's Festival (Bugle)

The date in bold indicates receipt of the Royal trophy

			Musical Director
1912	*Maritana* & "own-choice" hymn *Sandon*	1st	W Uren
1913	*Emilia* - Donizetti	1st	W Nuttall
	"own-choice" hymn *Sandown*	1st	
1914 to 1918	Contest suspended during First World War		
1919	*The Gondoliers* - Sullivan	1st	E J Williams
	"own-choice" hymn *Eventide*	1st	
1920 to 1923	Did not attend		
1924	*William Tell* - Rossini	3rd	E J Williams
	"own-choice" hymn	Unplaced	
	Recitative & Chorus (Open Section)	2nd	
1925	*Euryanthe - Weber*	1st	A W Parker
	Hymn *Calcutta* – T Clark (Open)	1st	
	Hymn to Music – Dudley Buck (Open)	1st	
1926	*Oberon* - Weber	2nd	A W Parker
	I heard the voice of Jesus say (Open)	Unplaced	
	Kyrie & Gloria – Mozart (Open)	Unplaced	
1927	Grand Selection *Halevy*	1st	A W Parker
	Hymn *Sennen* (Open)	1st	
	Behold and See - Lift up your heads (Open)	1st	
1928	*Il Travatore* – Verdi	2nd	A W Parker
	Hymn *Rhyd-y-Groes* (Open)	1st	
	Achieved is the glorious work (Open)	1st	
1929	*Lohengrin* - Wagner	3rd	A W Parker
	Hymn Tune *Sandon in G* (Open)	2nd	
	Chorus *We Bow our Head* (Open)	2nd	
1930	*Nabucco* – Verdi	4th	A W Parker
	March *Tannhauser* – Wagner (Open)	4th	
	Chorus *Amen* – Handel (Open)	4th	
1931	Grand Selection *Mendelssohn's Works*	2nd	A W Parker
	Bridal Chorus from Lohengrin (Open)	2nd	
	We never will bow down – Handel (Open)	2nd	
1932	Grand Selection *Donizetti*	2nd	A W Parker
	Processional March *Welcome* (Open)	3rd	
	Chorus *Worthy is the Lamb* (Open)	3rd	
	Deportment	1st	
1933	No contest held		
1934	*Der Freischutz* - Weber	3rd	A W Parker
	Largo - Handel	2nd	
	Deportment	2nd	
1935	*Grand Selection* - Haydn	3rd	A W Parker
	Intro & March from *William Tell*	3rd	
1936	*Roberto Il Diavolo* - Meyerbeer	1st	A W Parker
	War March of the Priests	1st	

1937	Grand Selection *Wagner's Works*	2nd	A W Parker
	Pomp & Circumstance No. 1	1st	
1938	*Grand Selection* - Spohr	3rd	A W Parker
	From Judas Maccabaeus - Handel	3rd	
1939	*L'Etoile du Nord* - Meyerbeer	1st	A W Parker
	By Babylon's Wave - Gounod	1st	
1940 to 1946	Contest suspended during Second World War		
1947	*Les Preludes* – Liszt	1st	A W Parker
	Hymn to Music- Dudley Buck	1st	
1948	*Themes from Symphony No. 5* Beethoven	1st	A W Parker
	Grand March *Tannhauser*	1st	
1949	*Coriolanus* – Cyril Jenkins	1st	A W Parker
	Worthy is the Lamb (Messiah)	1st	
1950	*Carmen* - Bizet	1st	A W Parker
	Coronation March from Le Prophete	1st	
1951	*The Royal Water Music* - Handel	2nd	A W Parker
	The Spirit of Pageantry – Percy Fletcher	1st	
1952	*The Valkyre* - Wagner	1st	F J Roberts
	La Reine de Saba - Gounod	2nd	
1953	*Overture for an Epic Occasion* – Wright	1st	F J Roberts
	Pomp & Circumstance No. 1 - Elgar	2nd	
1954	*Robin Hood* - McFarren	2nd	F J Roberts
	Grand March from Aida - Verdi	1st	
1955	*Eine Kleine Nachtmusik* - Mozart	2nd	F J Roberts
	And the Glory of the Lord - Handel	2nd	
1956	Grand Selection *Mendelssohn's Works*	2nd	F J Roberts
	Festival March	1st	
	Deportment	1st	
1957	*Grand Selection* - Haydn	1st	F J Roberts
	The Symphonic March Silvio - Mancini	1st	
1958	Grand Selection *Cavalleria Rusticana*	1st	F J Roberts
	The Hungarian March - Berlioz	2nd	
1959	*William Tell* - Rossini	1st	F J Roberts
	Thou Alone Art Holy - Beethoven	3rd	
1960	*Scheherazade* – Rimsky-Korsakov	3rd	F J Roberts
	Huldingungsmarsch – Grieg	3rd	
1961	Did not attend		
1962	From *Symphony No. 5* - Tchaikowsky	2nd	F J Roberts
	Pomp & Circumstance No. 4	1st	
1963	*Tintagel* - Dennis Wright	2nd	F J Roberts
	Choral Prelude *Deep Harmony*	3rd	
1964	*Resurgam* – Eric Ball	2nd	F J Roberts
	County Palatine – Maurice Johnston	1st	
1965 to 1970	Did not attend		
1971	*Rhapsody in Brass* - Dean Goffin	2nd	D Johnston
	Spring - Grieg	2nd	
1972	Symphonic Prelude *Blackfriers*	1st	D Johnston

	Grand March *Whitehall*	1st	
	Deportment	2nd	
1973	Overture *Le Roi d'Ys* - Lalo	1st	D Johnston
	Coronation March from Le Prophete	2nd	
	Deportment	Jnt 2nd	
1974	*Cornish Festival Overture* - Eric Ball	2nd	D Johnston
	Toccata from Suite Gothique	4th	
	Deportment	1st	
1975	*Diadem of Gold* - G Bailey	3rd	B Bygrave
	Hymn to Music - Dudley Buck	4th	
	Deportment	1st	
1976	*Peniel* - Eric Ball	4th	D A Greenwood
	Lament of the Captive Jews	3rd	
1977	*Triumphant Rhapsody* - Gilbert Vinter	4th	D A Greenwood
	Pilgrims' Chorus from Tannhauser	1st	
1978/79	Did not attend		
1980	*Journey into Freedom* - Eric Ball	3rd	D A Greenwood
	Toccata from Suite Gothique	3rd	
1981	*Freedom* - Hubert Bath	1st	D A Greenwood
	March *Molinnis Park* - Jon Hall	2nd	
1982 to 1985	Did not attend		
1986	*The Force of Destiny* - Verdi	2nd	M Cotter
	Homage March - Grieg	2nd	
1987	Did not attend		
1988	*High Peak* - Eric Ball	1st	Stephen Sykes
	British Bandsman - Derek Broadbent	1st	
1989	*The Corsair* - Berlioz	1st	Stephen Sykes
	Elegiac Melody No. 2 - Spring - Grieg	1st	
1990	*Benvenuto Cellini* - Berlioz	1st	Stephen Sykes
	Pilgrims Chorus from Tannhauser	1st	
1991	Did not attend		
1992	*Pageantry* - Herbert Howells	1st	D A Greenwood
	Lohengrin – Introduction to Act III	2nd	
1993	*Carnival Overture Op 92* - Dvorak	1st	D A Greenwood
	Lament of the Captive Jews - Verdi	2nd	
1994	*Journey Into Freedom* - Eric Ball	3rd	D A Greenwood
	Procession of the Nobles (Mlada)	1st	
1995	*James Cook, Circumnavigator* - Vinter	1st	D A Greenwood
	Grand March from Aida - Verdi	1st	
1996	*Variations on a Ninth* - Gilbert Vinter	2nd	D A Greenwood
	Toccato from Organ Symphony No. 5	1st	
1997	Did not attend		
1998	*The Wayfarer (Sinfonietta)* - Eric Ball	1st	Leonard Adams
	Senator - George Allan	2nd	
1999	*Festival Music* - Eric Ball	1st	Leonard Adams
	Worthy is the Lamb (Messiah)	1st	
2000	*The Land of the Long White Cloud*	1st	F Renton
	March *Huldigungsmarsch* (Homage)	2nd	

2001	Did not attend		
2002	*Diversions on a Bass Theme* - G Lloyd	1st	D Greenwood
	Centaur - Derek Broadbent	1st	
2003	*Paganini Variations* - Philip Wilby	1st	F Renton
	Ravenswood - Wm Rimmer	1st	
2004	*The Essence of Time* - Peter Graham	1st	F Renton
	Hymn *Praise My Soul*	1st	
2005	*Contest Music* – Wilfred Heaton	1st	F Renton
	Roll Away Bet – J Ord Hume	2nd	

Bugle Contest is synonymous with brass banding and those who started the festival, and those who continue to organise it, have performed a tremendous service to Cornish banding - long may it continue.

The National Brass Band Championship Festival was founded by John Henry Iles in 1900 and, apart from the war years of 1914 to 1919 and 1939 to 1944, it has been held every year since. During the early years the venue was the magnificent Crystal Palace, a building described as, *"Standing alone among the world's historic edifices – unique in its construction; universal in its fame; and diverse in its utilities"*. Originally built in Hyde Park for the Great Exhibition in 1851, it was moved to a new site, re-erected and extended. In 1936 the building was destroyed by fire and since then the contest has been held in a number of venues.

Regional Championships were initiated in 1945 and comprised eight Area Contests with qualification to the National Championship.

Camborne Town Band achieved Championship status in 1946 and has never relinquished it. Through some tough times the Band has maintained a consistently high standard and managed to retain its place among the elite of the brass band world and, on its day, has beaten them all.

In 1926 Camborne made the long trip to London to take part in the 26th Anniversary (21st Contest) of the Great National Band Festival at the famous Crystal Palace. Black Dyke was in the Great Championship Contest and was conducted by W Halliwell who also conducted seven other bands in that section. Camborne Town was competing in section three, the Junior Cup (A) Contest. Stenalees Silver and Falmouth Town, led by Tom Chainey, was also there; in section five; the Junior Shield (A).

Camborne Town and St Dennis were in the Second Section, the Grand Shield Contest, in 1928 and it is likely that St Dennis did the best as it moved up into the top section. Stenalees was in the Third Section and Falmouth Town and St Austell Town in the fifth.

St Dennis competed in the Championship Section in 1929, 1930, 1931 and 1932 but I have no results below the top six bands.

In the years up to 1922 the bands played standing, with the conductor in the centre. That year, in the Championship Section, "concert formation" was introduced with each player seated and using a separate music stand and with the conductor in front of the players rather than in the centre. At the 1923 contest, "concert formation" was adopted in all of the six sections.

At the 1922 contest the military band section was discarded in favour of an additional section for brass bands. This was the first of the "all brass" contests. Previously, there had been contests for military bands, boys' bands, reed bands and concertina bands.

The playing standard of Camborne Band had steadily risen throughout the 1930s and in August 1945, at Packer's Ground in Bristol, it qualified to compete in the Second Section National Final at Belle Vue, Manchester. Reg Toy played baritone at Bristol when the test piece was Beethoven's 5th Symphony but for the final, he moved to E flat bass.

Fred Waters said, *"I remember them getting off the night train from Manchester on the Sunday morning in September 1945 – they couldn't afford overnight accommodation"*. The Band was conducted by their resident Musical Director, A W Parker, and placed first out of the 14 qualifying bands to become the first Cornish band ever to win a National Championship. When the result was announced there was a spontaneous outburst of *Camborne Hill* and the organiser, Henry Iles, threatened to clear the hall (well, what did he expect?).

Gerald Fletcher recalled there being a problem with a certain entry so Mr Parker changed his style of conducting to give a beat to each note. To ensure that everyone remembered he wrote it down and stuck copies on the windows of each railway compartment; it obviously worked. *Kenilworth* was the test piece and knowing that a large number of Camborne players worked at Holman's, Mr Parker had a Foden's Band recording of the piece broadcast over the works' tannoy system for a few days prior to the contest.

Camborne Town Band was promoted to the Championship Section in 1946 and as there were no challengers at the West Country Area Contest automatically qualified for the National Championship. Somehow the committee managed to raise enough funds for the trip and the Band took its place amongst the top bands in the country.

At the first time of asking the Band achieved a tremendous result and we can only imagine the elation amongst the players at being placed sixth in the country. The adjudicators were agreed that the Band took a while to get into its stride and Henry Geehl, the test piece composer, wrote, *"A really poor start"*. Clearly the playing then improved sufficiently to lift the Band into the top six. Brighouse and Rastrick, with Fred Roberts as Principal Cornet, won the day but there were many famous bands placed behind Camborne. At the time of the 1946 Final Gerald Fletcher was playing baritone; he was inexperienced at playing at Championship level and was clearly nervous when the euphoniums and baritones took up the melody in the second movement. Without telling him what to do, Mr Parker took him to one side and told him that it's not always what's played but sometimes what's left out that counts. As it happens his nerves did get the better of him and he mimed the part. He said, *"I'll never forget the adjudicator's remarks, 'The second movement was beautifully played but the baritone could have been stronger'"*. The Band had made a very nervous start but a brilliant finish to the test piece and it is tempting to reflect on what might have been. The adjudicators clearly agreed when they awarded them sixth place with the comment, *"If only this band had started as they finished"*. Camborne Town Band has retained its championship status ever since.

Camborne was unopposed again in the 1947 Area Championship and took its place at the National Final in London when the test piece was *Freedom* by Hubert Bath.

In 1948 there was some local competition and it was necessary to compete for the Area Championship. In a much more satisfying way Camborne qualified for the National Final as West of England Champion.

Camborne was Area Champion again in 1949 with Falmouth Town Silver (A G Richards) in second place giving Cornwall two bands in the National Final. Falmouth was no one-year wonder as it also qualified in 1950 and 1951. George Hawkins conducted the Area Contest massed band concert comprising Camborne, Falmouth and Kingswood Evangel.

The British Bandsman Supplement of 12/11/1949 covering the National Championship Festival of 1949 makes interesting reading. *"Since 1945, when the great series of 'Daily Herald' contests started, each year has seen the introduction of some new measure, either in organisation, presentation or procedure, designed to ensure fair-for-all contesting under the best possible conditions. In 1945, the eight Area qualifying contests were inaugurated to reduce the cost of travelling and to create an Area Championship for all sections. Entries totalled 214. In 1946, it initiated the policy of staging contests in concert halls for Championship and top section bands so avoiding the many distractions of open-air performances. The well-known Adjudication Box was introduced. The 'Daily Herald' Brass Band Contesting Rules gave the movement its first national system of registration, with the Bandsman's Registration Card to certify he could play with only one band for national contesting. Entries totalled 320. In 1947, test pieces were specially commissioned, and the distribution of profits of Area Championships to competing bands and finalists was begun. Entries totalled 399."*

Under the heading *"Challenge from South and West,"* it continued. *"This will be the fourth time that Camborne Town has represented the West. Unopposed in the Area Championship in 1946 and 1947, it came first last year (1948) and again in May. In the forefront of West Country contesting bands for several decades, Camborne has broadcast more than 150 times. One is apt to overlook the fact that it won the National Second Section championship in the first year of the 'Daily Herald' contests. It would be unwise to overlook its chances of making the National Trophy go west for the first time."*

Camborne Town Band joined with Black Dyke Mills, Brighouse and Rastrick, Munn & Felton's Works, Clydebank Burgh, Harton Colliery, Foden's Motor Works, Cory Workmen's Silver and Morris Motors in the massed band concert under Sir Malcolm Sargeant. The programme included the *1812 Overture, Poet and Peasant, Introduction to Act III of Lohengrin and Slavonic Rhapsody No 2* and was broadcast on the BBC's Light Programme.

In the section entitled *Brass Facts* it said, *"Many trades are represented in the Camborne Town Band, among them tin miners, carpenters, builders, painters, office workers and a radio engineer."*

It was Camborne as Champions and Falmouth in runners-up-spot again in 1950 and although the points difference between them was quite considerable, Falmouth was "fielding" a fine band. The test piece in the National Final was *Pageantry* by Herbert Howells and Mr Parker had been taken ill just before going on stage to conduct. The players were already in position but could clearly see that he was in distress. Gerald Fletcher said, *"He went through the motions but the Band really had to play by itself"*. The contest is significant as it was the last time Mr Parker conducted the Band in the National Championship.

Because Camborne had automatic entrance to the National Final in 1951, having won the Area Championship three times in a row, the South-West, indeed Cornwall, had three bands competing – Camborne, St Dennis (W D Lawton) and Falmouth (J Fletcher). Many players who had provided long years of sterling service were about to retire around this time but had stayed on because they knew that Mr Parker was in terminally declining health. When he died, in early 1951, a number of key players retired. This left the new Musical Director, Mr F J Roberts, with a major problem but he took the Band to London and won an amazing sixth place. Only the big names had headed them - Black Dyke Mills, Foden's Motor Works, Brighouse & Rastrick, Fairey Aviation and CWS Manchester.

Camborne was on an tremendous run of wins at the Area Championship and took the title again in 1952 playing *Resurgam* by Eric Ball. The test piece at the National Championship was The *Frogs* by Bantock.

Another Area Championship in 1953 with Dean Goffin's *Rhapsody in Brass* and the Band was London bound once more where the reward was fifteenth place. This was John Berryman's first National Final and was held in the Empress Hall at Earls Court. The test piece was *Diadem of Gold* and at the tender age of 13 he was on flugel and had two important passages to play. Fred Roberts kept telling him to, *"Play a little louder"*. He did, and when they received the adjudicator's remarks it read, *"Flugel – much too loud"*.

The Grand Festival Concert was given by massed bands comprising; Fairey Aviation Works Band (1952 winners), Black Dyke Mills Band, Camborne Town Band, Creswell Colliery Welfare Band, Foden's Motor Works Band, Hanwell Silver Band, Park and Dare Workmen's Band, S H and W R Wallsend Shipyard Prize Band and Tullis Russell Silver Band. Sir Malcolm Sargeant, Harry Mortimer O B E and Frank Wright conducted and the concert featured the Trumpeters of the Life Guards. Camborne played in a number of these post-contest concerts at the National Championship and Reg Toy recalled, *"It was a marvellous opportunity to play under the top conductors but I remember one occasion when Harry Mortimer was not too pleased when our bass drummer jumped in too early during Finlandia"*.

In 1954 Camborne achieved its second hat-trick of wins in the Area Championship playing *Clive of India*.

The Band had been a competitor at every National Championship contest in London since 1946, twice finishing in sixth place. Eric Thomas recalled his first experience of contesting at the Royal Albert Hall. *"It was October 1954 and we left Camborne at 6.30am and travelled to the Crawford Hotel in Exeter for breakfast. From there we made our way to London, stopping at Andover for lunch. Our hotel was in Russell Square and once we had had something to eat a group of us made our way to the Adelphi Theatre to see The Dave Allen Show. A new singer was all the rage and we certainly enjoyed one of the early performances by Shirley Bassey. I remember, in particular, that Telfer Rule was quite taken with her."*

This was Monica Orchard's first appearance in the National Final. She recalled walking out onto the Royal Albert Hall stage, at the age of 11, *"It was scary - it seemed so big"*. For a little girl from Camborne the city seemed a fast and furious place where the traffic never stopped; even at night.

Although qualifying in 1955 by winning the Area Championship three years in a row, Camborne could not afford the cost of transport and accommodation and did not compete, leaving Falmouth & St Dennis as the South-West representatives.

In 1956 the Band travelled to Bristol by train and as they passed over the Tamar Bridge the players threw coins out of windows for luck. It must have worked as the Band came first. Clive Murton was playing second trombone and in his rush to get to one of the practices he forgot his music. He'd cycled from Wall so had no time to go back to fetch it but must have felt much better when Jack Berryman (first trombone) said, *"Freddie will be lived"*. Clive was known for the huge amount of home practice he put in and he placed his music pack on the stand and played the piece from memory. Luckily, Mr Roberts didn't notice and he got away with it.

Eric Thomas said, *"We were Area Champions again and back in London. A group of us, led by Jack Trounce, went to the Motor Show in the afternoon and to see the sights of London in the Evening – at the Windmill Theatre! I think there were four or five of us including Toni Volante and we made sure that we had good seats – in the front row upstairs."* In case you're wondering, the players did take time out to compete in the National Final!

The 1957 Area Championship was Alan Toy's first major contest on solo horn; he was 13 years of age. After negotiating a tricky cadenza he was congratulated by the senior players and felt that it was the point when he was fully accepted as a member of the "family".

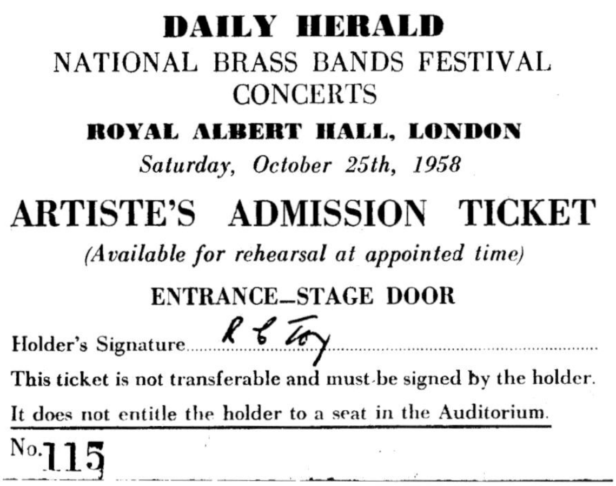
DAILY HERALD

NATIONAL BRASS BANDS FESTIVAL CONCERTS

ROYAL ALBERT HALL, LONDON

Saturday, October 25th, 1958

ARTISTE'S ADMISSION TICKET

(Available for rehearsal at appointed time)

ENTRANCE—STAGE DOOR

Holder's Signature R L Toy

This ticket is not transferable and must be signed by the holder.

It does not entitle the holder to a seat in the Auditorium.

No. 115

Camborne Town held the distinction of being undefeated at the Area Contest since its inception in 1945 and in 1958 it achieved its ninth West of England Area Championship win – in three groups of hat-tricks. One newspaper wrote, *"Camborne's nationally-famous conductor, Fred Roberts, was nearly as excited as the Band's youngest player, 14 year-old Monica Orchard"*. It was a Cornish clean-sweep; Camborne, St Dennis Silver and Falmouth Town occupied the top spots in the Championship Section and, just for good measure, Bodmin Town won the Second Section.

Camborne did not compete in the 1959 Area Contest leaving St Dennis to carry Cornish hopes on this occasion.

In 1960 a lack of funds made attendance at the Area Contest unlikely and Fred Roberts appealed to the General Committee saying, *"For morale and progress, contesting is essential"*. He outlined a scheme by which, *"If the Executive Committee agreed to send the Band to Bristol, the bandsmen would travel up and down in one day, thereby cutting expenses tremendously. Additionally, if the Committee would supply lunch, the bandsmen would buy their own tea."* This was approved with the Committee's appreciation for the gesture.

When they qualified, the General Committee agreed to the Band's attendance at the Final and the players, once again, offered to cut expenses to an absolute minimum. As it turned out the Band had to withdraw because of a shortage of four players, leaving St Dennis as the only Cornish band. This non-attendance clearly incurred the wrath of the Area Contest Committee and words like disgust, anger and discourtesy were bouncing about in the Camborne Committee Room. Members felt the Area Committee did understand the difficulties being experienced by the Band and the Secretary was asked to enquire if the number two and three bands of the Lancashire Area had also been banned from the 1961 contest.

Camborne had to be satisfied with the runners-up spot at the 1962 Area Contest but that was enough to see them on their way to the National Championship again. The test piece at the Final was the wonderful piece *La Forza del Destino* and the Band was placed fourteenth.

This was Reg Bennett's first National Final Championship. He said, *"I remember how daunting it was to walk onto the stage. Mr Roberts told us to squeeze together so that our chairs were touching. He also said not to look out at the audience but I couldn't help glancing and seeing this huge, black space. Despite sitting close together, I felt really alone and it seemed that the adjudicator would hear every individual note. Before we played I walked around the corridors under the stage and came across Black Dyke's dressing room - that certainly brought home to me the enormity of the occasion. Jack Pascoe was playing flugel and had such a busy part that he hardly had time to catch breath. I was told to cover the flugel part for two bars to help him out. I was playing repiano cornet and to achieve a softer tone I hung a blue beret over the bell."* George Ansell said, *"Jack Pascoe's performance was so good that a number of players from the top bands came over to congratulate him"*.

In 1963 Camborne returned to winning ways and won the Area Championship with Wagner's *Rienzi*. It's a testing piece for soprano but Roy Wearne had to play it twice. Cinderford's soprano player had been taken ill and in that event the rules allow a band to borrow a player from the band drawn immediately before them. Roy had the pleasure of winning with Camborne and coming second with Cinderford. This time there was a top 10 placing at London when, playing *Belmont Variations,* the Band took a superb ninth place. The other South-West qualifier was St Dennis under Eddie Williams.

Another Area Championship win, with *Symphony of Marches*, in 1964 and the Band was heading for London yet again. The lack of strength in depth was evident as, depleted by sickness, the Band was placed back in twenty-first place. Fred Roberts called for an increased drive to keep up the standard required at this level; that drive must also be through the learners' class which he considered should be equal to a Second Section band. Roy Wearne (soprano) left late in the year and Desmond Burley took over his role. The test piece was *Variations on a Ninth* and he only had six weeks to get used to the instrument and learn the music. Kenny Haynes (horn & baritone) was an ex Truro player and playing a cadenza he famously hid his instrument under his coat so that Freddie Roberts wouldn't see what valves he was using.

Camborne took part in the massed band concerts, one late afternoon and the other in the evening. Between the two concerts the players were supplied with refreshments and Dougie Piper (trombone) finished his in no time. He suddenly spied a spare plate on a window-sill and, not wishing to see good food go to waste, reached over and picked it up. As he munched through it a player from one of the other bands walked up and said, *"Bloody hell, somebody's pinched my sandwiches"*. Dougie turned round and said, *"Never mind boy, have one of mine."* The chap was very appreciative and must have thought, *"They boys from Cornwall are a generous lot"*.

St Dennis won the Area Championship in 1965 and Camborne qualified in second place and duly made its sixteenth appearance in the National Brass Band Championship of Great Britain. Funds were quite low at the time and it was decided to travel to London by sleeper train to avoid hotel costs. Alan Toy said, *"I remember Freddie in his dressing gown, walking up and down the carriage making sure everyone was in bed ready for the big day ahead; David Reed slept in the overhead luggage rack. We were a bit of a scratch band and I don't think we expected to do anything special. We were rehearsing in a brewery when Eddie Ashton said to Fred Roberts that we were cutting it a bit fine and ought to be on our way to the contest hall. A bit of panic set in. We arrived late, the stewards were looking for us and we had to go straight to registration and onto the stage; we had no time for nerves. We played after Faireys; a tough draw especially as they played well and won. We were absolutely delighted to take sixth place, ahead of Black Dyke! George Ansell had heard us play and he joined us after for a drink in a nearby pub. I remember him sitting next to Gerald Weeks who looked at George and said, 'You just drank my pint'. To which George said, 'Oh, sorry about that,' picked up his own and drank that as well. Everyone fell about laughing – except Gerald. On the night train home Freddie couldn't stop smiling about the result."*

St Dennis was Area Champion in 1969 and with Camborne back in third place it meant no London appearance for the fourth year in a row. As it turned out this was the last occasion when Fred Roberts conducted Camborne at a major contest. Barrie Trevena recalled attendance problems before the contest and Freddie being on the verge of withdrawing.

Playing the new Yamaha instruments Camborne achieved an emphatic win at Bristol in the 1972 Area Championship with *Concert Overture for Brass Band.* In what one newspaper described as, "*One of the strongest, most competitive championship for years,*" the Band was five points ahead of St Austell (F J Roberts), the other South-West qualifier. Conductor Derek Johnston attributed a good deal of the Band's win to the new instruments which, he considered, "*Had a better tone*". He said, *"It is not hard, but more mellow. I'm very happy with them. I get criticised by some people for deciding to use the instruments but now they have paid dividends."* The Band was heading for the London Final once again where it took fourteenth place out of the twenty-five competitors. Derek Johnston considered that, "*Youthful inexperience*" had proved a crucial factor in the Band's performance. He said, *"We know we could have played better"*.

The World Championship was discontinued in this year and the top bands returned to compete in the National Championship. Under the heading "*The 'National' Restored,*" the contest programme states – *"At the Royal Albert Hall, thousands of enthusiasts will see the restoration to its former glory of the title 'Champion Band of Great Britain'. The intriguing (and necessary) experiment with the World Championship over the past few years has shown that such an event, however attractive, cannot replace, in the affections of the bandsmen, the magic of the 'National'. The World Championship has been put 'on ice' in the meantime – to be revived in a new format at a later date."*

The Revd Basil Brown collected the cup when the Camborne players became Area Champions again in 1973 and received a splendid set of remarks from Geoffrey Brand as it headed the British Railways Staff Band, Stanshawe Band (W Hargreaves) and St Austell Band (F Roberts). The players must have headed for the National Final in good heart and it was to be rewarded as they chalked up fifth place, their best result to date; just four points behind the winners. A handwritten comment on one programme I've seen said, *"In with a chance"*. A comment, which is given credence as the writer was equally glowing in respect of the other top placed bands. This excellent result placed them ahead of such bands as Cory, Grimethorpe, GUS Footwear, Desford Colliery and Besses. In a newspaper report the Band Chairman, the Revd Basil Brown, said, *"Their performance was quite magnificent. They played their best .... we have no regrets about their performance"*. The only downside to the weekend was when the coach broke down on the return journey and their arrival back in Camborne was delayed until just short of midnight on the Sunday.

There was one other mishap but even that did not spoil a good performance and a tremendous result. Robert Cook said, "*I had a nose bleed while we were playing the test piece; I was on first horn at that time. I was okay apart from the blood running down on to my new uniform which was being worn for the first time. I kept playing as the Band was sounding beautiful and I didn't want to draw attention to my problem and cause any lapse of concentration. It was well worth it as we were placed fifth but my uniform was the first one to head for the dry cleaners. When we arrived back home Derek Johnson told the West Briton about the nosebleed and my determination not to let the Band down. I had my photograph on the front page of the newspaper the following Thursday."* The report said, *"He looked as though he had been involved in a boxing and not a band championship, with the front of his shirt red with blood."*

Following the excitement of the previous year, 1974 was a bit of a comedown. The Band failed to qualify in the Area Championship when it was placed third behind the five-year-old Stanshawe (Bristol) Band. Leonard Adams had been absent due to a road accident and another cornet player was missing through illness. St Dennis and Bodmin were unplaced but ex Camborne player,

Edward Ashton, conducted Helston Town Band to success in Section Three. The result was a huge disappointment to the Camborne players and a surprise to Derek Johnston who considered Camborne to be the best band there. St Austell (Fred Roberts) carried the Cornish Flag at the National Final and was placed fifteenth.

The Camborne (Derek Greenwood) players were Area Champions again in 1977 but that was not to be the extent of its achievement in this glory year. In what remains as the best result achieved by a Cornish band in the National Championship of Great Britain, Camborne Town Band was placed fourth. Black Dyke Mills was impressive with their rendition of *Connotations for Brass Band* and won the championship by five points. Grimethorpe Colliery was second; Yorkshire Imperial Metals third and then came Camborne, ahead of many well-known, previous winners. It was Leonard Adams' first contest as Principal Cornet. Eric Thomas recalled there being great concern regarding the lead-in to a three-in -a-bar section where the horns took up the melody. As it happens it was perfect but he was so relieved that he failed to count his 20 bars rest correctly and was not sure where to make his entry. He leant over to Gerald Weeks and whispered, *"Where are we Gerald?"* Gerald shook his head indicating that he didn't know either. As it happened all was well as Gerald was taking his cue from the baritones and he made a perfect entry with Eric a millisecond behind. Once the story got out the players picked up on the phrase, *"Where are we Gerald?"*

Writing in the Bandsman, Steve Walkley recalled the reception received on the march down through Camborne. He said, *"There were thousands of people from all over Cornwall who had turned out to congratulate 'their band' on its highest achievement to date - and we hadn't won, but we felt like winners with that reception...never have I experienced such celebrations"*. Steve (solo trombone) played in the Band for about three years.

In 1978 Camborne Town became Area Champion once again playing the test piece, *The Belmont Variations*. At the National Final the Band was unable to build on the success of the previous year but was placed a very creditable fourteenth. St Dennis (Eddie Williams), the other South-West qualifier, managed to keep a Cornish name in the frame with an impressive sixth place.

When taking part in the National Championship the Band often stayed at the Great Eastern Hotel, near Liverpool Street Station. The Manager had previously worked at the Tregenna Castle Hotel at St Ives and had some affinity with the Cornish. Not all of the instruments could be carried on the coach and Michael Weeks transported them to London in a van which he parked under the hotel, behind a locked gate. With an ever-present fear of terrorism the police became concerned about this strange van and alerted the hotel Manager who assured them it was bona fide. Perhaps they imagined that it was yet another Cornish rebellion!

Sun Life Stanshawe took first place in 1979 when Camborne failed to qualify.

Camborne qualified for the National Final in second place in 1980, one point behind Area Champions Bodmin Town (A C Jenkin). A good performance with *Carnival Overture* at London was rewarded with twelfth place; equal with GUS Footwear. Bodmin Town was drawn to play first and placed nineteenth.

1982 was another momentous year for the Band as it became Area Champion and picked up another fourth place at the National Championship. Adjudicators Arthur Butterworth, Noel Cox and Roy Newsome placed them fourth behind The Cory Band, the mighty Black Dyke Mills and Brodsworth Colliery. The Ever Ready Band was fifth and Fairey Engineering Works, sixth. Tim Joslin recalled, *"What a venue, what a performance, what a feeling and what a result. That was a day I shall never forget. Although it now sounds odd, I was a little disappointed because we were so used to winning and I was ignorant of the class and professionalism of the northern bands. Looking back, the result speaks for itself because since then neither Camborne nor any other Cornish band has even come close to fourth place."* Bodmin Town, the other South-West band, picked up a very commendable twelfth place.

Camborne was runner-up at the 1983 Area Championship when Sunlife, Bristol, was declared the winner. St Austell was in third place and a delighted group of Redruth players took fourth. This meant another trip to London for Camborne where the reward was sixteenth place for the test piece, *Ballet for Band.*

Another second place with *Waverley* at the 1984 Area Championship and the Band was on its way to London again where it came in a solid thirteenth. Sunlife was riding high and collected second place behind Champions, Cory.

Second place again at the Area Championship in 1985 but a superb ninth place at London for *Cloudcatcher Fells* put the Band ahead of many well-known names. About a month before the contest Lester Ashton (solo trombone) had been taken ill and rushed into hospital with appendicitis. *"It was Friday the 13th September and I knew I was going to miss the National Championship. Kevin Goninan came down to visit me and I remember thinking how nice that was. After a quick word about my health, however, he turned to Dad* (Eddie Ashton) *and asked if he would take my place at the contest – it was good to feel wanted."*

During rehearsals, Derek Greenwood detected a slight tuning problem with the trombones. It only occurred on one note, when the bass trombone player, Donald Cock, had his slide out to the seventh position. To overcome the problem Donald tied a length of binder twine to the trombone framework and the slide which limited its movement. It solved the problem but Derek Greenwood's comment was, *"He had to use orange binder twine, you could see the bloody stuff from a mile away!"*

In 1986 Camborne was accompanied by a large Cornish contingent in the Area Championship. Bodmin, Redruth, St Austell, St Dennis and St Keverne all made the journey to Bristol where Sunlife was crowned Champion Band with Camborne in second place. At the National Final, playing *Diversions for Brass Band,* Camborne was placed fourteenth, equal with Brighouse and Rastrick.

Ron Massey, in his British Bandsman column in 1987, discussed the merits of creating a, "New-style premier class". It's not that debate to which I wish to draw attention but to the league tables produced in support of his argument. In deciding the composition of this new "super league" he took the National Final results from 1972 to 1981 (10 years) and gave the winners 20 points, those in second place 19 points and so on down to the bands in twentieth place which received one point each; a sort of champion of champions table of the 10 years. Black Dyke had competed in nine of the years and was the clear winner with 175 points, Brighouse was second with 143 points and Cory was third. Camborne had played in five Finals and was in an impressive 15th place. In another table covering the period 1972 to 1986 (15 years) Black Dyke was still riding high in first place but Camborne (10 appearances) had risen to eleventh place, clearly helped by its fourth place in 1982.

Concerned that the early 1970s may be considered too out-of-date, a third table was produced for the ten-year period 1977 to 1986 (you can do anything with statistics!) and in that period Camborne (eight appearances) had reached the giddy heights of 9th place. Black Dyke was still supreme but this analysis shows that in the period 1977 to 1986 Camborne was the ninth most successful band in the National Championship of Great Britain.

In 1987 Camborne failed to qualify for the National Final but St Austell (Derek Greenwood), kept the Cornish flag flying with an outstanding sixth place.

In 1988 Cornwall was represented by five Cornish bands in the Championship Section of the Area Contest: Bodmin (5th), Camborne (2nd), Redruth (15th), St Austell (4th) and St Dennis (10th). Second place meant yet another appearance on the national stage against the "big boys" of the brass band world when the test piece was *Seascapes* by Ray Steadman-Allen; Stephen Sykes led the Band to a superb twelfth place.

For the more casual follower of brass bands it may be necessary to explain that to play in the National Championship is an achievement in itself. A band must win or be placed second in one of the eight Area Contests or have been in the top four at the previous year's National Final. Competing in the Final means playing against the top bands including the likes of Black Dyke, Brighouse and Rastrick, Fairey FP (Music) Band, Cory Band, Foden's and so on. These are the Manchester United and Arsenal of the brass band world and it is a huge achievement when our Cornish bands rub shoulders with them. Perhaps that brings into perspective what a top fifteenth or a top tenth National Championship result means but just move from there to appreciate Camborne's three sixth places, its fifth place and the two fourth places it achieved in 1977 and 1982 - giddy heights indeed.

Playing the test piece *Prisms* by Peter Graham, Camborne was second at the Area Championship in 1989 and was off to the London Final again. Stephen Sykes had conducted both Camborne

Town and Carharrack & St Day and both gained a second place in their respective sections. At the National Championship, Camborne again took twelfth place with *Odin* by Arthur Butterworth.

1990 was another good year for Camborne becoming Area Champions from Bodmin (Leonard Adams) and Flowers with St Austell placed tenth and Redruth seventeenth. An excellent result at the National Championship saw the Band take eighth place for the test piece *English Heritage* with Bodmin town, the other Cornish representative, in twenty-second position.

The following year the test piece for the Area Championship was *Journey Into Freedom* but it turned out to be a less than happy journey for Camborne. A disappointing tenth place left it in unfamiliar territory and a long way from qualifying for London.

Ask any Cornishman and he will tell you that Bristol is not a good location for South-West events; it is hardly central to the area. And so it was with the Area Championship and in 1992 Camborne Town Band again made the point that the contest involved Cornish bands in considerable travelling. In a letter to the organisers it was suggested that Plymouth, with its excellent facilities, should be considered. Whether it had anything to do with the distance or not, the Band had a disappointing result at Bristol and would be missing out on the National Final. Bodmin Town (Leonard Adams) qualified and went on to take an excellent seventh place in the National Final.

A better result in the 1993 Area Championship when second place was enough to see Camborne return to the national stage. Derek Greenwood was conducting at London as the Band took eighteenth place for *The Devil and the Deep Blue Sea.*

An almost identical result in 1994 gave Camborne a second at the Area Championship and seventeenth at the London Final playing *Theme and Cooperation.*

The following year brought a third place at the Area with the test piece *Un Vie de Matelot.* The SWEB Camborne Town Band was headed by two of its greatest South-West rivals, Sunlife and Flowers. Bodmin Town's fourth place and St Dennis' eighth meant no Cornish representation at the National Final.

A disappointing fourth place in 1996 meant that the Band had failed to qualify for the National Final again. Derek Greenwood referred to, *"A tremendous audience response to a good performance, which simply did not please the adjudicator".* A letter of thanks was sent to St Dennis who had lent the Band a euphonium when it was discovered that Stuart Butt's instrument had been left behind in the bandroom.

Thomas Wyss conducted at the Area Championship in 1997. It was felt that the Band did not give its best performance on the day and the fourth place result was a disappointment but not a surprise. Flowers and Bodmin Town represented the South-West in the National Final and were tenth and twelfth respectively. David Loukes (trombone) played for Camborne on this occasion; he later became Musical Director of St Austell Town.

Four Cornish bands represented the county in the Area Championship in 1998 but South West Trains Woodfalls took first prize. Camborne (Leonard Adams) headed the Duchy challenge and qualified for the Final by taking second place. The other Cornish bands were Bodmin (3rd), Mount Charles (5th) and St Austell (9th). Camborne went on to secure yet

Returning from the National Championships in 1998 with Leonard Adams (MD)

another top 10 placing in the National Final when Leonard Adams led it to an impressive ninth position.

The test piece for the Area Championship in 1999 was *Blitz* by Derek Bourgeois and the Band's failure to secure a first or second place meant it would not be appearing in the National Final. Bodmin qualified to represent Cornwall and was placed sixteenth.

The result at the 2000 Area Championship was hugely disappointing for the Camborne players but, looking on the bright side, there would be no expensive trip to London. Bodmin qualified for the second year in a row and took fifteenth place.

The Area Championship in 2001 was notable for its mixed emotions. Six players were due to leave immediately after the contest and morale was low. Jeremy Squibb said, *"The mood of the Band seemed to change part way through the test piece, 'Jazz'. We were sounding good and the result turned out to be a spectacular success as we took first place to become Area Champions."* Brian Grant conducted at the National Final when the Band was placed nineteenth.

Whitsun Wakes by Michael Ball was the test piece for the 2002 Area Championship when Camborne (Frank Renton) was placed second and on its way to compete with the elite again. Major Paul Murrell conducted at the National Final when it was placed nineteenth for the second year in a row.

2002 – At the National Championship with the Albert Memorial in the background
Back row: Jeremy Squibb, Chris Leonard, Chris Netherton, Andrew Mitchell, Rob Sandow, Mark Leigh, Ian Hooper, Sharon Hooper, Becky Richards, Tracy Abbott and Mo Whitehead.
Middle row: Nigel Chadd, Charlotte McCaffery, Wayne Brown, Graham Barker, Nick Abbott, Gareth Cottrell, Chris Wooding and Mark "Billy" Rosewarne (percussion - played from the 1990s to March 2005).
Front row: Jason Smith, Graham Boag, Stephen Thomas, Aldene Button, Major Paul Murrell (Conductor), Rachel Trudgeon, Robert Jose, Tim Joslin and Lee Trewhella.
(Photo by Marcus Dunstan)

It was another year as Area Champions in 2003 when Frank Renton conducted the Band to success with *Prague* by Judith Bingham. Major Paul Murrell conducted at the National Final and took a well-deserved eleventh place playing Eric Ball's wonderful arrangement of *Enigma Variations.*

At the 2004 Area Championship the Band took second place under Frank Renton. The London trip to the Final got off to a bad start when there were problems with both buses. However, with problems solved, the players and supporters were on their way "up country". The test piece for the National Final, *All the Flowers of the Mountain,* was for the purist. It could not be described as a concert piece but a test it certainly was. All went well and a St Piran's flag was waved in approval at a good performance. An excellent ninth place saw many familiar names finish below Camborne but, even so, the honour of top Cornish band went to Mount Charles in seventh place.

There was a gasp of surprise at the 2005 Area Championship as Camborne was placed back in fifth place. There was another when Mount Charles was placed fourth and yet another, when Flowers was given third. The three favourites were out of contention and would not represent the South-West at the National Final. I have never heard the word "unbelievable" used so much as the audience waited for adjudicator Roy Roe's decision. The St Austell players were ecstatic with second place and, to the surprise of almost everyone in the hall, newly promoted Bournemouth Concert Brass was declared the winners. Lanner & District Silver took a creditable eighth place and consolidated its status in the top flight but it was an occasion when many people were left to wonder if the results had really been announced in reverse order.

Camborne Town Band's results at the South-West Area Championship

Second Section

1945	*Beethoven's 5th Symphony*	1st	A W Parker

Championship Section

1946	Qualified unopposed		
1947	Qualified unopposed		
1948	*Fantasia in F* – Mozart/Sargeant	1st	A W Parker
1949	*Morning Rhapsody* – Eric Ball	1st	A W Parker
1950	*Festival Overture* – Henry Geehl	1st	A W Parker
1951	Rule-enforced absence – automatic entrance to final		
1952	*Resurgam* – Eric Ball	1st	F J Roberts
1953	*Rhapsody in Brass* – Dean Goffin	1st	F J Roberts
1954	*Clive of India* - J Holbrooke	1st	F J Roberts
1955	Rule-enforced absence – automatic entrance to final		
1956	*Orion* - Granville Bantock	1st	F J Roberts
1957	*Moor of Venice* – Alwyn	1st	F J Roberts
1958	*Themes from Symphony No 9*	1st	F J Roberts
1959	*Wuthering Heights* - Raynor		F J Roberts
1960	*Themes from Symphony No 5* - Tchaikovsky	2nd	F J Roberts
1961	Did not attend		
1962	*Salute to Youth* - Gilbert Vinter	2nd	F J Roberts
1963	*Rienzi* - Wagner	1st	F J Roberts
1964	*Symphony of Marches* - Gilbert Vinter	1st	F J Roberts
1965	*Themes From The 1st Symphony* Beethoven	2nd	F J Roberts
1966	*Blackfriars* - Cundell		F J Roberts
1967	*Festival Music* – Eric Ball	3rd?	F J Roberts
1968	*Themes from Symphony No 8* - Beethoven	3rd	F J Roberts
1969	*Diadem of Gold* - G Bailey	3rd	F J Roberts
1970	Did not attend		

1971	*A Joyful Noise* – Gordon Jacob		D Johnston?
1972	*Concert Overture for Brass Band*	1st	D Johnston
1973	*The Plantagenets* - Edward Gregson	1st	D Johnston
1974	*Variations on a Ninth* - Gilbert Vinter	3rd	D Johnston
1975	*Journey Into Freedom* - Eric Ball		B Bygrave?
1976	*Spectrum* – Gilbert Vinter		D A Greenwood?
1977	*Pageantry* - Herbert Howells	1st	D A Greenwood
1978	*The Belmont Variations* - Sir Arthur Bliss	1st	D A Greenwood
1979	*Variations for Brass Band* - V Williams	?	D A Greenwood
1980	*Beatrice and Benedict* - Berlioz	2nd	D A Greenwood
1981	*Variations on The Shining River* - Rubbra		D A Greenwood
1982	*Essay* - Edward Gregson	1st	D A Greenwood
1983	*Images* - John McCabe	2nd	D A Greenwood
1984	*Waverley* - Hector Berlioz	2nd	D A Greenwood
1985	*Contest Music* - Wilfred Heaton	2nd	D A Greenwood
1986	*Variations on a Theme by Hadyn* - Brahms	2nd	S Sykes
1987	*Diversions on a Bass Theme* - Geo Lloyd	3rd	S Sykes
1988	*Ballet for Band* - Joseph Horovitz	2nd	S Sykes
1989	*Prisms* - Peter Graham	2nd	S Sykes
1990	*The Beacons* - Ray Steadman-Allen	1st	S Sykes
1991	*Journey Into Freedom* - Eric Ball	10th	S Sykes
1992	*Frontier* - Michael Ball	5th	D A Greenwood
1993	*Of Men and Mountains* - E Gregson	2nd	D A Greenwood
1994	*Partita* - Philip Sparke	2nd	D A Greenwood
1995	*Un Vie de Matelot* - Robert Farnon	3rd	D A Greenwood
1996	*Sounds* - John Golland	4th	D A Greenwood
1997	*A Lowry Sketch* - Philip Wilby	4th	T Wyss
1998	*Montage* - Peter Graham	2nd	Leonard Adams
1999	*Blitz* - Derek Bourgeois	3rd	Leonard Adams
2000	*Variations on an Enigma* - Philip Sparke	6th	Leonard Adams
2001	*Jazz* - Philip Wilby	1st	Frank Renton
2002	*Whitsun Wakes* - Michael Ball	2nd	Frank Renton
2003	*Prague* - Judith Bingham	1st	Frank Renton
2004	*Tristan Encounters* - Martin Ellerby	2nd	Frank Renton
2005	*Rienzi* - Wagner	5th	Frank Renton

Camborne Town Band's results at the National Championship:

Junior Cup (A) Contest (equivalent to Third Section)

1926	*L'Arlesienne* – Bizet		A W Parker

Grand Shield (Second Section)

1927	?		A W Parker
1928	*Egmont* – Beethoven		A W Parker

Second Section

1945	*Kenilworth* - Arthur Bliss	1st	A W Parker

Championship Section

1946	*Oliver Cromwell* - Henry Geehl	6th	A W Parker
1947	*Freedom* – Hubert Bath		A W Parker
1948	*On the Cornish Coast* – Henry Geehl		A W Parker
1949	*Comedy Overture* – John Ireland		A W Parker
1950	*Pageantry* - Herbert Howells		A W Parker
1951	*Epic Symphony* – Percy Fletcher	6th	F J Roberts
1952	*The Frogs* – Granville Bantock		F J Roberts
1953	*Diadem of Gold* - G Bailey	15th	F J Roberts
1954	*Sovereign Heritage* - J Beaver		F J Roberts
1955	Did not attend		
1956	*Festival Music* – Eric Ball		F J Roberts
1957	*Variations for Brass Band* - V Williams		F J Roberts
1958	*Variations on the Shining River* – E Rubbra		F J Roberts
1959 to 1961	Did not attend		
1962	*La Forza del Destino* - Verdi	14th	F J Roberts
1963	*Belmont Variations* - Arthur Bliss	9th	F J Roberts
1964	*Variations on a Ninth* - Gilbert Vinter	21st	F J Roberts
1965	*Triumphant Rhapsody* - Gilbert Vinter	6th	F J Roberts
1966 to 1971	Did not attend		
1972	*A Kensington Concerto* - Eric Ball	14th	D Johnston
1973	*Freedom* - Hubert Bath	5th	D Johnston
1974 to 1976	Did not attend		
1977	*Connotations for Brass Band* - E Gregson	4th	D A Greenwood
1978	*Checkmate* - Sir Arthur Bliss	14th	D A Greenwood
1979	Did not attend		
1980	*Carnival Overture* - Dvorak	12th	D A Greenwood
1981	Did not attend		
1982	*Contest Music* - Wilfred Heaton	4th	D A Greenwood
1983	*Ballet for Band* - Joseph Horovitz	16th	D A Greenwood
1984	*Dances & Arias* - Edward Gregson	13th	D A Greenwood
1985	*Cloudcatcher Fells* - John McCabe	9th	D A Greenwood
1986	*Diversions for Brass Band* - D Bourgeois	14th	M Cotter
1987	Did not attend		
1988	*Seascapes* - Ray Steadman-Allen	12th	S Sykes
1989	*Odin Op 76* - Arthur Butterworth	12th	S Sykes
1990	*English Heritage* - George Lloyd	8th	S Sykes
1991/92	Did not attend		
1993	*The Devil and the Deep Blue Sea*	18th	D A Greenwood
1994	*Theme and Co-operation* - J Horovitz	17th	D A Greenwood
1995 to 1997	Did not attend		
1998	*Between the Moon and Mexico* - P Sparke	9th	Leonard Adams
1999/2000	Did not attend		
2001	*Albion* - Jan Van der Roost	19th	Brian Grant
2002	*Masquerade* - Dr Philip Wilby	19th	Major Paul Murrell
2003	*Enigma Variations* - Elgar	11th	Major Paul Murrell
2004	*All the Flowers of the Mountain* - M Ball	9th	Frank Renton
2005	Did not attend		

The Junior, Youth and "B" Bands

Reg Toy

Reg Toy joined Camborne Junior Band when it started in 1925 and stayed until 1933. Jack Eustace was its first conductor; he was a member of the Senior Band and later conducted at Perranporth. Reg recalled, *"The Junior Band was very popular and I think the Senior Band was a bit jealous of our success. Sometime around 1932, separate committees were formed and we became a bit more independent. We had lots of fun and when we went carol playing we split up and one half covered the town and the other half the local villages. I played baritone and for a while I was a member of the Melody Makers' Dance Band but that was frowned on by Jack Eustace and I had to give it up. I also played tenor horn in Redruth Opera Orchestra and I remember playing bass trombone at Marazion solo contest and winning a medal. I won another at St Stythians solo contest when I played Village Blacksmith."*

The 1930 Marazion Contest was the Band's first competition and it took first prize playing the march *Right Away* (Conductor Jack Eustace).

1929 - The Junior Band.

Backrow: Dick Tresidder, is on the left but for the other eight I only have six names - Bill Simmonds, Bill Harris, Bill Menheniot, Jack Hosken, Bill Rundle, unknown and Harold Pellew.
Middle row: Maurice Burrell, Ernie Yeoman, Rex Burrows, Bill Head, Jack Eustace (MD), Tom Pidwell (Chairman), Reg Toy, unknown, Jack Davey and Wilson Eustice.
Front row: Leonard Wills, ? Burrell, Donald Lampshire, Reg Pascoe, Yank Crewes, George Clements, Sid Townsend and Arthur Cornelius.
This information was recorded on the back of a photograph by Reg Pascoe who appears here aged twelve.

1932 – The Junior Band
Back row: W Menhenett, R Pascoe, G Alford, A Pellew, D Chinn, A Hosking, D Lampshire, J Sewell or Sowell, J Ray, B Yeoman, R Crewes and W Harris.
Middle row (standing): R Tresidder, F Head, M Burrall, F Pascoe (young cornet player standing in front row), E Yeoman, R Toy, J G Sewell or Sowell, J Eustace, T G Pidwell, W Head, J Jones, G W Eustace, J Rule (young cornet player standing in front row), C Toy and D Waters (standing in front row).
Front row (seated): A Cornelius, A Toy, I Oates, F Martin and F Weeks.

1932 Bugle Class "B" – Conducted by Jack Eustace, the Band was placed sixth playing *Maritana* and unplaced for the hymn tune *Lavinia* by Handel. It was third in Class D (Deportment) behind Camborne Town Band and Park and Dare Workmen's Silver.

1935 Bugle Class "B" – Competing against nine senior bands, it took fifth place playing the test piece *Gems of Old England* by William Rimmer and the hymn tune *Sunset* by Handel. Johnnie Bawden was conducting in Class "C" and, playing the march *The Premier* by S Cope, it received second prize behind St Stythians. This class had ceased to be an Open Section and was for Third Section bands. Johnnie Bawden, who was a grandfather of singer Ben Luxon, played cornet in the Senior Band. He helped tutor many young players including John Berryman, Fred Waters and Treve Jory.

William Arthur (Joe) Trounce (trombone) was tutor to the youngsters and brought on many good players. He was an excellent player in the Senior Band but always talked about his brother's (Jack) playing ability rather than his own. In 1968 he was awarded the British Empire Medal for services to youth in recognition of his work with apprentices at Holman's and with the Camborne Town Band young players. Despite his pride Joe couldn't see why he had to go to London to receive it. I get the feeling that his preference would have been to receive it from a Cornishman in Camborne but he was persuaded to compromise and brother Jack drove him to Bodmin where the High Sheriff of Cornwall undertook the presentation.

Jack Trounce, Joe's brother, also helped in teaching the younger players but on a one-to-one basis. He trained a number who went on to develop a career in music; Adrian King, John Berryman and Treve Jory all passed through his hands.

Telfer Rule was a fine soprano player and won many awards during his playing career. He was the Junior Band tutor for some time, when Cornwall County Council financed the class with an Education Grant. In March 1961 concern was expressed that young players were not progressing from the Training Class into the Senior Band. The situation was analysed and it was apparent that the lack

Circa 1935 - Dick Tresidder (bass drummer), Ernie Yeoman (trombone on left), Reg Toy (trombone on right), Jervis Rule (young lad on right in front row), Jack Eustace (MD holding baton) and Tom G Pidwell (Sec. of Jnr Band on right of three non-players).

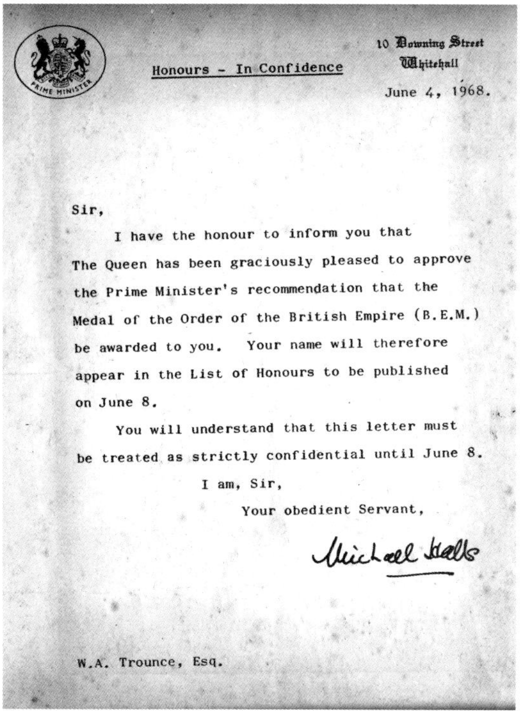

PRIME MINISTER

Honours - In Confidence

10 Downing Street
Whitehall

June 4, 1968.

Sir,

I have the honour to inform you that The Queen has been graciously pleased to approve the Prime Minister's recommendation that the Medal of the Order of the British Empire (B.E.M.) be awarded to you. Your name will therefore appear in the List of Honours to be published on June 8.

You will understand that this letter must be treated as strictly confidential until June 8.

I am, Sir,
Your obedient Servant,

Michael Halls

W.A. Trounce, Esq.

The British Empire Medal presented to Joe Trounce

Joe's letter relating to his British Empire Medal

of continuity stemmed from the increasing demands on younsters' time in following other activities. This problem still plagues bands everywhere. Later that year Telfer resigned and the position was advertised. There was difficulty in finding a replacement trainer and Fred Roberts took over the role with the authority to appoint a deputy if necessary.

Camborne Youth Band - Winners of the Cornwall Instrumental Group at a talent contest at Holman's Canteen in 1961

Standing: John Pooley (cornet - played in the early 1960s and went on to play trumpet in an Orchestra), Lawrence Polkinhorne, Monty Ray, unknown, unknown, unknown Reggie Bennett, David Bray and David Reed.

Seated: ?? Pryor, Michael Woods (played rugby for Camborne), Telfer Rule, David Boase (bass), unknown.

Clifford Bolitho was appointed Junior Class Instructor on the 25th March 1963. At that time there were only nine youngsters attending but by September this had risen to 22. He recalled a number of players who passed through his hands and graduated to the Senior Band. Dennis Treloar sticks in his mind as a particularly good bass player; he later joined the Guards. In 1965 Clifford left to conduct Carharrack & St Day Band and Mr Roberts took over the junior group again. David Bray recalled being taught by Clifford who he rated as one of the best trainers in Cornish brass banding. Clifford conducted the Senior Band on one occasion - at a Plymouth Argyle football match.

In 1967 the Band was advised by Cornwall County Council that future youth brass classes would be held at Redruth County School and that no funding would be available for tuition at Camborne. With no funding and reducing numbers, the Learners' Group was disbanded in January 1968 and for a few years there was no formal class.

Sid (Pop) Maidwell from Frogpool was an old-timer who played cornet at Carharrack & St Day. He helped lots of local bands including Camborne beginners from about 1969 to the mid 1970s. He rewarded each player with a Mars bar with the words, *"You've earned your pay"*.

John Phillips was on the scene during the 1970s and taught the juniors for about five years. He said, *"I realised the importance of the Band training its own youngsters and put in a lot of time with the beginners' group with lads like Robert Jose, Richard Knight, James Knight and many others, trying to give back the great enjoyment I received playing with a first class band"*.

Keith Rowe, music teacher at Pool School, conducted the "B" Band in the 1970s and a number of players were fed into the Senior Band. At this time the Youth and "B" Band seem to be one and the same – more or less!.

Bob Reason was in charge of the Junior Band in July 1972 and at the AGM he voiced his concern about the availability of the bandroom.

1973 Cornwall Brass Band Association Contest at City Hall, Truro, (under 19 yrs) - Keith Rowe conducted the "B" Band when it played the "own-choice" test piece, *Ceramic City Festival,* and was placed second behind St Dennis Youth. The Band also achieved a very impressive third overall in the concert contest.

In the early 1970s the Junior Band ("B" Band) was practising twice a week at the North Parade Methodist Church Sunday School.

Mr B Mabley was the leader of the beginner's class in 1976 and was desperately trying to retrieve instruments from youngsters who had ceased to turn up.

In 1978, at the CBBA Contest (under 19 yrs), G Goodale conducted in a section of eight bands but was unplaced playing *Three Songs Without Words* by Eric Ball.

At the 1979 Cornwall Brass Band Association Contest (CBBA) the Band was third in the under 16 yrs Section (Conductor Phil Tonkin).

1980 Kerrier Brass in Concert Contest – Conducted by Derek Greenwood the Band was first in the Junior Section.

1981 South West Brass Band Association (SWBBA) spring contest at Barnstaple – Placed first for the test piece and an "own-choice" march (Conductor Derek Greenwood).

1981 Kerrier Brass in Concert Contest – Placed first in the Junior Section ahead of Lanner & District (Conductor Derek Greenwood).

1981 Brass in Concert – Placed first in Junior Section.

1982 South West Brass Band Association (SWBBA) spring contest at Barnstaple – Placed first for the test piece and an "own-choice" march (Conductor Derek Greenwood).

1982 CBBA Contest – Placed second behind St Dennis (E Williams) in the under 19 yrs Section playing *Voices of Youth* by E Gregson. The Silver Cup for the best junior instrumentalist went to Camborne's horn player (Conductor Derek Greenwood).

Circa 1981 - The Youth Band

Back row: Tim Jeffrey (fifth right), 9th Robert Tanner (third right).

Middle row: Elizabeth Rowe (second left), Andrew James (third left), Neil Rutter (fourth left), Steven Weeks (right).

Front row: Jonathan Bond (left), Derek Greenwood (MD), John Hitchens (second right)

1983 South West Brass Band Association spring contest at Barnstaple – Placed first in the entertainment contest in which Robert Tanner won the soloist's award.

1983 CBBA Contest (under 19 yrs) – Placed second behind St Dennis in the under 19 yrs Section playing *Rural Suite* (Conductor Derek Greenwood).

1983 Brass In Concert – Placed first in the Junior Section (Conductor Reuben Long).

Ron Symons worked with the Band during the mid to late 1980s. He occasionally played bass with Lanner & District Band and also conducted Penzance Silver. He was married to Diana (née Commons) who was a playing colleague of mine at St Agnes Silver Band.

1984 South West Brass Band Association spring contest at Barnstaple – Reuben Long was due to conduct but the Band withdrew.

1984 CBBA Contest – Placed first, ahead of St Dennis and Lanner & District in the under 19 yrs Section playing *Bollin Hill Suite* by P Malbon. The best instrumentalist award was presented to Camborne's euphonium (Conductor Reuben Long).

In 1990, about 15 years after he had ceased playing, David Bray was approached by Michael Weeks and asked to help re-form the Youth Band. Jim Richards was appointed Musical Director and David, its Tutor. Before long, Sue Chandler (she later married Wayne Brown) was also on board and player recruitment in the schools was under way.

1992 (17th October) Penzance Contest – Placed first in both the Youth and the Fourth Section.

1993 CBBA Contest – Placed first ahead of St Dennis and Helston to become Cornish Youth Champions (under 19 yrs) playing "own-choice" test piece, *London River.* The best instrumentalist award was presented to Camborne's solo trombone (Conductor N J Richards).

The Youth Band was very busy with engagements as well as participating in contests and in May 1993 it gave a concert at Threemilestone School and played at a garden party at St Erth.

The lead team continued to the end of 1993 when Jim Richards left. The huge amount of work put in by him was acknowledged by the Society and a presentation made to show its thanks. The position was advertised but, in the interim period, David Bray continued as conductor and Alan Toy helped by taking some of the practices. Ray Grand then took over as Musical Director. David said, *"We were very good technically but Ray introduced an increased emphasis on style and dynamics".*

1991/1992 with Jim Richards, Sue Chandler & David Bray
Robert Sandow 3rd left, Andrew Mitchell – principal cornet.
(Photo Currah, Packet Newspapers)

Front row: extreme left is Andrew Mitchell, 3rd right is Vicky Kellow and 2nd right is Katie Tregenza. Centre is Jim Richards (MD) (photo by Phil Monckton/ CIOSP)

David Bray was assisting Ray Grand with the young players and Mrs Rowe was also helping with practices and in October 1994 there were 29 playing members in the Youth Band and 23 in the beginners class.

During the early part of 1994 the Trustees of the former Perranporth Band were trying to form a Youth Band and requested the return of numerous musical instruments and music stands which had been loaned to Camborne when it closed.

1994 CBBA Contest – Placed first in a section of four in the under 19 yrs Section playing the "own-choice" test piece, *Divertimento* (Conductor R Grand).

A Feast of Music was held on the 11th September 1994 at Marazion Community Centre featuring The Penzance Orpheus Ladies Choir and Camborne Town Youth Band. Ray Grand was conducting and Jeanette Eathorne of BBC Radio Cornwall compèred the concert. The programme notes state, *"The Band was formed (re-formed) in the spring of 1990 to support and eventually feed the very successful Championship Section Band. Our present Musical Director is Ray Grand who took over from Jim Richards in December 1993. Ray studied at the Royal Manchester College of Music and at the age of 11 he was appointed Assistant Principal Cornet of the National Youth Band of Great Britain. The band you will hear tonight has been together for four years and has an average age of 13 (excluding dads!). This Youth Band represents one of the few examples of an organisation contributing to the primary growth of brass banding in the county."*

The Youth Band took part in Penzance Contest in October 1994 when it was placed third in the Youth Section and second in the Fourth Section. The opinion was that the Band had not played well and there was a call for a discussion about its future. Ray Grand left in January 1995 and a couple of months later David Bray was asked to take over as Musical Director. He was in post until the end of 1995 when Francis Ralph took over. Mr Ralph was the Musical Director of Penzance Silver Band.

November 1993 - The winning quartet in the under 16 years class at the Camborne Music Festival. David Bray (Tutor) with Rachel Jenkin, Andrew Mitchell, Gavin Knowles and Sam Lewis.

1996 CBBA Contest at the Cornwall Coliseum, St Austell. - Placed third behind St Keverne and Mount Charles in the under 19 yrs Section playing the "own-choice" test piece *Suite de Ballet* (Conductor Francis Ralph).

1996 Bugle – Placed first in a section of six bands with Mount Charles Youth second and St Keverne Youth third playing *Northumbrian Suite*. Clare Jose (solo euphonium) won the best-player award (Conductor E F Ralph).

1996 SWBBA Contest (Torquay) – Placed third behind Mount Charles Youth and St Austell Youth playing *A Circus Suite* by Roy Newsome. Rachel Retallick won the Best Youth Player of the Day Award.

Francis Ralph resigned in September 1996 and Mr J Richards became Musical Director. At the end of 1996 there was a player shortage with some members transferring to other bands and it was agreed to advertise for players.

In March 1997 Mr Richards effectively resigned his position with the Youth Band and Ann Marsh, a Senior Band player, took over on a three-month's trial basis. In August 1997 a number of senior members left to join other bands, two players to Carharrack & St Day, Two to Lanner & District and one to Redruth. This outflow of talent was of great concern. Ann Marsh moved from the area and as a consequence of this she resigned.

Juliet Richards then took over on probation and in October 1997 she was appointed Youth Training Officer. She unfortunately sustained an injury and Leonard Adams took over until her return but her stay only lasted to December 1998.

In 1999 Alan Pope was appointed Youth Training & Development Officer. Alan was just five years old when he began his musical career - under Tommy Martin at Lanner. A couple of years later, in 1968, he moved to Carharrack & St Day under Clifford Bolitho. His father, Stanley Pope, said, *"We encouraged Alan to enter lots of solo contests when he was young and I remember driving him all over the place. In one year alone he won 38 first prizes and for each one Freddie Roberts' wife gave him 50p."* In 1972 he joined St Austell which was then conducted by Freddie Roberts. He was there for three years and moved to Camborne Town in 1975. After a couple of years he joined the Armed Forces and played in the Band of the $4^{th}/7^{th}$ Royal Dragoon Guards until 1993.

Apart from conducting Lanner Juniors for a year he then took a rest from banding but in 1998 he was enticed back into the brass band world by Leonard Adams. Alan had entered a quartet in

Alan Pope in the Royal Dragoon Guards (Photo by Eric Parsons)

the Camborne Music Festival and Leonard, who was conducting Camborne at the time, asked him if he would consider taking over the Youth Band. There were about eight members and seven beginners at that time and the idea appealed to him. Having decided to give it a go he went the whole hog and set himself up as a music teacher offering private tuition as well as taking over the responsibility for the Camborne Town Youth Band, Training Band and "B" Band. It was a brave move but one that has been hugely satisfying to Alan who is clearly very proud of his bands and the achievements of the young players.

Apart from his local involvement Alan is also a tutor with the Cornwall County Youth Brass Band and the Wessex Summer School Course which attracts about 180 players. In May 2003 he was presented with the Camborne Town Council plaque for services to youth music and in September 2004 he received the Treverva Shield at the Gorsedd in Truro for services to Camborne Youth Band.

On being appointed in 1999 Alan searched the bandroom for anything that looked as though it could make a noise like a brass instrument. A lot of work was needed on some of the old relics but he eventually ended up with 47 playable instruments. He then toured the local schools giving presentations to those children who seemed interested. Instruments and tuition were provided for a small weekly charge and the whole thing began to gather momentum. The process started in February 1999 but by May, with some schools still to visit, he was running out of instruments. Alan turned to Leonard Adams and Trevada Music for help and with a lot of Cornish ingenuity another 40 instruments were made available. They were soon put to good use with 87 instruments matched to 87 players.

With the help of some members of the Senior Band, a parents' evening was held when the youngsters played Alan's arrangement of *When the Saints*. Enthusiasm was growing and Bar-B-Qs, raffles and other forms of fund-raising began to swell the coffers. This was the forerunner of the *Brass on the Grass* evenings which became an annual event.

In November 1999, still in the first year of the resurgent band, a number of players took part in the Camborne Music Festival. Jean Graham was an encouraging adjudicator who described one group of youngsters as the "*Eager Beavers*".

In December 1999 a joint concert with the Senior Band was held at Camborne Wesley when, with an eye to presentation, both conductors – Leonard Adams and Alan Pope – wore matching waistcoats.

The Camborne Town Youth Band players were:
Chantelle Adams, Natalie Adams, Rachael Biscoe, Chris Butcher, Hannah Butcher, William Claydon, Luke Chappell, Kylie Clemence, Ben Cowburn, Sophia Cowburn, Danny Davies, Simon Dunstan, Sarah Edwards, Eleanor Edwards, Naomi Gendall, Matthew Glasson, Andrew Gool, James Gool, Jade Greenaway, Gareth Harris, Leanne Harvey, Peter Harvey, Martyn Hocking, Simon Hocking, Kattaliya Hollow, Grace Isherwood, Tanya Johnson, Sam Jones, Emma Kendall, Rosy Langley, Mark

Lowman, Sam Lowman, Thomas Martin, Matthew Medland, Laura Nicholas, Hannah Parsonage, Katie Poppelwell, Lisa Poppelwell, James Quintrell, Zoe Rail, Amber Roberts, Charlotte Roberts, Emma Roberts, Lauren Seymour, Rachael Stone, Kelly Symons, Jeremy Taylor, Grant Thurgood, Jessica Tredrea, Liam Vercoe, Anna Wade, Joseph Weeks, Natalie Weeks.
The Camborne Town Band players were:
Solo Cornets: Darren Hendy (Principal), Andrew Mitchell, Ian Hooper, Robert Cummings.
Soprano Cornet: Jeremy Squibb. Repiano Cornet: Chris Leonard.
2nd Cornets: Chris Netherton, Joanne Ryder-Pollard.
Third cornets: Marcus Dunstan, Sharon Hooper,
Flugel & Bandmaster: Stuart Chappell.
Horns: Graham Barker, Wayne Brown and Tracey Smith.
Baritones: Terry Sleeman and Stuart Butt who played from early 1990 to Aug 1997.
Euphoniums: John Hitchens and Tim Joslin.
Trombones: David Nicholas, Gareth Cottrell (tenor trom/bass trom/B flat bass - joined Oct 1997 and occasionally conducted at rehearsal and engagements) and Andrew Rice,
Basses: David Coad, Vic Ellis, Jason Smith and Simon Hooper.
Percussion: Mark Rosewarne, Nigel Chadd and Phil Trudgeon.

John Hitchens played the *Blue Bells of Scotland* by Arthur Pryor, Graham Barker played *Skelter* by Derek Broadbent and Terry Sleeman and Stuart Butt played *Deep Inside the Secret Temple* by Bizet.

1999 - The Youth Band with the two maestros with their matching waistcoats

Fundraising was going well and every opportunity was taken to make the Band self-sufficient so that it would not be a drag on the funds of the Society. At Christmas, the players spent an enormous amount of time playing carols in the town itself, at Sainsbury's in Truro and at Tesco in Redruth and Camborne. I mentioned Stanley Pope earlier in the book in the context of the Senior Band but he is also a very valued supporter and an avid fundraiser for the Youth Band. He and Rebecca Bond jointly organise the annual Wesley Concert. As Roger Merritt said, *"Stanley is never slow to come forward to shake the tin"*. Alan Pope demonstrated his perseverance in the year 2000 when he raised about £1000 for funds by completing the London Marathon.

Roger Merritt began his involvement in Youth Band affairs when his children, Rebecca (flugel) and Thomas (euphonium) joined in 2000. He became a member of the Youth Band management team with responsibility for funding opportunities including the Vice-President and Business

Partner Scheme. Tracy Abbott, who plays cornet in the Senior Band, looks after player registration and contest/concert arrangements, Ian Thompson investigates grant opportunities, Marcus Dunstan looks after the finance leaving Alan Pope to take care of the musical aspects.

During the year 2000, solo and quartet contest participation increased, as did the number of engagements with regular concerts at *The Shire* and the *Plume of Feathers* at Pool.

2001 was a landmark year when the Band first took part in a contest under Alan Pope. It was at the CBBA Contest at the Hall for Cornwall when it was unplaced in the under 20 yrs section.

2001 SWBBA Contest – Placed second behind St Dennis Junior playing the "own-choice" test pieces *Scenes from a Comedy* and the hymn tune *Great Soul.*

2002 CBBA Contest – Placed second behind JAG Mount Charles in the under 17 yrs Section playing the "own-choice" test piece *Rural Suite*. The best instrumentalist award was presented to Camborne's euphonium. It was unplaced in the under 20 yrs Section playing the "own-choice" test piece *Scenes from a Comedy.* JAG Mount Charles, St Austell and St Dennis took the first three places.

The reputation of the Youth Band was spreading and in 2002 it was invited to play a lunchtime concert in the College Gardens at Westminster Abbey. This was a prestigious event but the Band was faced with a huge obstacle – the cost of transport and accommodation would have to be met from its own funds. Nothing daunted, it was decided to travel up and back in one day and to raise the £1500 transportation cost. The concert was only three weeks after the date of the invitation but a hastily arranged sponsored walk raised £1700 – resourceful or what?

The CD, *Our Kinda Music,* was recorded in 2002. It was conducted by Alan Pope and included *Bohemian Rhapsody, Everything I do, Lady in Red, Y M C A, Unchained Melody, Hey Jude, The Wind Beneath my Wings,* and *One Moment in Time.*

2002 SWBBA Contest – Placed second behind JAG Mount Charles in the Junior Section playing *Youth Salutes a Master* and the hymn tune *Bursley.*

In October 2002 Camborne Youth Band joined forces with Champagne Cornwall Barber Shop for *Youth in Concert* at Camborne Wesley. The programme included a wide-ranging and entertaining programme; Alan Pope conducted the Band which had an average age of 11 years.

2003 CBBA Contest - A memorable occasion as the Band won the Junior Section (under 17 yrs) and became Cornish Junior Champions. The best instrumentalist award went to Peter Harvey (euphonium) who was later accepted into the National Youth Brass Band of Great Britain.

2003 SWBBA Contest – Placed first to become South-West Junior Champions (Conductor Alan Pope).

Anyone who attended the Last Night of the Cornish Proms at the Hall for Cornwall in 2003 will remember it as an excellent concert in which Camborne Youth Band excelled. It was a tremendous event; not only was the music appreciated, their professialism was also superb as they sat patiently while the other performers did their bit.

2004 CBBA Contest (under 17 yrs) – Placed first, followed by St Stythians Juniors, playing *Lydian Pictures.* The best instrumentalist award went to Jessica Tredrea (cornet) (Conductor Alan Pope).

In September 2004 Alan Morrison, Principal Cornet of Brighouse and Rastrick and former champion soloist of Great Britain, was appointed Professional Musical Adviser of the Youth Band. His remit was to work with the Musical Director in training the players and preparing them for contests.

2004 The National Youth Brass Band Championship of Great Britain – Placed first to become the Junior Champions of Great Britain. The age limit for the section was 16 and the players' average age was just 13 years.

The *West Briton* announced:

"Camborne Youth Band triumphant"

"The Cornish Flag flew proudly over The Royal Northern College of Music in Manchester last Saturday when the Camborne Youth Band, conducted by Alan Pope, won the title of Junior National Brass Band Champions of Great Britain."

The Western Morning News in April 2004 used the headline *"Youth Band a knockout"* and spoke of its triple achievement of becoming Cornish, South-West and National Junior Champions. It quoted one of the two adjudicators at the National Championship who referred to the top two bands as *"an absolute knockout"*. He said about Camborne Youth Band, *"Thank you for showing all the basic*

2004 - Camborne Youth Band – Junior Champions of Great Britain. Alan Pope (Musical Director)
Solo cornets: Chloe Abbott, Zoe Harris, Samuel Eddy, Jessica Tredrea (Principal), Simon Dunstan, Amber Roberts and Hannah Butcher.
Soprano: Emma Kendall. Repiano: Joe Weeks.
Second cornets: Christopher Bond, Daniel Lees, Emma Mallett and Michael Russell.
Third cornets: Rebecca Spinks, Matthew Brown and Cecilia Carlisle.
Flugel horns: Leanne Harvey and Rebecca Merritt.
Horns: Naomi Gendall, Matthew Glasson, Josh Lovelock, Alex Butcher and Ashley Williams.
Euphoniums: Peter Harvey and Simon Kendall.
Baritones: Ben King, Thomas Merritt and Jack Uterhark.
Trombones: Rosie Langley, Rachel Spinks, Alex Richards and Dominic Turner.
Basses: Sam Jones, Clifford Richards, Graham Griffiths and William Claydon.
Percussion: Rory Abbott, Jeremy Taylor, Chris Butcher and Tim Richards.
(photo by Umbrella Photography)

qualities of brass playing. Quality sound, no over-blowing, note value correct, balance and rhythm. Great percussion and a very, very good conductor."

Following its success in becoming the Junior Champions of Great Britain, Camborne Town Council presented the Band with a plaque for services to youth music and in July 2004 Kerrier Council did likewise.

2004 SWBBA Contest – Unplaced in the Youth Section playing *Scenes du Lac* by Roy Newsome. (Conductor Alan Pope)

Since January 2001 the Youth Band has organised an annual solo and quartet contest at Camborne School. A well-known musician is invited to adjudicate each year and then to provide a workshop the following morning. For the past two years the Senior and Junior Bands have concluded the event with a concert at the Penventon Hotel.

Adjudicators who have taken part:

2001 - Stan Lippeatt (flugel - ex Grimethorpe).

2002 – Richard Marshall (Principal Cornet - Grimethorpe).

2003 – Nick Hudson (trombone - ex Fairey's - became free-lance soloist).

2004 – Alan Morrison (Principal Cornet - Brighouse and Rastrick).

2005 – Stan Lippeatt who stood in for Peter Roberts (soprano - Black Dyke) who was unable to attend due to a family illness.

2005 The National Youth Brass Band Championship of Great Britain – Alan Pope took the Band to first place to become the Junior Champions of Great Britain for the second year in a row.

Against much stiffer opposition than in 2004, the Band was triumphant with a sparkling concert programme and to complete a perfect day, Jeremy Taylor (percussion) won the Best Soloist award. This was despite a nerve-twisting event just prior to the Band going on stage. One of the pieces featured Jeremy on Vibraphone, a sort of electric xylophone – so I'm told - which failed to work when it was plugged in. The contest organisers had supplied the instrument and playing had to be suspended for half-an-hour while they found a replacement.

When taking young players away for an engagement or contest the management team have to take the same precautions as a school on an educational trip. Forty-four players, aged nine to sixteen, made the trip to the Manchester Contest in April 2005 and with a required ratio of one adult for every six children, seven supervisors had to accompany them. Those adults have to be cleared as fit persons to supervise children and are required to have first aid training.

2005 - Camborne Youth Band – Junior Champions of Great Britain.

Alan Pope was Musical Director and the players taking part were:
Solo cornets: Chloe Abbott, Zoe Harris, Jessica Tredrea (Principal), Christopher Bond, Joe Weeks, and Hannah Butcher.
Soprano: Samuel Eddy and Rebecca Spinks. Repiano: Daniel Lees.
Second cornets: Emma Mallett, Michael Russell, Matthew Brown, and Lloyd Rowse.
Third cornets: Aimee Lees, Emily Brown, Katy Wilson, Lauren Mankee and Laureen Hodge.
Flugel horns: Rebecca Merritt. Cecilia Carlisle.
Horns: Naomi Gendall, Matthew Glasson, Amber Roberts, Alex Butcher and Ashley Williams, Kathryn McDermott
Euphoniums: Peter Harvey, Simon Kendall. Thomas Merritt.
Baritones: Ben King, Laura Weeks and Kayleigh Walker.
Trombones: Rosie Langley, Rachel Spinks, and Dominic Turner.
Basses: Sam Jones, Clifford Richards, William Claydon, Jack Carlisle and Matthew Julian.
Percussion: Rory Abbott, Jeremy Taylor, Jack Uterhark and Zoe Moore

The Youth Band is very much a part of the Camborne Town Band Music Society and as its ability to raise income has increased it has become less dependent on Society funds. It is in demand for engagements and it's interesting to hear that the Youth Band has been booked for three tea-treats this year; Townshend, Kehelland and St Ives. These annual gatherings have largely died out but, in the case of Townshend, the event is being held for the first time for some years.

In July 2005 the Youth Band made an exchange visit with Shadwell Youth Band from Tower Hamlets, London. The highlight was a performance at Canary Wharf when the audience was treated to a concert by the National Junior Champions. Alan Pope and the players were thanked by the Mayor of London, Ken Livingstone, and taken on a ride on the London Eye.

The young players are predominantly from the Camborne area and a number will eventually progress into the Senior Band while others will enjoy their playing elsewhere. Inevitably some will finish their banding activities when they become too old for the Youth Band but even if that is the case, they will have had a memorable and satisfying experience and I'll wager all of them will retain an affinity with the brass band world.

The "B" Band comprises some of the young players plus some ex-members of the Senior Band and a few parents who have followed their offspring into the brass band world. I have tried to distinguish between the bands but as they have often shared a Musical Director and players it has sometimes been a difficult decision where to slot the information.

1974 CBBA Contest – Placed first in the Fourth Section and fifth in the "Open" Concert Contest. Leonard Adams conducted and Keith Rowe, the joint MD, played tenor horn.

1974 Bugle – Placed third for the hymn tune *Cornwall* and fourth for *A Psalm for all Nations* in Class "C". Totnes Town received two first place awards and St Breward two seconds (Conductor Leonard Adams).

1975 Bugle – Placed third behind Lanner & District and Bideford in Class "C" playing *The Ancient Temple* by Eric Ball. The result was the same for the "own-choice" march when the Band played *Slaidburn*. Susan Rowe (euphonium) won the best-player award.

Some members of the "B" Band
Top left: David Roberts
Top right: Clr Tony Bunce
Bottom left: John Pinsent

1979 (I think) CBBA Contest – Placed second in a section of six bands playing *Devon Fantasy* by Eric Ball. The results I have are slightly confusing but it appears that Camborne was also the highest placed Third Section band in the concert contest. (Conductor K Rowe)

The "B" Band appears to have disappeared around this time which probably reflects the difficulty being experienced in appointing and retaining conductors.

In early 1988 Stephen Sykes signalled his intention to form a "B" Band and in April he held the first rehearsal. Several players turned up and he said he looked forward to the time when it would be able to undertake engagements and compete in contests. It seems that the "B" Band then took on a more discernable identity and at a meeting held on the 1st July 1992 it was proposed to register both the Youth Band and the "B" Band. This would enable adults to take part in future contests.

1993 CBBA Contest - Second behind the City of Truro Band in the Fourth Section playing the "own-choice" test piece *Rural Suite* (Conductor J Richards).

1994 CBBA Contest – Placed second in the Fourth Section playing the "own-choice" test piece *Divertimento* (Conductor Ray Grand).

In 1994 or 1995, the "B" Band was de-registered but in December 1996 plans were put in place to re-form it.

2002 South-West Championship – Unplaced with the first three positions going to the Cornish trio of St Dennis, Hayle Town and Pendennis Brass (Falmouth) playing the test piece *Suite in Bb* by Gordon Jacob (Conductor Alan Pope).

2002 SWBBA Contest - Unplaced in a section of eight bands playing *Little Suite for Brass No. 1* by Malcolm Arnold.

2003 CBBA Contest – Placed first ahead of the City of Truro, Constantine, Indian Queens and Wendron in the Fourth Section playing the "own-choice" test piece *Little Suite for Brass No 1.*

Like any group, the Band has its characters and Dominic Turner seems to self-select for special mention. He was marching through the town on Trevithick Day when the slide on his trombone fell off and dropped to the ground. When in a marching formation there is not a lot of time to retrieve anything and by the time he had made a few attempts to grasp it, the rest of the players were on him.

An excellent result in the 2003 South-West Championship as the Band was placed third out of 25 bands in the Fourth Section. Conducted by Alan Pope and playing *Lydian Pictures* by Simon Dobson it qualified for the National Final and members had to set about raising about £4000 to cover the cost of transport and accommodation in Dundee where the contest was to be held. Corporate sponsorship was sought for each player and a balloon race and a sponsored blow was organised. The people of Camborne responded well and the Band was on its way.

2003 National Championship – Placed fourteenth out of 21 Fourth Section bands playing the test piece *Call of the Sea* by Eric Ball - one of the leading figures of the twentieth century in the brass

2003 - The "B" Band setting off for National Finals in Dundee

band world. A commendable result considering that this predominantly youth band was playing in an adult section. Additionally, because of the results in the qualifying contests at Torquay in 2002 and 2003, it was promoted to the Third Section after only two years of contesting.

2004 CBBA Contest – Placed second behind Hayle Town in the Third Section playing the "own-choice" test piece, *Viscaya* by Gordon Jacob.

2004 South-West Championship – Unplaced in the Third Section playing the test piece *Viscaya.*

2004 Bugle – Placed third behind St Pinnock and Pendennis Brass in the Third Section for both *Lydian Pictures* and the hymn *Treskerby* by Monty Pearce (Conductor Alan Pope).

I mentioned Dominic Turner earlier and on this occasion he featured again. Alan Pope said, *"The tension on a contest stage is always high but not so with Dominic. He is a very laid back young chap but I'm sure this instance made, even him, panic a little. The Band was playing in the Third Section and was required to play two test pieces on its single visit to the platform; the hymn tune Treskerby and Lydian Pictures by Simon Dobson. All but one player placed the hymn tune on the stand and prepared to begin the quiet and tender music. One player had placed Lydian Pictures on the stand and prepared himself to make a bold and emphatic start. He made a very good, solid entrance and very quickly realised that something was wrong."* I asked Alan what went through his mind at that moment and it seems that it was something like, *"That'll be Dominic and that's the hymn tune gone".* The adjudicator, in his remarks, seems to have summed it up with the comment, *"I don't believe what I just heard!"*

A superb result at the 2005 Area Championship as the Band took fifth place playing *Tam O'Shanter's Ride*. Hayle, under former Camborne player Derek Johnston, was third, a heart-breaking position which meant promotion but left them just short of qualification for the National Final.

2003 Camborne "B" Band at the National Final in Dundee
Back row: Marcus Dunstan (centre) and Warren Bennett (right).
Front row: John Adams, Dave Roberts and Russell Kellow.
John Barnes (centre with trombone and Alan Pope (MD in suit)
(Photo by Brass Band World)

Camborne Town Band Today

David Roberts - President of Camborne Town Band Music Society

Michael Weeks - Chairman of Camborne Town Band Music Society

Brass bands have always had its share of characters – the bandroom is a place where they seem to abound – and Camborne, over the years, has had a few. We now move right up-to-date and take a look at the players who have inherited the rich heritage passed on by their predecessors.

Principal Cornet - Chris Leonard (Nobby)
Chris started playing at the age of seven with St Austell Youth Band before moving to St Dennis. He joined Camborne in 1995 and became Principal Cornet in the year 2000. Since then he has won many Special Awards and has the enviable record of leading the Band to three successive appearances in the National Championship at the Royal Albert Hall.

Soprano Cornet - Jeremy Squibb (Squibby)
Having started with St Stythians Youth Band at the age of six, Jeremy moved to St Austell under the guidance of Albert Chappell. After a brief spell with St Dennis he moved to Camborne in 1993. He turned down an invitation to join Sunlife in 1995 and moved back to St Austell in 1996. He won the best soloist award at Bugle Contest in 1997 and immediately moved west again to rejoin Camborne. He has won the best soprano award at Bugle a record six times. Jeremy's sister, Karen, also played at St Austell and their father had played with Gweek and St Stythians during the 1970s to 1980s. With his fiancée, Rachel Trudgeon (baritone), he managed the Camborne Town Band web site until 2005 when he also relinquished his roles of Society Vice-Chairman and Band Manager.

Solo Cornet - Mark Leigh (Pob)
Having started with Carharrack and St Day at the age of seven, in 1983, Mark moved via Lanner & District and Bodmin Town to Camborne in 1993. After a couple of years back with Bodmin he returned to Camborne circa 2001. He has been Principal Cornet of Cornwall Youth Band and narrowly

Chris Leonard , Mark Leigh, Jessica Powell (guest), Vicky Kellow and Zoe Alexander (guest).

missed becoming Principal Cornet of The National Youth Brass Band of Great Britain when a second audition placed him in second position. Mark suffers from mild asthma which the breathing techniques required in playing a brass instrument helps to control. He also suffers from migraines and, just two days before the 2003 National Championship, he had to be taken home but recovered in time to take his place in the competition. He is the Engagement and Contest Registration Secretary.

Solo Cornet - Vicky Kellow
Vicky started her music career in Porthleven Band and moved to Penzance where she was Principal Cornet before transferring to Camborne in 2002. This is a big year in her life; in addition to being promoted to the front row she married Musical Director, Steve Thomas.

Solo Cornet - Ian Hooper
Ian began his playing career at Redruth in 1975 when he was nine years old. He joined Camborne in 1988 but left to play with Lanner & District from 1992 to 1998 before returning to Camborne again. His wife, Sharon (cornet), joined in the late 1980s having previously played with Truro and St Agnes. She left in October 2004, to have a baby. Ian took a temporary break from banding at the beginning of summer 2005.

Repiano - Katie Bullock
Katie, who had started her playing career in St Austell Youth Band, soon established herself as a cornet soloist. After several successful years, picking up many soloist awards and contest specials along the way, Katie moved to Bodmin Band. As soon as the flugel position became available she jumped at the opportunity and established herself as a fine soloist. She joined Camborne in October 2004.

Second Cornet - Chris Netherton (Spike)
A product of Indian Queens Band, Chris played with St Austell for a few years before making the move to Camborne in 1993. He played in the Cornwall County Youth Band for three or four years and toured Austria under Derek Greenwood. Although he had a brief spell on solo cornet with the Band, Chris prefers his role as the anchor man of the back row.

Jeremy Squibb, Katie Bullock, Chris Netherton, Marcus Dunstan and David Barnes (guest)

Second Cornet - Jessica Tredrea
Jessica is a product of the Youth Band. She was taught by Alan Pope and has already led the Junior Band to two consecutive National Titles, and the "B" Band to the National Final, followed by promotion to the Third Section. She won a best player award in 2004 playing *Lydian Pictures* and remembered one of the highlights of her career - when she tripped over the pavement, marching in the Trevithick Day parade.

Mo & Jo

Third Cornet - Jo Ryder-Pollard
Jo comes from a banding family and joined a number of her relatives at Redruth Town when she was nine years old. Following short periods at Bodmin Town and St Dennis Silver she joined Camborne in 1995 and, apart from some breaks for other commitments, has been there ever since. Her uncles Leonard Dunstan and Ralph Kenward played during the 1960s when Freddie Roberts was Musical Director. Her daughters also play at Camborne - Jasmine in the Junior Band and Emily in the Training Band. Jo is described is an excellent utility player who can find herself in almost any seat on the cornet section. Mo Whitehead and Jo played at the Cambridge contest and recalled the fire alarms sounding in their travel lodge. They had to assemble outside - in their pyjamas!

Third Cornet - Tracey Abbott
Tracey commenced her playing in Appledore Band and, after moving to Cornwall and getting the bug for it again, she joined the Band in May 2001, just a few months after her husband, Nick. They have three

children amongst the young players at Camborne - Chloe (cornet), Rory (percussion) and BJ (percussion). Tracey is a member of the Youth Band Management Group.

Flugel Horn - Andrew Mitchell (L Plate)

Andrew has been described by Frank Renton as one of the young lions of the Band. He's not really sure what this means but thinks it could be because he is usually in the midst of the fun. His musical career began with Carharrack & St Day in 1988 at the age of six from where he moved to Camborne Youth Band and then to Redruth where he was Principal Cornet. He joined Camborne Town Band in 1998, initially playing cornet, and took the principal role for a while. He now plays flugel and is often called on for solos at concerts.

Solo Horn - Mark Letcher (Letch)

Mark commenced playing at Lostwithiel Youth when he was eight years old and moved to Bodmin Town in 1984. Having spent 20 years at Bodmin, initially on cornet and then on tenor horn where he won many awards, Mark moved to Camborne in 2004. An established soloist in his own right he now regularly features as one of the Band's concert soloists.

First Horn - Wayne Brown (Captain)

Wayne began playing at the age of 10, in 1970, with Lanner & District. He moved to Camborne in 1981 and has played there ever since - on cornet and flugel before moving to tenor horn in 1998. His wife, Sue, plays for Pendennis Brass and their children, Matthew and Emily, play in Camborne Junior Band. He has played in three hat-tricks of wins at Bugle and in 15 Albert Hall appearances including in 1982 when the Band took fourth place. With 24 years service he must be one of the longest serving members in the Band's history.

Second Horn - Cath Lovegrove

Cath has been referred to as a super-sub as she mixes her commitments with St Stythians Band and Camborne. She has played with Bugle, Bodmin, St Austell and Mount Charles and brings an expanse of knowledge to the highly experienced horn section. Amongst the highlights of her career are a tour of Germany with Mount Charles and a tour of France with Lostwithiel.

Principal Euphonium - Robert Jose (Josey)

Robert started playing at the age of 11 and was taught by Albert Chappell and Steve Sykes. After three years he joined the National Youth Brass Band of Great Britain and held the principal euphonium position for six courses. He won the Junior and Senior Soloist Awards at the age of 15 and became the Junior Slow Melody Champion of Great Britain. He retained this title the following year and was also Radio Cornwall's Musician of the Year. He successfully competed in all major music festivals and soloist contests throughout the country and played in many of the best concert venues including the London Barbican, the Queen Elizabeth Hall and the Royal Albert Hall where he enjoyed playing with Camborne and with the National Youth Band in a Henry Wood Promenade Concert.

Second Euphonium - Steve Thomas

Steve is also the resident Musical Director and appears earlier in the book.

First baritone - Gavin Knowles

Gavin began his playing career in 1993, with Camborne Junior Band, and has recently returned to his roots after a few years playing for Bodmin Town. In 1996, he won the Albert Chappel Memorial Shield – possibly the only baritone player to win it. I was pleased to hear that as I've always felt that the baritone is one of the unsung heroes of a band (of course, that's got nothing to do with the fact that I played first baritone!) Gavin has a number of family connections in the Band; Nigel and Donald Cock were his uncle and great uncle and his grandmother was Sylvia Dunstan who, with her friend Christine Dale, worked hard on the committees.

Second Baritone - Rachel Trudgeon

Rachel started playing euphonium with St Austell Youth Band when she was 12 years old and won the best euphonium player award at the CBBA Contest in 1999 and the best player award at the National Youth Championship at Salford. She progressed into St Austell Town Band and then to Camborne in 2000. Bugle Contest 2005 was the first time that brother Phil and Rachael had played together for Camborne at that particular competition.

The trombone section: Chris Wooding, Neil Murley and Nick Abbott.

Solo Trombone - Nick Abbott
From humble beginnings with Appledore Band at the age of 10, Nick made the meteoric leap to Camborne in 2001 as the Band's solo trombone player. His wife Tracy and their three children also play at Camborne.

Second Trombone - Neil Murley (Nally)
Neil has been playing for 25 years, having been a member at Hayle, Redruth, Penzance and the Cornwall County Youth. Another former pupil of Albert Chappell, Neil passed his grade five at the age of 10 and is a fully accomplished musician on a range of instruments including the electric organ, drums and didgeridoo (I'm still not sure if he was pulling my leg). Neil provides organ music at a range of functions including wedding receptions and dinner dances. He joined Camborne in 2003 and says the thrill he derives from playing in Bugle Square is as good as it gets. He is the Band's web-site manager.

Bass Trombone - Chris Wooding (Woody / Party Boy)
Chris started his musical career with Mount Charles Youth. He moved to St Austell Youth and eventually took up his first Senior Band posting with Camborne in 2001. Always the "introvert", he recalled having one or three drinks with Andrew Mitchell, another Camborne "introvert", at the All England Masters at Cambridge in 2004 and being applauded by David King, the conductor of Yorkshire Building Society, as they walked the streets singing *"We're goina win London"*.

Kevyn Caddy, Eric Thomas & Tim Joslin

Principal E flat bass - Tim Joslin

Tim is another product of Carharrack & St Day Band where he started playing at the age of six. From there he moved to Illogan and then to Camborne, in 1982. After many successful years on 1st baritone, Tim moved to E flat bass after a short spell on euphonium.

His first year included the National Championship, when Camborne came fourth, and the Pontins' Final at Prestatyn. He said, *"What a year 1982 was and what an introduction to Championship brass banding. In the years since then I have had a wonderful time, visited many places and met hundreds of people. I have had two visits to Paris and many excellent contest performances which is really why we all participate in this great 'hobby' of ours."*

E flat bass - Kevyn Caddy

Kevyn played at Camborne during the mid 1970s before leaving and returning in 2005 - on E flat bass. In the meantime he played with Lanner & District, Constantine and Pendennis and was a part of the successful Redruth Town Band of the 1980s.

Principal B flat bass - Eric Thomas

Eric is the most senior member of the Band, joining Joe Trounce's beginners group in 1952, at the age of 15, and playing under the baton of the late Freddie Roberts. He played with the National Youth Band of Great Britain when it was founded in 1955, under the legendary Eric Ball. He was a member at the same time as Barry Tresidder, Toni Volante, John Berryman, Adrian King and John Roberts.

His first period at Camborne finished in 1957 and it was not until 1971 that he resumed playing – with Hayle. In the mid 1970s he joined Camborne "B" Band under Leonard Adams and Keith Rowe and after a couple of years, moved back into the Senior Band where he stayed until 1982 and played in the 1977 and 1982 National Championships when Camborne enjoyed their best results. After periods with Hayle Town and Penzance Silver, Eric rejoined Camborne in 2003.

He first played at the National Championship in 1954 and an article in the *brass band world* of October 2003 said *"49 years on, Eric limbers up for another National final".* Of course, since then, he has notched up the extra year. In the article Eric recalled that the test piece in 1954 was *Sovereign Heritage* and that coming from "down Camborne," playing at the Royal Albert Hall was a great experience.

B flat bass - Jason Smith (Gormo)

Jason commenced playing in St Ives Band in 1976, at the age of nine. About four years later he moved to Hayle Town Band, when Alan Toy was the conductor, and was involved in forming a musical group *St Ia brass ensemble.* Then followed a move to Camborne Youth Band in 1982 under Keith Rowe and promotion to the Senior Band the following year. This was a time when, *"The experiences really started,"* for Jason.

He was a member of the Cornwall County Youth Brass Band and took part in its tours of Luxembourg, Switzerland and Austria when he met his future wife, Tracey, who played tenor horn for Lanner & District Band before moving to Camborne Town Band.

Jason "retired" in 2001 but maintains his registration and played with the Band at the Area Championship, the Spring Festival Senior Trophy and the CBBA Contest in 2005. He is described as a veteran bass player, yet still a young man, and the Band are delighted to have him as a corner stone in the bass section.

B flat bass - Lee Trewhella
Lee started playing at the age of five - on E flat bass at Breage and District Silver. He transferred to Helston before attending university and playing with the Nottingham City Transport Band, Horsham Brass Band (principal euphonium) and Desford where he took part in the 1997 British Open. He returned to Cornwall in 2001 and played with St Keverne before achieving his ambition of joining Camborne Town Band.

Principal Percussionist - Jeremy Taylor
Jeremy originally started on trombone in the Youth Band but quickly found that he preferred the accuracy of tuned percussion rather than the guesswork of a trombone. Having said that, he continued to glide the slide as well as playing the piano. Another product of the excellent youth system, he was crowned best player of the section at the National Junior Championship in 2005 when he brought the house down with a virtuoso performance of *Czardas.*

He claims to be a bit of a show-stopper – ever since he kept the band and the audience waiting for a couple of minutes while he hunted for his xylophone sticks at the 2003 CBBA Contest at the Hall for Cornwall – the silence was deafening!

Percussionist - Phil Trudgeon
Phil started his musical career on tenor horn with St Austell Youth Band but decided to turn his hand to percussion and, after a few years, he moved to Camborne where his sister, Rachel, also plays. He joined the Royal Marines in 2000 and is based at Portsmouth. Because of this, he now takes a part-time role with the Band but always returns whenever possible to play in his own enigmatic style.

Percussionist - Nigel Chadd
Nigel commenced playing at Bude in 1977 and after a couple of years he moved to Launceston where his father, Nick Chadd, was Musical Director. He joined Camborne in 1994 and played regularly until April 2004 but still returns to help the Band in the "kitchen sink" department. Nigel said two events stand out in his memory, the *Cry of the Celts* Concert and the Pendennis Castle Concert at the time of the Tall Ships event.

Just prior to publication, there were a few changes in the ranks of the Band:

Graham Boag, former MD and player returned to the bass section after a period with Lanner & District.

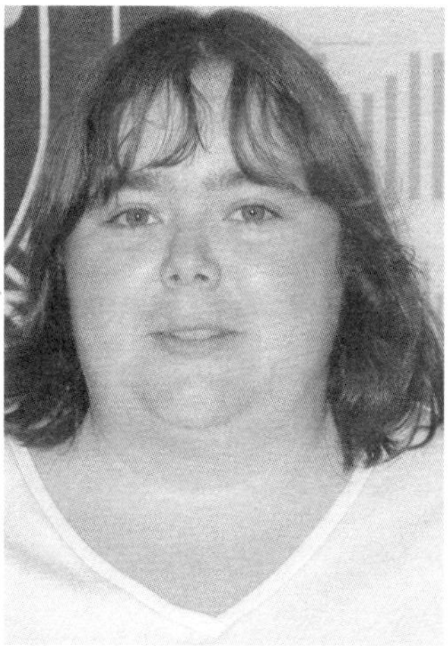

Alison Farr (née Richards) joined from Newquay Town - she replaced Rachel Trudgeon who had left to join Helston Town Band.

Jeremy Willcock played with St Dennis and a number of other brass and orchestral groups - he replaced Jeremy Squibb who had left to join Helston Town Band.

****

Camborne Town Band has been at the forefront of Cornish brass banding for over 100 years. It has been in the National Championship Section for 60 years and earned a top ten result at the National Finals on, at least, 11 occasions. Although it currently has some healthy competition it has seen many other bands rise and fall and has often had to carry the reputation of Cornish Championship brass banding on its own. We may well ponder why it has had this unprecedented run of success. Perhaps it relates to the community or its willingness to employ top conductors; recognizing that the music making comes before everything else. Whatever the reason, the beneficiaries have been the enthusiasts throughout Cornwall because no band has done more to improve the standard of brass banding in the Duchy.

No book can hope to reproduce the magical and distinctive music of a brass band but I hope that you will occasionally "hear" the sound of a familiar piece as you read through the pages. It was always my aim to set pulses racing, revive memories and capture the joy of making music. My enthusiasm for banding is deep in my roots – I hope it comes through.

This exploration into the history of Camborne Town Band has been a journey of discovery, perhaps a longer journey than I imagined when Tom Ruse first approached me with the idea of producing this book. My intention, as ever, has been to paint a picture with words. In this case, a picture that recreates the uniqueness of the brass band world and in particular, the history of Camborne Town Band. I hope that Tom, and all those people who I have met along the way, will feel that I have portrayed their band in the way that they would wish.

May Camborne Town Band go on producing music of the highest quality
and continue to be an excellent ambassador for Camborne and Cornwall.

Acknowledgements

I have interviewed many past and present players, committee members and supporters of Camborne Town Band and appreciate the co-operation and help I have been given. I have enjoyed the chats and cups of tea and from the reaction received, have a sneaking suspicion that most people have enjoyed the chance to reminisce in front of an eager listener. My thanks go to all those people who have been so generous in giving their time to make this book possible. Their memories have been sorely tested in trying to identify the people in the photographs and I sincerely hope that we have got it right.

Leonard Adams, George Ansell, Eddie Ashton, Lester Ashton, Reg Bennett, Courtney Berryman, John Berryman, Clifford Bolitho, John Brush, Desmond Burley, Colin Butson of St Agnes, David Bray who died before this book was published, Stuart Chappell, Roma Cock, Robert Cook, Dudley Currah re Billy Moyle, Captain Pete Curtis, Lieutenant Colonel Chris Davis, Monica Dean née Orchard, Marcus Dunstan, Ian Facey, Pat Farr, Ray Farr, Gerald Fletcher who died before this book was published, Alan, Dennis & Gordon Floyd, Derek Greenwood, Melba Hale née Roberts, Melville Hancock who provided information about Bugle Contest, Darren Hendy, John Hitchens, Kingsley Hitchens, Mike Hocking, Phillip Hunt, Russell Kellow, Adrian King, Brian Leigh, Ron Matthews of St Agnes, Roger Merritt, Roy & Dorothy Nancarrow, Angela & Roy Netherton, J Arthur Osborne, Wathew Parker (nephew of A W Parker), Jack Pascoe, John Phillips, Alan Pope, Stanley Pope, David Reed, Frank Renton, Mike Rosewarne, Tom Ruse, David Saunders, Cora Seddon née Trounce, Bob Seymour, Gordon Simpson from Edinburgh who provided information about the Area and National Championship, Jason Smith, Jeremy Squibb, Ian Sutton, Robert Tanner, David Thomas, Alan Toy, Reg Toy, Barrie Trevena, Eric Trerise, Barry Tresidder, Rachel Trudgeon, Toni Volante, Fred Waters, Michael Weeks, Ashley White, Stephen White, Lorna Williams (wife of Eddie Williams), Barbara Yeoman. To the above list must be added the members of the current band and the Musical Director who provided information about themselves and, in some cases, about their colleagues as well!

It is always dangerous to identify specific people for special thanks but it would be wrong of me not to acknowledge the exceptional and pro-active help received from Marcus Dunstan, Brian Leigh, Phillip Hunt, Roy Nancarrow, Angela Netherton, Alan Pope, Tom Ruse, Jeremy Squibb, Alan Toy and Michael Weeks.

A special thanks, yet again, to my good friend and mentor Alan Murton of Goonhavern for proof reading and correcting any English mistakes - he must have worn out a few pencils!

The photographs appearing in this book are from many sources and I have tried to trace the photographers but in some instances this proved impossible. I hope that they will accept my apologies and understand that no photograph has been included without extensive efforts to identify who took it and to obtain approval to its inclusion. Of the people who I have been able to find, the following have kindly agreed to their photographs appearing:

Donald Bennetts of Troon on behalf of W J Bennetts & Son of Camborne, Brass Band World, Sam Bennetts of St Ives, The Clive Benney Collection (Clive is my co-author in some joint projects), The Cornwall Centre, Redruth, for the use of photographs by George W F Ellis, Marcus Dunstan, Brian Errington Photographer, Geoff Hichens Photography, Mike Saynt James Photographer, Malcolm Jenkin of Portreath, Clive Letcher, Phil Monckton of Cornwall & Isles of Scilly Press (CIOSP), Roy Netherton, Eric Parsons Photographer, Donald L Williams of St Ives and Umbrella Photography of Manchester.

References

Books:

The Archive Photographs series Camborne by David Thomas
Mithian in the parishes of St Agnes and Perranzabuloe by Tony Mansell
St Agnes and its Band by Tony Mansell
Victorian and Edwardian Camborne by J Arthur Osborne and David H Thomas

Sundry articles and extracts from:

The *Cornish Post and Mining News*
The *Packet Newspapers*
The *Royal Cornwall Gazette*
The *West Briton*

The meeting minutes of Camborne Town Band
The meeting minutes of Camborne Town Band Music Society

Contest programmes from the various named organisations

The Bugle Band Contest Internet web page
The Camborne Town Band Internet web page
The 4barsrest Internet web page

Other books by the Tony Mansell:

Mithian in the Parishes of St Agnes and Perranzabuloe
St Agnes and its Band
With St Agnes in Mind
A History of Blackwater and its Neighbours (co-author Clive Benney)